Getting Smart

Critical Social Thought

Series editor: Michael W. Apple
Professor of Curriculum and Instruction and Educational Policy Studies, University of Wisconsin-Madison

Already published

Critical Social Psychology Philip Wexler
Reading, Writing and Resistance Robert B. Everhart
Arguing for Socialism Andrew Levine
Between Two Worlds Lois Weis
Culture Wars Ira Shor
Power and the Promise of School Reform William J. Reese
Becoming Clerical Workers Linda Vali
Racial Formation in the United States Michael Omi and Howard Winant
The Politics of Hope Bernard P.Dauenhauer
The Common Good Marcus G. Raskin
Contradictions of Control Linda M. McNeil
Social Analysis of Education Philip Wexler
Keeping Them Out of the Hands of Satan Susan D. Rose
Primary Understanding Kieran Egan
Capitalist Schools Daniel P. Liston
The New Literacy John Willinsky
Becoming a Woman Through Romance Linda Christian-Smith
Growing up Modern Bruce Fuller

PATTI LATHER

Getting Smart
Feminist Research and Pedagogy With/in the Postmodern

ROUTLEDGE
New York •
London

Published in 1991 by

Routledge
An imprint of Routledge, Chapman and Hall, Inc.
29 West 35 Street
New York, NY 10001

Published in Great Britain by

Routledge
11 New Fetter Lane
London EC4P 4EE

Printed in the United States of America

Library of Congress Cataloging in Publication Data

Lather, Patricia Ann, 1948—
Getting smart : feminist research and pedagogy with/in the postmodern / Patti Lather.
p. cm. — (Critical social thought)
Includes bibliographical references and index.
ISBN 0-415-90377-7; ISBN 0-415-90378-5 (pbk.)
1. Feminist theory. 2. Feminism—Research. 3. Women's studies.
I. Title. II. Series.
HQ1190.L38 1991
305.42′072—dc20 90-37449

British Library Cataloging in Publication Data also available.

Contents

Series Editor's Introduction

Positivism has been displaced, or so we hope. The program of making everything knowable through the supposedly impersonal norms and procedures of "science" has been radically questioned. The hope of constructing a "grand narrative," either intellectual or political, that will give us the ultimate truth and will lead us to freedom has been shattered in many ways. Reality it seems is a text, subject to multiple interpretations, multiple readings, multiple uses. Accepted paradigms and language games—to borrow from Kuhn and from Wittgenstein—have been relativized and politicized. As the saying goes, all have been "decentered." What does this mean for social research in a "postmodern age"?

There are few words more often used—and abused—in discussions of contemporary culture than "postmodernism." It manifests itself in a multitude of fields from architecture, literature, film and cultural studies in general to philosophy, sociology, and education. It is hard in fact to find an area of study where it has *not* had an impact. In general terms, the form postmodernism takes is that of the self-conscious, self-contradictory, self-undermining statement.[1] It wants to provide a thoroughgoing "denaturalizing" critique, to "de-doxify" our cultural representations and to show their undeniable political importance.[2] All of our discourses (a word used to signify the system of relations between parties engaged in communicative activity and a concept that is, hence, meant to signal the inescapably political contexts in which we speak and work) are "politically uninnocent." They occur within a shifting and dynamic social context in which the existence of multiple sets of power relations are inevitable.[3] Discourse and politics, knowledge and power, are, hence, part of an indissoluble couplet. This has had a profound impact on the growth of critically oriented work in a variety of fields.

In critical educational studies, for instance, the last two decades have witnessed a veritable flowering of research on the relationship between knowledge and power. Beginning with a vague recognition that what was counted as legitimate knowledge (and our research on it) was a social construction,[4] we moved to more economically rooted and structuralist appraisals where the distribution and production of knowledge was seen as dependent on a mode of production.[5] The conceptual, historical, and political weaknesses of this latter position soon became apparent. Progress on understanding the "relative autonomy" of culture and politics led to considerably less economistic and reductive approaches.

At the same time that there was movement away from such base/superstructure models, there was also a challenge to explanations of the relationship between knowledge and power based totally on class dynamics. While not wishing to eliminate the profound import of class relations, it was clear that no account of exploitation and domination that rested its case solely on class could be successful. Gender and race came center stage,[6] as did questions of the very constitution of subjectivity. This movement toward more subtle and inclusive positions can be traced out in my own work, for example: from the culturally oriented but still somewhat functionalist and class based arguments in *Ideology and Curriculum* to the considerably more flexible analysis of the contradictions among and within economy, culture, and politics in *Education and Power* to, finally, the arguments about the constitutive power of gender and race, not only class, in *Teachers and Texts*.[7]

Throughout all of this emerging literature—one that is mirrored in many other fields—there has been a growing tendency to recognize the multiplicity of relations of power. Out of this recognition has come an expanded influence of postmodern theories.

Reactions to postmodernism have of course been more than a little varied. For some, postmodernism is simply a reflection of the cultural logic of late capitalism. For others, it leads only to cynicism and political despair. And for still others, its act of calling into question notions of totality, of certainty, truth and neutral technique, and its focus on how our discourses creates "Others" have radical political potential.[8]

While sensitive to the contradictions in the postmodern project, *Getting Smart* takes many of its arguments, deconstructs and reconstructs them, and employs the results to provide us with a new basis for research and pedagogy in the "human sciences." The book stands between the teleological assumptions of orthodox marxism and the cynicism that characterizes a good deal of postmodernism. It is firmly grounded as well in a feminist appraisal of how power operates. Thus, feminist, neo-marxist, and postmodern theories and practices are blended together here in a unique and insightful manner.

Responding to the critics of postmodernism, Lather writes that postmodernism can give feminism and neo-marxism ways of avoiding both dogmatism and their tendency to reduce everything to a single cause. In this way, they can "produce knowledge from which to act and . . . diffuse power as a means to take advantage of the range of mobile transitory points of resistance inherent in the networks of power relations."

The issue of power is crucial here since one of the book's most pressing questions is "How do our very efforts to liberate perpetuate relations of dominance?" In order to answer that, it must analyze how research and researchers function in relations of unequal power.

Part of Lather's project is evident in the following.

> While the dispersal of authority engendered by the breakdown of positivist hegemony creates liminal space for new ways of doing social inquiry to arise, it also calls into question the role of critical intellectuals concerned with using knowledge and engagement in potent ways. Much has been written about the role of intellectuals in social change . . . . What postmodernism adds to this long-running debate is its focus on how power works via exhibition, observation, classification. To make something available for discussion is to make of it an object. This suspicion of the intellectual who both objectifies and speaks for others inveighs us to develop a kind of self-reflexivity that will enable us to look closely at our own practice in terms of how we contribute to dominance in spite of our liberatory intentions. Within this self-reflexive context, the central question becomes: what would a sociological project look like that was not a technology of regulation and surveillance?

The project becomes simple to say, but not always easy to carry out. Lather shows us a way. We must shift the role of critical intellectuals *from* being universalizing spokespersons to acting as cultural workers whose task is to take away the barriers that prevent people from speaking for themselves.

It is feminism that will enable us to find a way through this maze. In

Lather's terms, even with the varied strands of feminist discourse, at their very center lies an "appeal to the powers of agency and subjectivity as necessary components of socially transformative struggle." Because of this, contemporary feminism can assist us in dealing with "the alleged impotence of the subject in the face of social/political forces and situations." Because feminism has had long experience in self-reflexivity and in making commonsense problematic, it also can provide the basis for the development of practices of self-interrogation and critique.

Using a framework developed out of the integration of feminism, neomarxism, and postmodernism to analyze both praxis oriented critical research and contemporary radical educational theory, Lather helps us answer a significant question. What is an empowering approach to generating knowledge? For her, all critical inquiry is fundamentally dialogic and involves a mutually educative experience. It must respond to the experiences, desires, and needs of oppressed peoples by focusing on their understandings of their situations. Its ultimate goal is to stimulate "a self-sustaining process of critical analysis and enlightened action" at the same time that it is not impositional. Coming close to Paulo Freire, Lather proposes a new, more emancipatory way of validating critical research, what she calls *catalytic validity*. Rather than researcher neutrality, she argues for a more collaborative, praxis oriented and advocacy model that acts on the desire for people to gain self-understanding and self-determination both in research and in their daily lives.

The influence of feminist research and pedagogy is clear here. As Alison Jaggar, for instance, argues the goal should be to make theory, method, and praxis inseparable from each other, especially in their aim to transform women's subordinate positions in our dominant institutions. Combining theory and practice in this way is successful when the "representation of reality" is tested "constantly by its usefulness in helping women transform that reality."[9] Theory, research, practice, and pedagogy—and all overlap with each other—are democratized. The ultimate aim is action on the everyday world by women as subjects and objects of their own experiences. The norms guiding such work involve openendedness, dialogue, explicitness, and reciprocity.[10] And as Lather so cogently puts it, research must be premised on a deep respect for the intellectual and political capacities of the dispossessed. The implications of all this for work not "only" with women but with all people involved in unequal power relations are profound.

In enabling us to think more cogently about the issue of emancipatory research and pedagogy, other questions seem naturally to surface. What does it mean to know? What is science? How does one do "human science" in a postfoundational context? How do we deal with the issue of relativism? How do we understand the person, the subject? On the issue of relativism, *Getting Smart* offers a stinging critique to those who fear that by challenging the status of our accepted notions of science and knowing, we lose the foundations for saying anything. As Lather puts it, "Fears of relativism and its seeming attendant, nihilism or Nietzschean anger, seem to me an implosion of Western, white male, class-privileged arrogance—if we cannot know anything, then we can know nothing." It is her very ability to combine theoretical answers to these questions with political argument that sets Lather's work apart from many others who may have taken the postmodern turn but have forgotten the multiple sets of emancipatory politics for which it must work.

While *Getting Smart* provides an insightful and provocative theoretical account of where we might turn our conceptual energies in research and pedagogy, it does not remain at the level of theory. Lather gives us a self-reflexive account of her own and her students' experiences in a women's studies course when she put these theories into practice. Her analysis of the moments of puzzlement, questioning, and even exhilaration shows us the contradictory dynamics and possibilities at work in building a liberatory pedagogy in existing institutions.

It is evident here that *Getting Smart* recognizes the connections between critical research and liberatory pedagogy. In demonstrating these connections, it illuminates some of the possibilities and problems of creating teachers not as "masters of truth and justice [but] more as creators of space where those involved can act and speak on their own behalf." Just as importantly, it helps us see that this can be done without romanticizing people and their experiences.

Some readers may still have doubts about postmodern theory. After all, the debate about its politics and tendencies is still far from settled. But there can be no doubt that Patti Lather's feminist reworking of it here challenges all of us to reflect on where we stand and what we can do in a society so deeply structured by multiple relations of power.

Michael W. Apple
The University of Wisconsin, Madison

Acknowledgments

For the very material support that makes a book possible, especially release time from teaching, thanks to Ohio State University, the Bush Foundation of Minnesota, Mankato State University, and the New Zealand-United States Educational Foundation and the Universities of Auckland and Waikato for sponsoring a Fulbright which made it possible for me to present these ideas in draft form to New Zealand colleagues. A special thanks to Dean Bill Webster, Mankato State University, who supported this project at a crucial time in its development; to Michael Apple for smoothing the way to publication; to the goddess of word processing with whom all things are possible; to everyone I ever talked with: students, research participants, conference connections, women's studies teachers, progressive cultural workers involved in multi-sited struggles, and my down-to-earth family. I especially appreciate my O.S.U. feminist reading group, PMS (Postmodern Studies), with whose dozen or so members since 1988 I have engaged in practices of "epistemological *jouissance*" (Bordo, 1989:144).

I have functioned as a sieve in these encounters. I have tried to give credit where credit is due. My thanks to all who feed my head and my spirit and make it possible for me to say, in the words of Bruce Springsteen, "I was never much of a cynic, myself" (quoted in Marsh, 1987:208).

Chapter 3 is a revision of papers originally presented at the Sixth Annual Curriculum Theorizing Conference, Dayton, October 1984, sponsored by the *Journal of Curriculum Theorizing* and the University of Dayton, and the annual meeting of the American Educational Research Association, Chicago, March 1985. It was first published in the *Harvard Educational Review,* 56 (3, 1986), 257–277 and reprinted in the 1987 volume of *Evaluation Studies Review Annual,* (Beverly Hills: Sage).

Chapter 4 is a revision of papers presented at the annual meeting of the National Women's Studies Association Conference, Champaign, Illinois, June 1986, the Eighth Annual Curriculum Theorizing Conference, sponsored by the *Journal of Curriculum Theorizing* and the University of Dayton, October 1986, and the annual meeting of the American Educational Research Association Conference, Washington, D.C., April 1987. An earlier version is published in *The Women's Studies International Forum,* 11 (6, 1988), 569–581.

Versions of chapter 5 were presented at the Ninth Annual Curriculum Theorizing Conference, Dayton, October, 1987, sponsored by *The Journal of Curriculum Theorizing* and the University of Dayton, and the annual meeting of the American Educational Research Association, San Francisco, 1988. A later version of it is forthcoming in the Spring, 1991 issue of *Educational Theory*.

Chapter 6 is a revision of a paper originally presented at the Alternative Paradigms for Inquiry Conference, co-sponsored by Indiana University and Phi Delta Kappan, San Francisco, March 25–26, 1989, and included in the published proceedings of that conference, *The Paradigm Dialog: Options for Social Science Inquiry,* Egon Guba, ed. (Beverly Hills: Sage 1990). Sections of early versions were published in *Educational Foundations* and *The Journal of Curriculum Theorizing*. A later version is published in *The Humanistic Psychologist,* special issue on Psychology and Postmodernity, 18 (1, Spring 1990), 64–84.

Preface

> A book, even a fragmentary one, has a center which attracts it: a center which is not fixed but is displaced by the pressure of the book and the circumstances of its composition. Yet it is also a fixed center which, if it is genuine, displaces itself, while remaining the same and becoming always more central, more hidden, more uncertain and more imperious. [S]He who writes the book writes it out of desire and ignorance of this center. The feeling of having touched it can very well be only the illusion of having reached it. (Maurice Blanchot, quoted in Warminsk, 1987:xxvii)

Believing strongly that in our action is our knowing, my central focus in the writing of this book is how research and teaching methods can better challenge the relations of dominance. The book expands on work I have done over the last few years regarding the implications for critical practices of the conjunction of the various feminism*s*, neo-Marxism*s* and poststructuralism*s*[1] which characterize contemporary critical theory. It draws on these three critical discourses[2] in an exploration of the possibilities and limits of oppositional theory and practice regarding approaches to research and teaching. By oppositional, I mean those discourses/practices seeking to challenge the legitimacy of the dominant order and break its hold over social life. As such, this book is the result of my longtime interest in how to turn critical thought into emancipatory action.

The audience I address is the transdisciplinary array of those concerned with the politics of research, teaching and theory building, especially how one develops theory based on the open-endedness of practice and struggle. I write to those who question how such work might be brought to bear on the wider context of challenges to power and authority and serve as a basis for political action. I write particularly to those who ask such questions within the study and practice of emancipatory education.

Such questioning does not take place in some academic vacuum apart from the outside world. Curriculum, research methods, pedagogy: all are much contested cultural terrain. Current directions in American culture are full of contradictory voices. On the one hand, we have those self-designated guardians of orthodoxy who want permanent boundaries and unquestionable canons. All of their perceived enemies—feminists, minoritarians, structuralists, poststructuralists—"in one way or another . . . pose critical challenges to an increasingly embattled elitist, monolithic, and unitary conception" of culture (Scott, 1989: 689).

I read this as *a dinosaur culture* of master narratives struggling to retain dominance against what is perceived as the splintering, disintegrating and fragmenting effects of the partiality and plurality of contesting voices, all of which are presented as threatening chaos/anarchy. The "crisis" these high priests of Western culture perceive is to their continued hegemony over the production and legitimation of knowledge in the name of national heritage and the legacy of Western civilization.

To see culture as neither fixed nor finite but as dynamic, expansive and intrinsically shaped by power and the struggle against it is to occupy a very different position in this "crisis" of authority over what is to count as legitimate knowledge. There are other ways to read the pervasive questioning of established notions and forms of thought occurring across the disciplines. Rather than as "crisis," such questioning of basic assumptions might be seen as an effort to break out of the limitations of increasingly inadequate category systems and toward theory capable of grasping the complexities of people and the cultures they create—theories outside of binary logics of certainty, non-contradiction, totality and linearity.

In the wake of poststructuralism, "intellectual workers" can no longer remain oblivious to what has been brewing for so long, evidencing itself perhaps earliest in quantum mechanics and the ushering in of the reality crisis in physics. We live in both/and worlds full of paradox and uncertainty where close inspection turns unities into multiplicities, clarities into ambiguities, univocal simplicities into polyvocal complexities. As but one example, upon close inspection, "women" become fragmented, multiple, and contradictory both across groups and within individuals (Riley, 1988).

Whether one views the challenge of such complexity as crisis or opportunity depends very much on where one is located in the apparatuses of what Foucault (1980) refers to as "power/knowledge" systems. The various feminisms, Marxisms and minoritarianisms have long argued that to politicize means not to bring politics in where there were none, but to make overt how power permeates the construction and legitimation of knowledges. What the addition of poststructuralism foregrounds in critical theory is the inescapability of how our invested positionality shapes our rhetoric and practice, and that this very much includes the discourse of those of us who embrace the term "oppositional" to describe the work we do in the name of liberatory politics. To complicate issues even more, Lyotard writes "oppositional thinking . . . is out of step with the most vital modes of postmodern knowledge" (quoted in Schrift, 1990:102). Hence, my central movement in the book is a turning away from a focus on dominant power to a focus on oppositional discourses of criticism and resistance (Cocks, 1989), especially as they play out in the arena of empirical inquiry, in a time when truth/falsity oppositions are being displaced altogether.

With all of this in mind, I have three aims for the text that follows: 1) to mark the development of what philosopher of science Brian Fay (1987) terms "a critical social science" in what is more generally referred to as "the postpositivist intellectual climate of our times" (Fiske and Shweder, 1986:16); 2) to contribute to the theory and practice of liberatory education; and 3) to explore the implications of feminism, neo-Marxism and poststructuralism for developing inquiry-approaches in the human sciences[3] that move us toward ways of knowing which interrupt relations of dominance and subordination.

Each of these aims is grounded in the belief that "getting smart" about the conditions of our lives and the means necessary for change requires some "housecleaning" at the site of intellectual work, a belief arising out of my location in the two worlds of women's studies and critical educational theorizing. From this double vantage point, I have become especially intrigued with what happens to the neo-Marxist concept of resistance in trying to understand the shortcomings of theories of political transformation, including first-world feminist theories.

Many have noted the lack of audience for critical theories, theories intended to "enlighten," "empower", "emancipate" people from oppression (e.g., Fay, 1977; Aronowitz, 1981). While the receptiveness to critical theories grows in the academy, "the estrangement of critical theory from its audience" (Cocks, 1989) characterizes its impact on policy and its resonance in the lives of people outside the academy (Wexler, 1987; Lauder and Kahn, 1988; Bromley, 1989; Shapiro, 1989). While feminist thought and practice is the more successful of the critical theories at reaching large numbers of people outside the academy it, too, evokes much resistance.

Resistance to critical theory is multi-sited; understanding it requires much attention to the intersection of "individual consciousness" and social context. Living in these two worlds of women's studies and critical educational theorizing, however, foregrounds for me what Kipnis calls "the absences that constitute first-world radical theory at this juncture" (1988: 154), especially those aspects of critical theorizing over which we as theorizers do have some control. I speak here of those parts of how we do our work that are rooted in a hubris at play in our creation of theory which fails to touch the audience for whom it is intended: the oppressed whose overthrow of "the culture of silence" lies at the root of social transformation (Freire, 1973, 1985).

It is here that critical educational theorizing can learn from feminist praxis. Feminism's grassroots, "no more experts" credo is premised on the sturdy sureness that, given enabling conditions, every woman has something important to say about the disjunctures in her own life and the means necessary for change. Such feminist tendencies against vanguardism problematize the position of those "transformative intellectuals" (Aronowitz and Giroux, 1985) who assume a hegemony over what theory is and themselves as the locus of what can be known and done. But feminist academics themselves suffer from a tendency to do theory "for" instead of "with" people. Lugones and Spelman (1985), in a much noted article on the challenges of Third World women to white academic women, write that the deck is stacked when one group takes it upon itself to develop the theory and then have the "others" criticize it.

Better ways of examining "otherness" and the relationship between "self" and "other" are increasingly central to both feminism and poststructuralism. Additionally, poststructuralism's suspicion of totalizing theories and expert prescriptions seems well-taken as we attempt to generate ways of knowing that can take us beyond ourselves. We have much to learn about why some people move from privatized discontent to struggle toward a more broad based cultural renewal. But efforts "to identify the emancipatory potential in the present" (Flax, 1978) and to generate what Habermas called "catalytic theory" (1971) can never be more than an academic exercise until we face the underlying hubris of much of our intendedly liberatory approaches to research and teaching.

As a first-world woman—white, middle-class, North American, heterosexual[4]—my self-described positionality shifts from "post-Marxist feminist" to "postmodern materialist-feminist".[5] Such hybrid forms of feminism reflect Haraway's observation that, "It has become difficult to name one's feminism by a single adjective" (1985:72). Additionally, I have learned my lesson from the "new French feminisms":[6] that I am a constantly moving subjectivity. This book, then, marks the place from which I presently speak as I wrestle with what it means to do research and teaching in a time noteworthy for broadbased questioning of the foundational assumptions of Western knowledge.

After an introductory chapter which frames the issues, Chapter 2 portrays the challenges provided by the varied feminisms, neo-Marxisms and poststructuralisms both to one another and to approaches to inquiry and teaching that diversify the possibilities of struggle. I then unfold the book in a sequence of chapters that evokes my journey through these three critical discourses as I have sought to both track and contribute to the emergence of more emancipatory ways of generating social knowledge. In Chapter 6, I present the challenges of poststructuralism to what Haraway (1988) terms "knowledge projects we call science." This includes a focus on the charge of "relativism" which is used now to debunk poststructural moves in the sciences, as "lack of objectivity" was used to debunk earlier efforts to do openly politicized empirical work. The final chapter presents an effort toward deconstructivist empirical inquiry where the methodological issues laid out in the preceding parts of the book are brought to bear on my three-year study of student resistance to liberatory curriculum in an introductory women's studies course.

As I write, I face the inescapability of reductionism. Language is delimitation, a strategic limitation of possible meanings. It frames; it brings into focus by that which goes unremarked. While the silences of my own writing are subject to some comment in what follows, I am keenly aware that I write in a time when the formerly unsaid/unheard are becoming increasingly visible and audible. Historical "others" move to the foreground, challenging and reshaping what we know of knowledge. Centers and margins shift (Hooks, 1984). Foucault (1980) speaks of "subjugated knowledges" arising; deconstructionists speak of the "decentering" brought about by the silenced coming to voice. Mexican poet, Octavio Paz, writes, "Now the center or nucleus of world society has disintegrated and everyone, including European and North American—is a peripheral being. We are living on the margin . . . because there is no longer any center . . ." (quoted in Cleveland, 1985:194–195).

Both my desire for and experience of writing this book have been to amplify a discourse already much in the air, to tap into a *Zeitgeist* that is suffusing academic thought and practice, to open myself up so that it can come through me. While this may be overstating the passivity/receptivity in the act of writing which is this book, there has been a sort of "channeling" experience at play here.

As I read across the disciplines, participate in the transformative work of women's studies, and struggle to make sense of the poststructuralist debates ranging across the academy, what Derrida calls "the as yet unnamable" begins to proclaim itself (1978:293). As such, the varied moments in the conjunction of feminism, neo-Marxism and poststructuralism so evident in recent academic discourse feel to me a harbinger of a shift in the ways we think about what we know. While fully acknowledging the amazing capacity of Western culture to absorb oppositional, counter-hegemonic movements (Wexler 1987), we seem somewhere in the midst of a shift away from a view of knowledge as disinterested and toward a conceptualization of knowledge as constructed, contested, incessantly perspectival and polyphonic. It is from the place of such a shift that I write this book.

Finally, while I do not much subscribe to theories of the invisible writer, I believe more that "*in the text only the reader speaks*" (Barthes, quoted in Ulmer, 1985:296, original emphasis). My hope is to create a text open enough, evocative enough on multiple levels, that it will work in ways I cannot even anticipate.

Patti Lather
Hamilton, New Zealand

1
Framing the Issues

> What is really happening, then, is itself a function of frames, which are a kind of fiction. (Hassan, 1987:118)

By way of introduction, let me briefly state the many strands of this book. One is my research into student resistance to liberatory curriculum. As one cannot talk of students learning without talk of teachers teaching, I also look at empowering pedagogy. Another strand of the book is my exploration of what it means to do empirical research in a postpositivist/postmodern era, an era premised on the essential indeterminancy of human experiencing, "the irreducible disparity between the world and the knowledge we might have of it" (White, 1973). A final strand is my desire to write my way to some understanding of the deeply unsettling discourses of postmodernism in a way that doesn't totalize, that doesn't present emergent, multiply-sited, contradictory movements as fixed and monolithic. To write "postmodern" is to simultaneously use and call into question a discourse, to both challenge and inscribe dominant meaning systems in ways that construct our own categories and frameworks as contingent, positioned, partial. My struggle is to find a way of communicating these deconstructive ideas so as to interrupt hegemonic relations and received notions of what our work is to be and to do.

As elaborated in what follows, I continue to share with many academics an ambivalence about the politics of postmodern thought and practice. At present, I align with those attempting to create "a cultural and adversarial postmodernism, a postmodernism of resistance" (Huyssen, 1987:xvi; Foster, 1985). This "critical appropriation of postmodernism" (Hutcheon, 1988b) grows out of the dilemma of those intellectuals who, while committed to emancipatory discourse and modernist strategies (e.g., consciousness-raising), are yet engaged by postmodernism to try to use it in the interests of emancipation.[1] It is this intersection of postmodernism and the politics of emancipation that I put at the center of my attempt to explore what it might mean to generate ways of knowing that can take us beyond ourselves. This chapter provides background for such a project by sketching the basic assumptions which guide my work.

The failure of positivism. My first basic assumption is that a definitive critique of positivism has been established and that our challenge is to pursue the possibilities offered by a postpositivist era. The critique that has amassed over the last 20 years or so regarding the inadequacies of positivist assumptions in the face of human complexity has opened up a sense of possibilities in the human sciences. We live in a period of dramatic shift in our understanding of scientific inquiry, an age which has learned much about the nature of science, its inner workings and its limitations (Kuhn, 1970). Few corners of social inquiry have been impervious to the great ferment over what is seen as appropriate within the boundaries of the human sciences.

Within educational research, while positivism retains its hegemony over practice, its long-lost theoretic hegemony has been disrupted and displaced by a newly hegemonic discourse of paradigm shifts. Interpretive and, increasingly, critical "paradigms"[2] are posited and articulated (Bredo and Feinberg, 1982; Carr and Kemmis, 1986; Popkewitz, 1984). Unsettlement and contestation permeate discussion of what it means to do educational inquiry. Some talk of crisis (e.g., Phillips, 1987); others talk of a dissemination of legitimacy and an openness to "an experimental moment in the human sciences" (Marcus and Fischer, 1986).

The value-ladenness of inquiry. My second assumption is that ways of knowing are inherently culture-bound and perspectival. Built upon Gramsci's (1971) thesis that ideology is the medium through which consciousness and meaningfulness operate in everyday life, and Allthusser's (1971) focus on the materiality of ideology, I conceptualize ideology as the stories a culture tells itself about itself. Within post-Athusserean Marxism or cultural Marxism, ideology is viewed as something people *inhabit* in very daily, material ways and which speaks to both progressive and determinant aspects of culture (Apple, 1982; Wexler, 1982; Giroux, 1983). Such a stance provides the grounds for both an "openly ideological" approach to critical inquiry (Lather, 1986b) and the necessity of self-reflexivity, of growing awareness of how researcher values permeate inquiry.

Harding (1986) distinguishes between "coercive values—racism, classism, sexism—that deteriorate objectivity" and "participatory values—antiracism, anticlassism, antisexism—that decrease distortions and mystifications in our culture's explanations and understandings" (p. 249). This second assumption, then, argues that change-enhancing, advocacy approaches to inquiry based on what Bernstein (1983:128) terms "enabling" versus "blinding" prejudices on the part of the researcher have much to offer as we begin to grasp the possibilities of the postpositivist era. As we come to see how knowledge production and legitimation are historically situated and structurally located, "scholarship that makes its biases part of its argument arises as a new contender for legitimacy."[3]

The possibilities of critical social science. A third assumption that guides my work concerns the possibilities for a critical social science (Fay, 1987). Within the context of the Frankfurt School of critical theory, *critical* reason was used as the interlocutor of *instrumental* reason, the driving force behind modernism. What Van Maanen (1988) calls "critical tales" ask questions of power, economy, history and exploitation. In the words of Poster (1989), "critical theory springs from an assumption that we live amid a world of pain, that much can be done to alleviate that pain, and that theory has a crucial role to play in that process" (p. 3). The various feminism*s*, neo-Marxism*s* and some of the poststructuralism*s*, then, become kinds of critical theories which are informed by identification with and interest in oppositional social movements. While in practice not unknown to have *instrumental* moments, critical theories are positioned in relation to counter-hegemonic social movements and take as their charge " 'the self-clarification of the struggles and wishes of the age' " (Marx, quoted in Fraser, 1987:31). As critical practices derive their forms and meanings in relation to their changing historical conditions, "a position of resistance can never be established once and for all, but must be perpetually refashioned and renewed to address adequately those shifting conditions and circumstances that are its ground" (Solomon-Godeau, 1988:204).[4]

The politics of empowerment. My fourth assumption is that an emancipatory, critical social science must be premised upon the development of research approaches which empower those involved to change as well as understand the world. My usage of empowerment opposes the reduction of the term as it is used in the current fashion of individual self-assertion, upward mobility and the psychological experience of feeling powerful.[5] Drawing on Gramsci's (1971) ideas of counter-hegemony, I use empowerment to mean analyzing ideas about the causes of powerlessness, recognizing systemic oppressive forces, and acting both individually and collectively to change the conditions of our lives (Bookman and Morgan, 1988; Shapiro, 1989). It is important to note that, in such a view, empowerment is a process one undertakes for oneself; it is not something done "to" or "for" someone: "The heart of the idea of empowerment involves people coming into a sense of their own power, a new relationship with their own contexts" (Fox, 1988:2).

This raises many questions about vanguard politics and the limits of consciousness-raising. The historical role of self-conscious human agency and the efforts of intellectuals to inspire change toward more equitable social arrangements are precisely the aspects of liberatory politics most problematized by postmodernism (Cocks, 1989). Derrida (1982), for example, deconstructs "enlighten" as a light-based metaphor or heliocentric view of knowledge which positions the emancipators as "senders" and the emancipated as passive "receivers" of rays. These problems are at the center of this book which is written from within but against the grain of the emancipatory tradition given its foregrounding of the questions raised about that tradition by postmodernism.

The challenges of postmodernism. Hence, the central assumption undergirding this work is that postmodernism profoundly challenges the politics of emancipation sketched out in the preceding basic assumptions. In terms of definition, throughout the book I sometimes use *postmodern* to mean the larger cultural shifts of a post-industrial, post-colonial era and *poststructural* to mean the working out of those shifts within the arenas of academic theory. I also, however, use the terms interchangeably. This conflation of postmodern with poststructural is not popular with some cultural critics (e.g., Grossberg, 1988b:171), but another, in the same edited collection, divides postmodernism into "neoconservative postmodernism" and "poststructural postmodernism" (Foster, 1988:251). Hall (1985) adds the term "discourse theory" to the confusion and describes it as follows:

> The general term, "discourse theory," refers to a number of related, recent, theoretical developments in linguistics and semiotics, and psychoanalytic theory, which followed the "break" made by structuralist theory in the 1970s, with the work of Barthes and Althusser. Some examples in Britain would be recent work on film and discourse in *Screen,* critical and theoretical writing influenced by Lacan and Foucault, and

> post-Derridean deconstructionism. In the U.S., many of these trends would now be referred to under the title of "post-modernism." (p. 113)

Any effort at definition domesticates, analytically fixes, and mobilizes pro and contra positions. Lattas (1989) suggests that a way to diffuse this is to get rid of the progressivist idea of history encoded in the "post" of postmodernism (p. 92). As a conjunction of debates and circulating ideas, postmodernism is not positioned as a "successor regime." Both/and and neither/nor the disease and the cure of modernist excesses and failures, postmodernism is "the horizon of our contemporaneity" (Arac, 1988:vii). Rather than a progressive development, it is movements which "cross each other and give rise to something else, some *other* site" (Derrida, quoted in Kearney, 1984:122), a conjunction of often contradictory ideas and practices which has come to be coded with the name "postmodern."

Spanos (1987) advises that remarks *toward* a definition be used to displace the desire to comprehend, to "clearly understand." In that spirit, I offer Fraser's and Nicholson's (1988) definition which draws on Lyotard's (1984) identification of modernism with "grand narratives":

> The postmodern condition is one in which "grand narratives" of legitimation are no longer credible. By "grand narratives" Lyotard means . . . overarching philosophies of history like the Enlightenment story of the gradual but steady progress of reason and freedom, Hegel's dialectic of the Spirit coming to know itself, and, most importantly, Marx's drama of the forward march of human productive capacities via class conflict culminating in proletarian revolution. (p. 86)

What is foregrounded in this definition is the postmodern break with totalizing, universalizing "metanarratives" and the humanist view of the subject that undergirds them. Humanism posits the subject as an autonomous individual capable of full consciousness and endowed with a stable "self" constituted by a set of static characteristics such as sex, class, race, sexual orientation. Such a subject has been at the heart of the Enlightenment project of progress via education, reflexive rationality, and human agency (Bowers, 1987; Peller, 1987). Such a subject has been de-centered, refashioned as a site of disarray and conflict inscribed by multiple contestatory discourses. "Grand narratives" are displaced by "the contingent, messy, boundless, infinitely particular, and endlessly still to be explained" (Murdoch, quoted in Spanos, 1987:240). In Lyotard's (1984) already classic definition, postmodernism is "that which, in the modern, puts forward the unpresentable in presentation itself; that which denies itself the solace of good forms . . . that which searches for new presentations, not in order to enjoy them, but in order to impart a stronger sense of the unpresentable" (p. 81).

Hence, contemporary intellectuals work within a time Foucault argues is noteworthy for its disturbing of the formerly secure foundations of our knowledge and understanding. Foundational views of knowledge are increasingly under attack (Bernstein, 1983; Smith, 1984; Sheridan, 1980; Gergen, 1985; Haraway, 1985, 1988; Harding, 1986). It is the end of the quest for a "God's Eye" perspective (Smith and Heshusius, 1986) and the confrontation of what Bernstein calls "the Cartesian Anxiety" (1983), the lust for absolutes, for certainty in our ways of knowing. It is a time of demystification, of critical discourses which disrupt "the smooth passage of 'regimes of truth' " (Foucault, quoted in Smart, 1983:135), "not to substitute an alternative and more secure foundation, but to produce an awareness of the complexity, contingency and fragility of historical forms and events" (Smart, 1983:76).

In this context of ferment, educational inquiry is increasingly viewed as no more outside the power/knowledge nexus than any other human enterprise. Lincoln and Guba have a chapter in their *Naturalistic Inquiry* (1985) entitled, "Is Being Value-Free Valuable?" The pages of the *Educational Researcher* increasingly pay attention to issues of subjectivity (Peshkin, 1988) and the politics of method (Eisner, 1988). Postmodernism implodes the concepts of "disinterested knowledge" and the referential, innocent notions of language that continue to haunt the efforts of educational inquiry to move away from positivism and to loosen the grip of psychologism on its theories and practices. As such, educational research is another site where postmodernism exacerbates an already felt erosion of basic assumptions.

The following chart[6] brings all of this definitional work together and presents an image of positionality regarding the project that I have been involved with over the last few years concerning the methodological implications of the various critical theories. This chart is grounded in Habermas' (1971) thesis of the three categories of human interest that underscore knowledge claims: prediction, understanding, emancipation. It assumes postpositivism, the loss of positivism's theoretic hegemony in the face of the sustained and trenchant criticisms of its basic assump-

Postpositivist Inquiry

Predict	Understand	Emancipate	Deconstruct
positivism	interpretive	critical	poststructural
	naturalistic	neo-Marxist	postmodern
	constructivist	feminist	post-paradigmatic diaspora
	phenomenological	praxis-oriented	
	hermeneutic	educative	
		Freirian participatory action research	

tions. I have added the non-Habermasian column of "deconstruct."[7] Each of the three postpositivist "paradigms" offers a different approach to generating and legitimating knowledge; each is a contender for allegiance. I place my work in the emancipatory column with great fascination with the implications of deconstruction for the research and teaching that I do in the name of liberation.

The chapters which follow will go into greater detail regarding the above chart; what is of note here is the plethora of terms used to describe postpositivist work. Whether heard as cacophany or polyphony, such profusion attests to the loosening of the grip of positivism on theory and practice in the human sciences. An explosion has transformed the landscape of what we do in the name of social inquiry. This explosion goes by many names: phenomenological, hermeneutic, naturalistic, critical, feminist, neo-Marxist, constructivist. And now, of course, we have the proliferation of "post-conditions," including "post-paradigmatic diaspora" (Caputo, 1987:262) which undercuts the very concept of paradigm itself. All of these terms question the basic assumptions of what it means to do science. Each contributes to a transdisciplinary disarray regarding standards and canons. This proliferation of contending approaches to inquiry is causing some diffusion of legitimacy and authority.

Within this unprecedented cross-disciplinary fertilization of ideas which opens up possibilities, it is not easy to sort out the seduction of "the glamor of high theory" (JanMohamed and Lloyd, 1987:7) from what is useful for those of us concerned with what it means to do research and teaching in an unjust world. Wexler (1987), for example, warns of "a kind of discursive status consumerism and academic fashion consciousness" (p. 5) that is anything but anticipatory in form of a new politics of society. While such concerns about usefulness are central to what follows, it is my primary thesis that this time of foundational uncertainty is an opening for we who do our research and teaching in the name of liberation to make generative advances in the ways we conceptualize our purposes and practices.

The remainder of this introduction will explore the way I use language/ the way language uses me and then address three questions at the heart of this book: Why praxis? Why research? Why pedagogy? It concludes with an outline of the chapters that follow.

Language and power: marking a place from which to speak

> this is the oppressor's language
> yet I need it to talk to you. (Rich, 1975)

> . . . by "fixing" the world conceptually, language at once frees thought to think and permits it to think in only one of an infinite number of logically possible ways. (Cocks, 1989:29)

Language is the terrain where differently privileged discourses struggle via confrontation and/or displacement. Like all discursive politics, this book is positioned in the language/power nexus. To position my own discourse is to mark a place from which to speak.

As I look at what I have written here, that position seems much more reflective than interruptive of conventional norms of academic writing. For example, Van Maanen (1988) calls for "readerly texts" which foreground "the reference-and-footnote games" (p. 26) we play via our use and abuse of "metatheory tuned to the intellectual fashions of the day" and the "authority by association and authority by theory" (p. 68) that we create in our texts. While I make some effort to take Van Maanen's call into account, I expect this book will not be perceived as especially "readerly" by those outside of postmodern discourse.[8]

As such, postmodernism is easily dismissed as the latest example of theoreticism, the divorce of theory and practice. This tendency is compounded by the desire of those who write in these areas to want to "interrupt" academic norms by writing inside of another logic, a logic that displaces expectations of linearity, clear authorial voice, and closure. Luce Irigaray, for example, a key player in the new French feminisms, writes: "How to master those devilries, those moving phantoms of the unconscious, when a long history has taught you to seek out and desire only clarity, the clear perception of (fixed) ideas?" (1985:136). Additionally, Morris (1988) rails against "the pressure of the same old calls for plain-speaking, common sense, hard facts, immediate practicality . . . the tendency to say that things are too urgent now for serious people to be bothered with idle speculation, wild theorizing and lunatic prose" (p. 186). What Morris calls "the blackmail to urgency" describe/inscribes this tendency to insist that poststructuralism make clear its practicality before it has barely begun to develop (p. 180). Things are too urgent to give up our probing of "the mystery of correspondences between discourse and the world" and "the teasing flight of the object" (p. 191) Morris writes, as she points out Lyotard's paradoxical observation that postmodernism is the master narrative of the end of master narratives.

If what we are about here is a fundamental turning point in social thought, an epochal shift marked by thinking differently about how we think (Flax, 1987), the following advice from Lacan is well taken. For anyone beginning to play with what all of this might mean for our interventions in the world, Lacan cautions, ". . . to read does not obligate one to understand. First it is necessary to read . . . avoid understanding too quickly" (quoted in Ulmer, 1985:196).

Within postmodern textual practice, "the fiction of the creating subject gives way to frank quotation, excerpation, accumulation and repetition of already existing images" (Hutcheon, 1988a:11). For example, to re-photograph photographs of other works of art is to create a textual practice which undermines notions of originality, authenticity and presence (Solomon-Godeau, 1988). This de-centering of the author via *intertextuality* is a demonstration of how the author is inevitably inscribed in discourses created by others, preceded and surrounded by other texts, some of which are evoked, some not. In my own writing, the accumulation of quotes, excerpts and repetitions is also an effort to be "multi-voiced," to weave varied speaking voices together as opposed to putting forth a singular "authoritative" voice.[9] "The homage of quotation is capable of strengthening not self-effacement but rather a strengthening or consolidating resolve," Rosler writes in regard to the extensive and often eclectic quotation, a tissue of quotations, that characterizes postmodern writing (quoted in Hutcheon, 1989:106).

The deconstructive text is a point of interrogation where binary notions of "clarity" are displaced as the speaking voice uses its authority to disperse authority. It positions itself as other to a call for a "plain-speaking" voice of reason which assumes that accurate information and clear messages will bring about desired behavioral change (Treichler, 1989). The deconstructive voice especially asks what roles a reader might play other than that of being "convinced" of the author's right to serve as "The Great Interpreter" (Dreyfus and Rabinow, 1983) or "the master of truth and justice" (Foucault, 1977:12). The postmodern text is *evocative* as opposed to didactic; extended argument is displaced by what Barbara Johnson (1987) refers to as "a much messier form of bricolage [oblique collage of juxtapositions] that moves back and forth from positions that remain skeptical of each other though perhaps not always skeptical enough" (p. 4). Pastiche, montage, collage, bricolage and the deliberate conglomerizing of purposes characterize postmodern art and architectural styles.

Forms such as cyclic fragmentarity work against authorial imposition of a monolithic direction of meaning and purposefully operate at the very limits of intelligibility. In writing of Irigaray, Grosz (1989) notes how "[h]er writings perform what they announce" by "resonat[ing] with ambiguities that proliferate rather than diminish meanings" (pp. 101–102). Derrida (1984) writes of "the text [that] produces a language of its own, in itself, which while continuing to work through tradition emerges at a given moment as a *monster,* a monstrous mutation without tradition or normative precedent" (p. 123). One example is the provocative use of typographic spacing, textual upheaval and intersecting surfaces of Sollers' "explicitly heterogeneous and discontinuous text: quotations, parentheses, dashes, cuts, figures, and Chinese characters" (Johnson, 1981:xxix).

Given such an articulation of postmodern textual practice, this text that I have created feels more traditional than not, no radical departure from the tradition that it interrogates As but one example, it clearly does not break with a profusion of references and footnotes in its creation of textual authority. I have, however, attended to what Derrida (1978) speaks of as "writing under erasure." What this means to me is that to write "postmodern" is to write paradoxically aware of one's complicity in that which one critiques. Such a movement of reflexivity and historicity at once inscribes and subverts. Provisionality and undecidability, partisanship and overt politics, replace poses of objectivity and disinterestedness (Hutcheon, 1989:74). Additionally, while I in many ways inscribe the conventional and provoke conditioned responses, I attempt, via making explicit my authorial agendas, to subvert those responses by foregrounding how they were induced. Finally, the text I have created also "performs what it announces" in the use of introductory quotes for which the reader "must come back to the text again and again; [s]he must brood on it. . . ." (Bannett, 1989:9). Such a self-conscious use of difficult and indeterminant passages "prevents the reader from consuming them at a gulp and throwing them away" and, instead, demands the active participation of readers in the construction of meaning (ibid.:8).

My strategy for such a textual practice in this book is to trace my journey through the discourses of feminism, neo-Marxism and poststructuralism in an effort to understand what these sometimes complementary, sometimes contestatory critical practices have to contribute to more emancipatory ways of generating social knowledge. In doing so, I take Ebert's (1988) words to heart: "If one is always situated in ideology, then the only way to demystify these ideological operations . . . is to occupy the interstices of contesting ideologies or to seek the disjunctures and opposing relations created within a single ideology by its own contradictions" (p. 27). Located at the conjunction of the feminisms, neo-Marxisms and poststructuralisms, my interest is in the processes by which theories and practices of meaning-making shape cultural life, specifically how research and pedagogy might be positioned as fruitful sites in which to pursue the question of a postmodern praxis.

Why praxis?

> For us the intellectual theorist . . . has ceased to be a subject, a representing and representative consciousness . . . there is no longer any representation, there is only action, theory's action, the action of practice in the relationship of networks. (Deleuze, quoted in Kritzman, 1988:xii)

The question of praxis is at the heart of "getting smart." According to *A Dictionary of Marxist Thought* (Bottomore, 1983), praxis is the self-creative activity through which we make the world; it is, in my favorite part of the exegesis, *the* central concept of a philosophy that did not want to remain a philosophy, philosophy becoming practical (p. 386). The requirements of praxis are theory both relevant to the world and nurtured by actions in it, and an action component in its own theorizing process that grows out of practical political grounding (Buker, forthcoming).

Postmodernism, however, raises questions that press at our efforts toward transformative praxis. Many talk in terms of the failure of emancipatory objectives, not the least being the failure of critical research to impact on policy (Gitlin et al., 1988; Lauder and Kahn, 1988). Neo-Marxists and feminists speak of the need for both better explanations and better strategies (Fay, 1977; Aronowitz, 1981; Weedon, 1987; Hartsock, 1987). In this search for praxis, the varied emancipatory projects are destabilized from a variety of directions: feminists skeptical of Marxism, Marxists skeptical of identity politics focused on race, gender or sexual orientation, poststructural suspicion of all who claim to be on the outside of regimes of truth. Regardless of these philosophical debates, "The question ultimately is *What is to be done?*" (Deleuze, 1988:30, original emphasis). The question of action, however, remains largely under-addressed within postmodern discourse. As Caputo (1987) so clearly frames the issue: "We are faced with the problem of not only what we can know but also of what we are to do" (p. 236).

For those committed to using the present to construct that which works against the relations of dominance, interventions in the arenas of research and pedagogy can illuminate the intersection of postmodernism and the emancipatory projects. In Ulmer's (1985) hopeful words: "Theoretical fictions organized into a pedagogy that would collapse the distinctions separating teaching, research, and art might also have the power to guide transformation of the lived, social world" (p. 27). The juxtaposition of Ulmer's "theoretic fictions" and the concept of praxis, perhaps *the* central category of Marxist thought (Bottomore, 1983:384), foregrounds the ways cultural Marxism and postmodernism both parallel and interrupt one another, a topic to be elaborated upon in the following chapter. Suffice it to say here that to speak of theoretic *fictions* organized into a pedagogy that can effect social change is to salvage praxis in a way that denies both teleological Marxism and a postmodernism of cynicism (Sloterdijk, 1987).

To salvage praxis is an interruptor strategy, an intervention of "willful contradiction" that, while not teleological, is unabashedly committed to both the open-endedness of the struggle over truth and reality, and the transcendence of the "postenlightenment schizocynicism" (Huyssen, 1987:ix) assumed by many to be inherent in non-foundational, post-metaphysical philosophy. Such refusal of the totality of the radical negation of the Enlightenment aims to salvage the discourse of emancipation. This reconfiguration uses strategies of displacement rather than strategies of confrontation in order to multiply the levels of knowing and doing upon which resistance can act (Spivak, quoted in Harasym, 1988).

Strategies of displacement are grounded in deconstruction, "not a method," according to Derrida, but a disclosure of how a text functions as desire (1984:124). Rather than an exposure of error, deconstruction is "a way of thinking . . . about the danger of what is powerful and useful. . . . You deconstructively critique something which is so useful to you that you cannot speak another way" (Spivak, 1989b:135,151). While impossible to freeze conceptually, deconstruction can be broken down into three steps: 1) identify the binaries, the oppositions that structure an argument; 2) reverse/displace the dependent term from its negative position to a place that locates it as the very condition of the positive term; and 3) create a more fluid and less coercive conceptual organization of terms which transcends a binary logic by simultaneously being both and neither of the binary terms (Grosz, 1989:xv).[10] The goal of deconstruction is neither unitary wholeness nor dialectical resolution.[11] The goal is to keep things in process, to disrupt, to keep the system in play, to set up procedures to continuously demystify the realities we create, to fight the tendency for our categories to congeal (Caputo, 1987:236).[12] Deconstruction foregrounds the lack of innocence in any discourse by looking at the textual staging of knowledge, the constitutive effects of our uses of language. As the postmodern equivalent of the dialectic, deconstruction provides a corrective moment, a safeguard against dogmatism, a continual displacement.

As noted by Spivak (Harasym, 1988), such a strategy cannot ground a politics. The courage to think and to act within an uncertain framework, then, emerges as the hallmark of liberatory praxis in a time marked by the dissolution of authoritative foundations of knowledge. Additionally, the "interpretive praxis" (Atkins and Johnson, 1985:2) that is deconstruction includes the development of a Foucauldian awareness of the oppressive role of ostensibly liberatory forms of discourse. Strategically, reflexive practice is privileged as the site where we can learn how to turn critical thought into emancipatory action. This entails a reflexivity where we learn to attend to the politics of what we do and do not do at a practical level, to learn, in Nancy Hartsock's (1987) words, "to 'read out' the epistemologies in our various practices" (p. 206).

Postmodernism demands radical reflection on our interpretive frames. Rajchman (1985) terms self-reflexivity "the new canon" as we enter the "post-enlightenment culture" where the myths of universality, progress and the autonomy of science are debunked. Uncovering the particularity and contingency of our knowledge and practices is at the core of whatever generative advances we might make regarding our purposes and practices.

Why research?

This is a both exciting and dizzying time in which to do social inquiry. Given the postmodern foregrounding of the ways we create our worlds via language, for perhaps the first time, the complex question of political commitment and its relation to scholarly inquiry can be seriously addressed. While the concept of advocacy research remains as oxymoron to the many who take scholarly objectivity as both a possible and desirable goal in the human sciences, the mantle of objectivity which largely shielded the sciences from such questions has been irreparably rent. Contemporary history and philosophy of science, sociology of knowledge, and movement in science itself, all have combined to impress upon us the interdependence of method, theory and values (Mishler, 1984:14).

An enormous counterpoint has arisen to positivist hegemony. While the purpose of method traditionally has been to provide some standards of logic and evidence, the controls of logic and empirical validation are weakening (Harding, 1982; Nelson et al., 1987). A variety of incompatible directions are available in the culture of science, all competing for allegiance. Within this array of alternative ways of knowing, focus has shifted from "are the data biased?" to "whose interests are served by the bias?" Neo-Marxism and feminism, for example, have had an uneven but nonetheless remarkable impact on stretching the parameters of post-positivist inquiry. Questions of how to do "good" openly value-based inquiry can be seriously entertained, a discourse unheard of outside marginalized circles such as feminist and Freirean participatory research until very recently (Reason and Rowan, 1981; Mies, 1984; Lather, 1986b).

While the dispersal of authority engendered by the breakdown of positivist hegemony creates liminal space for new ways of doing social inquiry to arise, it also calls into question the role of critical intellectuals concerned with using knowledge and engagement in potent ways. Much has been written about the role of intellectuals in social change (e.g., Aronowitz and Giroux, 1985; Gramsci, 1971; Foucault, 1977). What postmodernism adds to this long-running debate is its focus on how power works via exhibition, observation, classification. To make something available for discussion is to make of it an object (Haug, 1987). This suspicion of the intellectual who both objectifies and speaks for others inveighs us to develop a kind of self-reflexivity that will enable us to look closely at our own practice in terms of how we contribute to dominance in spite of our liberatory intentions. Within this self-reflexive context, the central question becomes: What would a sociological project look like that was not a technology of regulation and surveillance?

Why pedagogy?

Like Spivak (1989b), I position pedagogy as a fruitful site for learning about strategies of a postmodern praxis. In the interests of accessible language, I had given thought to replacing the word pedagogy with the word teaching in the title of this book until I read David Lusted's 1986 article in *Screen* entitled, "Why Pedagogy?" Lusted defines pedagogy as addressing "the transformation of consciousness that takes place in the intersection of three agencies—the teacher, the learner and the knowledge they together produce" (p. 3). According to Lusted's definition, pedagogy refuses to instrumentalize these relations, diminish their interactivity or value one over another. It, furthermore, denies the teacher as neutral transmitter, the student as passive, and knowledge as immutable material to impart. Instead, the concept of pedagogy focuses attention on the conditions and means through which knowledge is produced.

Arguing for the centrality of the issue of pedagogy to both cultural production and the popularization of critical analyses, Lusted sees the disattention, the "desperately undertheorized" (p. 3) nature of pedagogy as at the root of the failure of emancipatory objectives. While he cites Stuart Hall and Michael Young, Lusted appears unfamiliar with the American literature on radical pedagogy, a small but vibrant literature in both feminism (e.g., Culley and Portuges, 1985; Bunch and Pollack, 1983; Shrewsbury, 1987) and neo-Marxism (Giroux, 1983; Shor, 1980; Freire, 1985). Nevertheless, Lusted brings to the center stage of cultural studies the interactive productivity as opposed to merely transmissive nature of what happens in the pedagogical act.

While liberatory pedagogies have argued many of the same points, they have not clearly enough seen themselves as one of many conflicting voices in a context of semiotic bombardment. Additionally, tied to their version of truth and interpreting resistance as "false consciousness," too often such pedagogies fail to probe the degree to which "empowerment" becomes something done "by" liberated pedagogues "to" or "for" the as-yet-unliberated, the "other," the object upon which is directed the "emancipatory" actions (Ellsworth, 1989). It is precisely this question that postmodernism frames: How do our very efforts to liberate perpetuate the relations of dominance?

Chapter overviews

The remainder of this book explores how we can position ourselves in the interstices and disjunctions of the varied critical theories in order to expand our understanding of what it means to do change-oriented research and teaching.

Chapter 2, "Postmodernism and the Discourses of Emancipation: Precedents, Parallels and Interruptions," surveys the challenges offered to the production and legitimation of knowledge by the various critical theories. It focuses especially on the challenges of postmodernism to the discourses of emancipation. Additionally, I begin to probe how postmodernism might serve as a point of interrogation for educational theory and practice.

Chapter 3, "Research as Praxis," explores the methodological implications of critical theory by focusing on the developing area of emancipatory research. The concept of "research as praxis" is defined and examined in the context of social science research. The primary objective of this chapter is to help researchers develop a democraticized process of inquiry characterized by negotiation, reciprocity, empowerment—research as praxis.

Chapter 4, "Feminist Perspectives on Empowering Research Methodologies," outlines feminist efforts to create empowering and self-reflexive research designs. Three questions are addressed: What does it mean to do feminist research? What can be learned about research as praxis and practices of self-reflexivity from looking at feminist efforts to create empowering research designs? What are the implications of poststructuralist thought and practice for feminist empirical work? I explore this last question by attempting a self-reflexive critique of my research into student resistance to liberatory curriculum in an introductory women's studies course.

Chapter 5, "Deconstructing/ Deconstructive Inquiry: The Politics of Knowing and Being Known," traces the parameters of deconstructive inquiry by looking closely at examples of empirical work which take the deconstructive impulse into account. After another effort to map the boundaries of the postmodern moment, three problems in deconstructivist inquiry are raised: description and interpretation, the textual staging of knowledge, and the social relations of the research act. Multiple exemplars of deconstructivist empirical practice are then presented as concrete illustrations of these points. The chapter concludes with an attempt to sketch the parameters of deconstructive inquiry.

Chapter 6, "Reinscribing Otherwise: Postmodernism and the Human Sciences," interrogates the values underlying the cultural practices we construct in the name of the human sciences. After playing with the definition of "science," I present three possible framings of the human sciences. Each of the three framings is looked at regarding method, ideology, relationship between researcher and researched, and the attitude toward language. I then wrestle with two key issues in the project of reinscribing science: the issue of relativism, and the continued lack of an adequate poststructuralist theory of the subject. Both are surveyed by looking more closely at the varied moves in feminist receptions of postmodernism.

Finally, Chapter 7, "Staying Dumb? Student Resistance to Liberatory Curriculum," illustrates what a deconstructivist feminist practice might look like within the context of researching liberatory teaching. Beginning to probe the implications of postmodernism for pedagogy, this chapter deconstructs my three-year empirical study of student resistance to liberatory curriculum in order to illustrate how poststructuralist debates are restructuring approaches to knowledge production and legitimation across the disciplines. By addressing a series of methodological questions raised by poststructuralism, I use the data amassed in this study to explore the parameters of what might be called deconstructivist empirical work. In such work, questions of interpretive strategy, narrative authority and critical perspective go far toward blurring the lines between "the humanities" and "the social sciences."

Conclusion

This book is positioned somewhere in the midst of what Habermas (1975) refers to as a "legitimation crisis" of established traditions in intellectual thought. The orthodox consensus has been displaced; post-positivist philosophies of science focus more and more on the interpretive turn, the linguistic turn in social theory. Social science is increasingly polarized as the political content of theories and methodologies becomes apparent. On the one hand, a sense of experimentation and breaking barriers pervades.[13]

On the other hand, well represented by D. C. Phillips (1987), self-termed "closet Popperian/Hempelian" (p. 111), are those who warn that the post-Kuhnian ship of science has run aground on the shoals of relativism (p. 22).[14] In his recent book, Phillips asks, do "the apparent demise of positivism" (p. 80) and "the new philosophy of science run rampant" lead to "the end of social science as it is currently known? (p. 82). While I suspect that my arguments may be seen by Phillips as one of the "startling flights of fancy" (p. 80) occasioned by the postpositivist era, the answer I put forward in this book is, "It already has."

2

Postmodernism and the Discourses of Emancipation: Precedents, Parallels and Interruptions

> Journals, conferences, galleries and coffeehouses are spilling over with talk about postmodernism. What is this thing, where does it come from, and what is at stake? (Gitlin, *New York Times Book Review,* Nov. 6, 1988:1)

In essence, this book is an exploration of the links between knowledge and power. The refusal to separate knowledge from power may well be apotheosized in the French poststructural philosopher, Michael Foucault. But Foucault's focus on the power/knowledge nexus has precedents, parallels and interruptions in work that ranges across that of sociologists of knowledge to the more overtly politicized work of feminists, neo-Marxists and the increasing number of those committed to what Spanos calls "a forwarding, a postmodern critical practice" (1987:12). I bring these three critical discourses together to focus on my primary concern: the possibilities and limits of liberatory theory and practice regarding approaches to research and pedagogy. Within this project, I frame the varied critical discourses as differing practices and impulses that both weave together and interrupt one another rather than as fixed, contrasting positions.

This chapter provides background for such a project by exploring the intersection of postmodernism and the discourses of emancipation. I begin, once more, with definitions, a slippery business given the post-modern tenet that any effort at definition is not so much *description* as *inscription,* marking with words that impress investments of privilege and struggle. As Calinescu writes, "There is not one but many possible theories of modernism and postmodernism, defined by the strategic objectives of those who articulate them" (1987:305–306). I end this chapter on the politics of postmodernism by probing its implications for efforts in education to develop emancipatory thought and practice.

As some effort to unmask authorial agendas in what follows, I foreground the textual strategy upon which I have settled. My desire is to construct a non-agonistic narrative which proceeds otherwise than by thinking via oppositions (de Lauretis, 1989). Using Gitlin's questions that preface the chapter, I weave a position of "surveying" the movements of poststructuralism across the fields of Marxism, feminism and emancipatory education with the subtext of my intense personal engagement with the issues. This engagement positions me such that "I have been writing for and of my life" (Richardson, forthcoming:20). Trying to absorb, reflect upon and codify the rapid changes that characterize contemporary cultural theory raises many issues in regard to doing critical and oppositional work. Given the postmodern tenet of how we are inscribed in that which we struggle against, how can I intervene in the production of knowledge at particular sites in ways that work out of the blood and spirit of our lives, rather than out of the consumerism of ideas that can pass for a life of the mind in academic theory? Given the ways the text works against itself, how can I communicate my always-in-process ideas and practices in order to expand a sense of the possibilities of oppositional cultural work? As a feminist attempting to incorporate the work of the fathers and take it where they cannot go, how much should I be about the business of "feeding feminism to the fathers?" (Snitow, 1989:14). In posing these questions, I take heart from Martin Luther King's caution regarding paralysis of analysis. In an era of rampant reflexivity, just getting on with it may be the most radical action one can make.

What is this thing?

> Empires in retreat get into some pretty weird stuff (David Byrne, *Guardian,* Nov. 19, 1986:20).

The term "postmodern" first gained widespread currency in the United States in architectural criticism (Klotz, 1988). It is now widely used as a periodizing concept and as a descriptor for both a cultural aesthetic and a philosophical movement (Jameson, 1984). More properly pluralized in order to encompass the varied positions termed "postmodern," postmodernism*s* are responses across the disciplines to the contemporary crisis of representation, the profound uncertainty about what constitutes an adequate depiction of social "reality." Philosophically speaking, the essence of the postmodern argument is that the dualisms which continue to dominate Western thought are inadequate for understanding a world of multiple causes and effects interacting in complex and non-linear ways, all of which are rooted in a limitless array of historical and cultural specificities.

Historically speaking, the argument is that the technologies of communication profoundly shape human experience. Just as the printing press of the sixteenth century transformed the human landscape, so in the twentieth century the complex multi-directionality and simultaneity of the electronic media constitute a different kind of subject in a different kind of social mileau. To quote from historian Mark Poster, in his essay on Foucault:

> The electronic means of communication explode the space-time limits of messages, permit the surveillance of messages and actions, complete the process of the automation of production, despatialize certain kinds of work, enable signifiers to float in relation to referents, become a substitute for certain forms of social relations, provide a new relation between author and text, expand infinitely human memory, and undermine the Cartesian ontology of subject and object. In these ways "reality" is constituted in the "unreal" dimension of the media. In this domain, there are no longer pure acts, only linguistically transformed representations, which are "acts" themselves. (1987–88:121)

Poster concludes by stating that those committed to the project of emancipation must take into account both the information explosion which is the ground of postmodernism, and the resultant interactive complexity, shifting-centered, and multi-sited constructedness of our selves and our worlds.

As an historical moment, there is also no small debate as to whether postmodernism is the latest stage of the Enlightenment or whether it is, in fact, a rupture with that era and the beginning of a new age.[1] Sloterdijk, for example, sees postmodernism as the latest incarnation of the demythologization of the world of metaphysical consciousness and universal concepts, a demoralization, a "twilight state" necessary for realization of the Enlightenment project of transformation through rational consciousness (1987:82). I find this the least interesting aspect of the postmodern debates. The question of periodization, however, does surface the issue of how the various emancipatory projects intersect with postmodernism, a topic receiving much attention in cultural theory these days.[2] Whether the Enlightenment project of human emancipation via reason is to be abandoned or re-visioned is precisely the question. I will illustrate this intersection by exploring the concepts of "post-Marxism" and "post-feminism."

Post-Marxism?

> The Enlightenment is dead, Marxism is dead, the working class movement is dead . . . and the author does not feel very well either. (Smith, quoted in Harvey, 1989:325)

> In those halcyon days I believed that the source of enigma was stupidity. Then the other evening . . . I decided that the most terrible enigmas are those that mask themselves as madness. But now I have come to believe that the whole world is an enigma, a harmless enigma that is made terrible by our own mad attempt to interpret it as though it had an underlying truth. (Eco, 1989:95)

The points of departure for an interrogation of Marxism are many. In such questioning, it is important to position Marxism as a heterogeneous and conflictual movement, what Bennington calls "that shifting and unstable consensus called 'Marxism' " (1987:18) where there are "almost as many marxisms as there are marxists" (Smart, quoting Bobbio, 1983:4). Such a non-totalizing view of Marxism avoids becoming mired in fixed positioning and stabilizing meaning in ways that obscure the continual contestation that so characterizes twentieth-century Marxist thought.

In rethinking what Marxism might mean within a postmodern context, it is also important to not position it as the "demonic other" of postmodernism. Given Marxism's status as the "master discourse of the left" (Patton, 1983:53) and the principle intellectual resource for movements of social and political emancipation (Benton, 1984), it is the primary object of the postmodern questioning of Enlightenment thought and practices. But much of postmodernism is an implicit if not explicit dialogue with Marx (Ashley, forthcoming). French post-Marxism, for example, can only be understood in relation to the dominance of Marxism in French intellectual life (Grosz, 1989).

In French social theory, shortly before and after World War II, mechanistic (scientific) and humanistic (phenomenological and existential) Marxism fought for supremacy over the terrain of radical politics. Both were displaced in the 1960s by Althusser's antihumanist and antireductionist structuralist Marxism which challenged the phenomenological vision of the subject as the master of meaning and source of knowledge. Cutting across the disciplines as a formal method of systemic analysis for uncovering underlying, non-observable relations between empirical elements, structuralism assumed precise rules and conventions. It displaced consciousness with language and choice with the production and reproduction of social subjects and formations. It increased attention on the concrete material practices which produce ideology, culture and subjectivity in the relations of dominance and resistance.

The political and social upheavals of 1968 created a disillusionment with established left orthodoxies, especially the communist party as the vanguard of change. "A politics of spontaneity and specificity" emerged in France (Grosz, 1989:17), a non-hierarchical uprising against all of the "experts" who proposed to speak for or on behalf of others. Truth, objectivity and certainty were displaced by a focus on "regimes of truth," deconstruction of the binary, linear logics of Western rationality, and a foregrounding of ambiguity, openness and contingency. This movement eventually came to be characterized with the terms "postmodern" in the United States and "poststructural" more globally.

The "crisis of Marxism" is nothing new. The Frankfurt School responded to an earlier version with an internal critique of its fundamental categories. Feminist theory has long been suspicious of Marxism's category systems and vanguard politics. Long-noted problems include the failure of actually existing socialisms, inadequate concepts of base/superstructure, power/politics, and the relation between structure, action and consciousness as well as the epistemological issue of the scientific status of Marxism (Smart, 1983:5).

Poststructuralism positions Marxism as a movement of controlling, labelling, and classifying which denies its complicity and investment in dichotomy at the expense of the Other. Transforming difference into dichotomous oppositions, it reduces multiplicities and plurality into a single oppositional norm. Hence, the crisis of Marxism is not only of effectivity, organization and popular appeal but of theory in terms of claims to truth, will to knowledge, and the primacy of reason (Campioni and Grosz, 1983:121). Overly cognitive in its conception of the dynamics of subordination and emancipation, ensnared in phallocentric and logocentric assumptions, it relegates practice to an object of theory, history to a teleology where each age is a stepping stone for the next, agency and structure to dualistic categories, and strategy to the masculinist myth of "the One Big Revolution" (Patton, 1983:57). Campioni and Grosz speak of such theoretical closures as invested with a desire for power: "Why is it necessary to unify/solidify what may be fluid, diverse and changing, if not in order to block and control it? Diverse, changeable, strategic knowledges pose a potential threat that must be minimized—that of the incapacity of theory, of *any* theory to capture reality in its entirety or in its essence" (1983:127).

Is Marxism too reluctant to accept dispersion and fragmentation to be useful? Is its ideal of a global, totalizing prospect of emancipation, some new historical bloc, some new counter-hegemonic alliance, some new archimedean standpoint too intrinsic to be done away with and still have Marxism? Is it too irredeemably structuralist, too tied to a premise that adequate knowledge grasps underlying structures and totalities of reality, a reality and a reason conceptualized as amenable to such understanding? At what point does the constant revision of the explanatory and predictive claims of classical Marxism exhaust it, creating a situation where Marxism no longer speaks to contemporary times? What is at issue here is "[t]he presumed ability of marxism to indefinitely extend itself beyond the parameters of its original paradigm," (Campioni and Grosz, 1983:118) as opposed to Harvey's (1989) position that Marxism is as useful now as it has ever been in understanding the conditions of our lives.

What is the Marxism that comes after structuralism? A Marxism beyond scientism which no longer occludes its own discursivity and textuality? A Marxism beyond origin, what Spivak calls "the lurking reductionist last instance" (in Bennington, 1987:41); a Marxism beyond the telos so unsettled by Derrida's "the always already"? To abandon or renew, that is the question raised by the postmodern crisis of representation in regard to Marxism.

The crisis of representation is an erosion of confidence in prevailing concepts of knowledge and truth. Whatever "the real" is, it is discursive. Rather than dismissing "the real," postmodernism foregrounds how discourses shape our experience of "the real" in its proposal that the way we speak and write reflects the structures of power in our society. In post-representational theory, language is a productive, constitutive force as opposed to a transparent reflection of some reality capturable through conceptual adequation. To move from establishing the "real" to how what we see is constituted by our very pursuit of it is to move into *a post-Marxist space*[3] where claims to totality and certainty, claims central to Marxist explanatory systems, are severely undercut. Within such a space, all of the varied forms of Marxism, neo-Marxisms included, are marked as "a patriarchal discourse of 'mastery/transparency/rationalism,' a master code issuing from a transcendental point of view" (Kipnis, 1988:161).

Inglis writes "the moment of Marxism is past, its revolutionary possibilities dissolved into a different order" (1988:13). Unworkable constructs like "false consciousness" (Hall, 1985), the absence of what Haraway calls "the fetishized perfect subject of oppositional history," including the essentialized "Third World woman" of much feminist discourse (1988:586), inquiries into language and meaning and the consequent problematizing of the lust for totalities, universals, certainties—all have "uncouple[d] Marxism from necessity" (Inglis, 1988:245).

Fekete defines a "post-Marxist" impulse as "wish[ing] to do more and other than reversal/displacement, it wishes to make a difference" (1987:xiv). Such an interventionary impulse propels oppositional intellectuals who, while recognizing the contingency and historicity of values, nevertheless, take a stand, act, assess, "self-consciously situating themselves at vulnerable conjunctional nodes of ongoing disciplinary discourses where each of them posits nothing less than new objects of knowledge, new praxis of . . . activity, new theoretical models that upset or at the very least radically alter the prevailing paradigmatic norms" (Said, 1986:226).

In this post-Marxist space, the binaries that structure liberatory struggle implode[4] from "us versus them" and "liberation" versus "oppression" to a multi-centered discourse with differential access to power. Here, nothing is innocent. As Foucault (1980) makes clear, overtly oppositional work, while at war with the dominant systems of knowledge production, is also inscribed in what it hopes to transform. Patton, for example, writes of "The Academicisation of marxism" which seems tied to its "divorce from oppositional political struggles" (1983:48). He sees the renewal of Marxism as accompanied by its dispersal. Given its pretension to unify the field of oppositional politics, "the difference crisis" challenges its very status as the center of leftist discursive practices. What Campioni and Grosz (1983:140) point out as the claim to difference as a strategy of defense against a levelling process decenters the call to unity upon which Marxist practice is based.

It is my argument that this decentering is post-Marxism, a decentering that is not anti-Marxist but a repositioning of Marxism as one among many, a no longer dominant discourse of opposition. Such a relational view of post-Marxism takes into account Smart's (1983) argument that Marxism is not so much dead as limited within a context so changed from Marx's day that it needs to be supplemented with other modes of analysis. It also heeds Foucault's prophecy that, "It is clear, even if one admits that Marx will disappear for now, that he will reappear one day" (Kritzman, 1988:45).

Post-feminism?

> For as long as the sexes are socially distinguished, "women" will be nominated in their apartness, so that sexual division will always be liable to conflation with some fundamental ontological sexual difference. So feminism, the reaction to this state of affairs, cannot be merely transitional, and a true post-feminism can never arrive. (Riley, 1988:111)

Regarding "post-feminism," Nancy Cott points out that the term was used as early as 1919 by a Greenwich Village female literary group: "We're interested in people now—not men and women" (1987:282). The term has been much picked up by the popular media and even academic discourse in such books as *Woman, Native, Other: Writing Postcoloniality and Feminism,* by Trinh T. Minh-ha (1989), advertised as the "first full-length study of Post-Feminism." What is one to make of such a concept? In exploring this question, I will especially remark on how postmodernism re-situates the relationship between feminism and Marxism, a relationship much commented upon since Hartmann's (1981) classic essay, "The Unhappy Marriage of Marxism and Feminism."

Kroker and Cook state: "*Feminism is the quantum physics of postmodernism*" (1986:22, original emphasis). Quantum physics opened up another world, a world otherwise than Newtonian linearity, subject-object duality and universal covering laws. Hence, I read the metaphor of quantum physics as a movement of displacement rather than origination. Feminism displaces the articulation of postmodernism from the site of the fathers and opens up the possibility of a heteroglot[5] articulation premised on multiplicities and particularities. Full of contestatory and contradictory theories and practices "while still producing solidarity and concerted action" (Smith, 1988:155), feminism is, at this particular historical juncture in North American culture, "the paradigmatic political discourse of postmodernism" (Kipnis, 1988:60). I will construct three framings of feminism to advance such a claim.

First, of the three critical discourses under study here, feminism is the site where the theory/practice nexus is being most creatively interrogated. Reiss (1988), for example, argues that while the discourse of feminism has been deeply embedded in popular practice which seeks to transform the world and where its own development and self-criticisms were responsive to that practice, Marxism has moved into theoreticism, the divorce of theory and practice. Contrary to the overarching concern on the part of the varied strands of Marxism with theoretical refinement, it has been the demands of political practice that have fueled the development of feminist theory to explain gender-based oppression (Fraser and Nicholson, 1988).

The production of grand social theories, which by definition attempt to speak for *all* women, was disrupted by the political pressures put upon such theorizing by those left out of it—poor and working-class women, women of color, lesbians, differently-abled women, fat women, older women. For example, the work of women of color documents resistance to the universalizing tendencies of feminist theorizing, resistance that grew out of desire not for better theory but for survival (e.g., Lorde, 1984; Smith, 1983; Hooks, 1984; Moraga and Anzaldua, 1983; Lugones and Spellman, 1983; Lugones, 1987). In sum, the tendencies toward practice-based theorizing in American feminism interrupt theoreticism in ways that efforts toward a postmodern praxis cannot afford to ignore.

Secondly, contemporary feminism is the cultural site most effectively disruptive of the alleged impotence of the subject in the face of social/political forces and situations. While the varied strands of feminism can be categorized in many ways,[6] all feminisms appeal to the powers of agency and subjectivity as necessary components of socially transformative struggle. It is feminist discourse that has raised the most questions about the fractured, fragmented subject postulated by poststructural discourse. Fox-Genovese, for example, writes: "Surely it is no coincidence that the Western white male elite proclaimed the death of the subject at precisely the moment at which it might have had to share that status with the women and peoples of other races and classes who were beginning to challenge its supremacy" (quoted in Yudice, 1988:233; see also, Hartsock, 1987).

Such a refusal to go along with the "death of the subject" grows out of the feminist dilemma of accounting for the specificity of gender without reifying one particular definition of femaleness, without falling into an essentialist discourse on gender. Hence, feminism has, for some time now, been wrestling with the question of difference. Especially lesbians and Third World women pushed feminism away from the assumption that there is a generalizable female experience (and, of course, generalizable "lesbians" and "Third World women"). Such women well knew the experience of being positioned in the midst of multiple and contradictory discourses. For example, rising out of "the paralyzing position of being the spoken" (Gwin, 1988:23), women of color have confronted white women "with what black women have learned as a result of their experience in this country, that the noun 'Woman' cannot stand alone. All people, female or male, belong to one racial group or another. In other words, neither gender nor racial categories are pure ones; instead they are always interactive" (Christian, 1988:36).

The move in feminist theories away from essentialism and toward a *constructed* subject is evoked in Alice Walker's 1977 essay on going to Cuba. Exemplifying Alcoff's point that, "One does not have to be influenced by French post-structuralism to disagree with essentialism" (Acoff, 1987:413), Walker anticipates many aspects of what will come to be known as postmodern theory and textual practice. In the form of pastiche or collage of fragments of multiple voices and mixed genres that "is neither definitive nor complete" (p. 203), she comes "face to face with my own prejudice. . . . My own perverted categorization" (pp. 211, 212). The salience of race is relational, she decides, as she watches Cuban children and then, later, the distress of a woman "because we black North Americans want to claim her as one of us, exclusively, whereas she has been brought up to believe she belongs to the world" (p. 219). Walker's essay well illustrates the material grounding of the outsider discourses of feminism from which most often come breaks with hegemonic meaning systems: "Her oppression and that of her people have opened them to an unfixity delimited by the unboundedness of struggle" (Yudice, 1988:229).

While the subject of contemporary feminism is not single, unified or static, neither is she utterly determined. Positioned as both the Other of patriarchy and the construction of feminism's internally heterogeneous discourses about identity, subjectivity and agency, she is theorized in ways that offer hope for sustained contestation and resistance (Smith, 1988). Transcending both biological essentialism and the linguistic determinism of the dispersed, fragmented poststructural subject, she moves between several positions "in which the necessity of adopting a position in a given situation . . . include[s] simultaneously calling it into question" (Rabine, 1988:27).

This brings me to a third possible framing in my unpacking of what it might mean for feminism to function as the quantum physics of postmodernism. Feminism's long-standing tendencies toward self-reflexivity provide some experience of both rendering problematic and provisional our most firmly held assumptions and, nevertheless, acting in the world, taking a stand. Women's simultaneous experiences of positions of both privilege and marginality is the material ground for the development of practices of self-interrogation and critique. Let us return, for example, to the concept of essentialism.

Just when the theoretical tide turns away from essentialized categories, Spivak urges that we "take the risk of essence in order to increase the substantive efficacy of feminist resistance" (quoted in Smith, 1988:148). Grounded in the needs of feminist politics to make a difference by forging the identity "Women," such a contradictory doubled strategy both assumes and then immediately problematizes its subject positions. Riley (1988), for example, calls into question the cultural centrality of gendered subjectivity, noting the unevenness of its saliency and the problems in its articulation, while, simultaneously, striving for a brief foothold, a place from which to act. Deconstructing feminist usage of its central term, "women," Riley advises "foxiness" and "versatility" in negotiating between awareness of the indeterminancy of the terms of "women" and a strategic willingness to speak

> "as if they existed"—since the world behaves as if they unambiguously did. . . . Sometimes it will be a soundly explosive tactic to deny it, in the face of some thoughtless depiction, that there *are* any "women." But at other times, the entrenchment of sexed thought may be too deep for this strategy to be understood and effective. So feminism must be agile enough to say, "Now we will be 'women'—but now we will be persons, not these 'women.' " And, in practice, what sounds like a rigid opposition—between a philosophical correctness about the indeterminacy of the terms, and a strategic willingness to clap one's feminist hand over one's theoretical mouth and just get on with "women" where necessary—will loosen. (pp. 112–114)

The ground for such a doubled movement is knowing what West terms "a reality *that one cannot not know*" if you have been positioned as the Other (interview with Stephanson, 1988:277, original emphasis). Feminism becomes, then, not a veering between the passive, dispersed subject of deconstruction on the one hand, and, on the other hand, the transcendent subject of most emancipatory discourse, but "the site of the systematic fighting-out of that instability" (Riley, 1988:5).

The topic of essentialism is given yet another "spin" in an early issue of *differences*. In that journal, Spivak (1989b) problematizes her earlier problematizing of anti-essentialism with her urging to "take the risk of essence." Suspicious of the way such advice has been picked up and celebrated "in a personalist, academic culture" (p. 128), she characterizes "all the noise about anti-essentialism" (p. 132) as "not doing one's homework" (p. 133) regarding "the necessity of essentialism and how careful we must be about it" (p. 134). Using the concept of essence to illustrate the ways in which deconstruction critiques that which is so useful that you cannot think without it, "what one learns from deconstruction is the importance of essences, how useful they are" (p. 150) as Spivak moves "sort of soldiering on in my own way to bring anti-essentialist metaphysics to crisis" (p. 151). As Fuss (1989) warns, work which "rashly jettisons" (p. 79) essentialism takes away an interventionary strategy of the oppressed who can use it in an Irigarayian move "to undo by overdoing" (p. 86), a "displacement and *redeployment* of essentialism" which thinks through the body (p. 80, original emphasis). Such movement demonstrates what Spivak terms "this endless wave of my thinking" (1989b:151), a characteristic of feminist theorizing which uses deconstructive strategies to avoid both dogmatism and the construction of winners and losers in "the feminist theory contest" (de Lauretis, 1989:7).

Like Hutcheon (1989), I argue that feminism has pushed post structuralism in directions it might otherwise not have gone in terms of political engagement. In doing so, I have tried to heed de Lauretis' caution regarding the dangers of positioning poststructuralism as the theory and feminism as "just a practice" (1989:10). While both feminist and Marxist thought share aspirations to be theories in the service of a politics, my argument for foregrounding feminist thought and practice in the inscribing of postmodernism displaces both the concept of post-feminism and the hegemony of Marxism over left discourse/practices. This is not to conflate feminism and postmodernism, given the politics of the one and the irredeemable political ambivalence of the other. Nor is it a move to do away with Marxism. It is, rather, to position Marxism, feminism and poststructuralism as "persistent interruptions of each other" (Spivak, 1987:249) in the struggle to do cultural change work in a post-foundational context.

Where does it come from?

The postmodern questioning of totalizing, universalizing theory is situated within a post-imperialist world where colonial "others" have emerged as subjects in their own right. Postmodernism is positioned within the loss of a confident and secure national mood brought on by a deflation of Enlightenment beliefs under the cumulative pressure of historical events such as the atomic bomb, the Holocaust, and the war in Vietnam. Spivak sees its rise as a "response to the problem of practice in the discourse of the human sciences" (1987:284). Merck (1987) credits its ascendence to a cross-fertilization of Althusserean Marxism, semiotics, Lacanian psychoanalysis and feminism. Finally, Frederic Jameson argues that postmodernism must be confronted "as a historical situation rather than as something one morally deplores or simply celebrates" (Stephanson, 1987:37). Jameson sees postmodernism as a mediating concept, a new cultural logic based on lives experienced as "synchronic multiplicities" and "existential bewilderment" (ibid.:33) at our inability to position ourselves and understand this world of multinational hyperspace and Baudrillardian simulacra.[7]

What follows will foreground two dimensions of the material ground of postmodernism: "post-Fordism" (as in post-*Henry* Ford; see Gramsci, 1971) and the "ex-centrics," a Lacanian term appropriated by Hutcheon (1988a) to characterize the uprising of the marginalized.

Post-Fordism

The explanatory and strategic incapacities of orthodox Marxism propelled Althusser's break with economism; Althusser's structuralism helped focus the attention of social theorists on ideology and culture. This reversal of orthodox Marxist theories of base/superstructure causality often positions culture as the new dominant. The postmodern focus on language exacerbates this denial of political-economic processes that become ever more global and powerful. The concept of post-Fordism attempts to address this valorization of language and the cultural. I draw largely from Harvey (1989) in this summary.[8]

Post-Fordism is a "new regime of accumulation" characterized by the pursuit of the consumption dollars of the rich, a shift from Fordist assembly line production models to flexible accumulation, including geographical dispersal to zones of easier labor control and a consequent new international division of labor. Notable characteristics include mergers, intensified rates of innovation, imploding centralization (e.g., 2% of publishing companies control 75% of books published in the U.S. [Harvey, 1989:160]), paper entrepreneurism, and a de-centering of corporate, state and personal financing with the increased autonomy of banks and financial systems where finance capital is increasingly autonomous from production and the nation state. All of this results in trouble for the welfare state and the social wage, forms of neo-imperialism, areas of conflict between nation-states and transnational capital given the internationalization of money power, benefits to the "already privileged": in essence a major transition in capitalism's dominant regime of accumulation. The mechanisms that have evolved for controlling the crisis tendencies of capitalism have been overwhelmed since the early 1970s due to the oil crisis plus the shift into transnationalism via the computerization of the big stock markets. The cash nexus and the logic of capital circulation expand. Capitalist social relations widen and deepen. The crisis tendencies of capitalism are rescheduled into the twenty-first century. "Fictitious capital" and asset inflation grow more hegemonic.

Such developments in the workings of capitalist expansion both undergird the "postmodern turn" (Hassan, 1987) and form the backdrop for forms of cultural struggle that hope to make a difference. To think outside the binaries of materialism/idealism is to find a place of both/ and and neither/nor. Whatever that means, it does not mean positioning culture as the sole locus for expansion and struggle. While "[t]he word is now as 'material as the world' " (Hall, 1988:28), this does not mean disregarding the growing global maldistribution of power and resources.

The Ex-centrics

It has been the ex-centrics who laid the groundwork for the present focus on the politics inherent in any act of interpretation. As Said points out, it is "the formidable difficulties of empire" (1989:225) that are at the root of the crisis of representation and the consequent paradoxes of producing and legitimating knowledge in a post-foundational context. To challenge canons, to expose systems of power which authorize some representations while blocking others—this has been part of the self-proclaimed task of the uprising of the marginalized, the silenced, the ex-centrics. Both cause and effect of the loss of patriarchal/colonial authority, the formerly silenced have come to voice. What Hartsock calls "the diverse and disorderly Others beginning to speak and beginning to chip away at the social and political power of the Theorizer" (1987:195) create a plurality of sites from which the world is spoken. While by no means monolithic, either within or across categories of marginalization, the voices of women, men of color, the economically oppressed, post-colonials, lesbians and gays, all create a powerful and no longer ignorable conjunction of critical voices in social theory. In the human sciences, the result is a displacement of an objective scientific reason by a consciously political and social reason. To quote from a report on the 1988 conference of the American Anthropological Association: "If we agree that there are no neutral observers, . . . if we agree that we all take sides, the question is, then, how far do you go in taking sides? . . . [T]he more we acknowledge our political positions, the freer we are to take a stand and become an advocate, the more we confront some very difficult ideas" (*The Chronicle of Higher Education,* Nov. 30, 1988:A8).

The marginalized discourses of the ex-centrics exposed the perspectivity and partiality of "official" accounts and problematized "imperial" categories in ways that resonated experientially and illuminated culturally. Out of "concrete experiences of exclusion" (Bordo, 1989:138), the ex-centrics cleared a semiotic space by challenging disciplines at the level of the basic categories and methods involved in the possibilities for knowledge.

This is not to say that the ex-centrics are the origins of postmodernism. Spanos disrupts the debate about origins by arguing that "the impulse informing the postmodern occasion is not fundamentally a chronological event in a developing plot but rather an inherent mode of human understanding that has become prominent in the present (de-centered) historical conjuncture" (1987:194). Spanos redirects attention away from a contest for originary position and toward what appears to be an important cultural formation emerging across disciplines and theoretical affiliations. Rather than arguing about who "invented" postmodern discourse, he argues us to view it as a situation where, speaking in different voices about different concerns, this conjunction arises out of an interplay of a multiplicity of factors and forces. Rather than a grab on the part of white, male academics to appropriate the insights of feminism, for example, he argues for postmodernism as an emerging coherency fed by a variety of currents which are sometimes overlapping, sometimes quite distinct. Factors that cut across these distinctions are a suspicion of generality and authoritarian insight into "reality," coupled with an attunement to interpretive multiplicity, indeterminacy and heterogeneity of cultural meaning and meaning production (Bordo, 1989).

Spanos terms this a situation where "equiprimordial" sites are "competing for authority to interpret the contemporary historical conjuncture they have collectively unsurped from the metaphysical discourse of humanism" (1987:247). Wherever one situates oneself, whether at the site of language, economics, culture, politics, race or gender, etc., one is "always already"[9] addressing other aspects of a moving field. While each of these sites of cultural theorizing has as tendency to see itself as the determining ground, Spanos argues, instead, for a framework which implodes base/superstructure models in its positing of multiply-sited, shifting, interactive forces and impulses (ibid.:249).

From this anti-originary position, it is interesting to look at the theoretical and strategical centrality given to the politics of gender in the work of some male postmodernists. Stephen Heath, for example, writes, "Any discourse which fails to take account of the problem of sexual difference in its own enunciation and address will be, within a patriarchal order, precisely indifferent, a reflection of male dominance" (1978–79:53). Additionally, feminism is seen by many male theorists of the postmodern as a central site of resistance to capitalism (Ryan, 1982; Culler, 1982; Owens, 1983; Arac, 1986). Scholes (1989) goes even further in positioning feminism as "the angel in the house of critical theory" (Fuss, 1989:80) which needs to be rescued from the mastering impulses of deconstruction: "In its handsome deconstructive sheepskin, isn't this the same old wolf after all?" (p. 101).

de Lauretis (1987), on the other hand, argues that, while feminism and poststructuralism have worked on a common nexus of problems, the feminist contributions are frequently marginalized. Like de Lauretis, Newton asks, "Why has feminist theory been so hard to see, especially for men and even for those in sympathy with feminist politics?" (1988:94). She goes on to note that, given the invisibility of feminism's theoretical labors, what happens is that "feminist scholars and theorists read each other and male theorists, while 'they' do not by and large read 'us.' 'We' have two jobs, and 'they' have one" (p. 106). Morris also discusses "the basic *exclusion* of women's work from a highly invested field of intellectual and political endeavor" (1988:15), even though feminism is, she argues, one of the enabling conditions of postmodern discourse (see, also, Jardine and Smith, 1987; Huyssen, 1987).

While postmodernism remains dominated by Eurocentric male discourses, the various feminisms and post-colonialisms increasingly wrestle with how to live in the postmodern world that they have helped create.[10] Rather than a contest over origins, the struggle is praxiological: the issue is not so much where postmodernism comes from, but what it will be. For example, *Feminism/Postmodernism,* a collection of essays edited by Nicholson (1990) asks the following questions. "Is postmodernism a theory whose time has come for men but not for women?" (p. 6). Can "the category of gender survive the postmodern critique"? (p. 8). "Are coherent theory and politics possible within a postmodern position?" (p. 9). The following section broaches these questions.

What is at stake?

> Unless there is this understanding, there will be divisiveness in the radical camp. Crisis management in the global economy

> will, in fact, act according to these productive interruptions, and we, on the other side, like stupid fools will take the interruptions as divisive positions so we are at each other's throats. . . . [We must not forget] that we can pull together even if we bring each other to crisis . . . [because] any really "loving" political practice must fall a prey to its own critique. (Spivak, interviewed in Harasym, 1988:68)

Current debates over the meaning and value of postmodernism flood the academic journals. A growing number of academics embrace "the postmodern turn" (Hassan, 1987). These academics range from feminists (Weedon, 1987) to neo-Marxist (Laclau and Mouffe, 1985) to "critical pragmatists" (Cherryholmes, 1988). Witnessing and participating in this engagement, I wonder about the seduction of postmodernism. Does it let us imagine anew what a radical politics might be? For example, might a more generous critical cultural politics emerge from the recognition of our own collusion with what we contest (Morris, 1988)? Is it a theoretical movement which will enable us, "finally, to escape the patriarchal paradigms of Western thought?" (Moi, 1988:5) Or is it more logocentrism,[11] more class privileged, Eurocentric, white male discourse, "the last ruse of the patriarchal university trying for power to fix the meaning, and contain the damage, of its own decline" (Morris, 1988:15)?

To what extent is this seeming rush to postmodernism in academic circles a case of "fiddling while Rome burns"?[12] It is important, I think, to frame oppositional intellectual work against the backdrop of what goes unasked and undone in order to wrestle with these arguably escapist, elitist academic concerns with theoretical refinement.[13] Does postmodernism provide greater power to generate more effective explanation and strategy, or is it more theoreticism, more construction of theory unmoored in any specific cultural practice which could serve to ground that process dialectically and/or deconstructively?

There is cause for pause in all of this. Regardless of where one positions oneself, postmodernism raises compelling questions regarding emancipatory efforts. For example, the politics of liberation are questioned as such central categories in identity politics as race, class, gender, and sexual orientation are seen as "constantly being produced anew within different and competing discourses . . . more fluid and drifting than had previously been assumed" by reproduction theorists (Haug,

1987:17). Such undercutting of foundational Enlightenment tenets causes many intellectuals with emancipatory concerns to question the politics of postmodernism.

Yet while many advances have been made, the fault lines in European Enlightenment rationality grow increasingly evident. On the one hand, many of us are more able than ever before to act as agents, to produce rather than reflect meanings. While we are born into the "always already," we negotiate more outcomes, produce ourselves out of a range of possibilities, position ourselves as "constantly moving subjectivities." On the other hand, the Enlightenment project of emancipation via reason has been marked by degeneration into social engineering and rationalist planning (Aronowitz, 1981; Sholle, 1988). What Foucault (1980) calls "the technologies of normalization" result in an increase of homogenizing surveillance, regulation and programming. The revolution as predicted by Marx is a long time coming and, as witnessed by the fall of the Berlin Wall, comes about in most unexpected ways.[14] Much critical social theory seems short on both explanatory and practical levels. All of this combines into what Bernstein terms "a rage against humanism and the Enlightenment legacy" (1985:25), a post-Enlightenment frame of mind which has come to be coded with the term "postmodern."

In his diatribe against the contemporary American academy, Allan Bloom (1987) writes amazedly of what he calls, "the Nietzscheanization of the Left." In Bloom's view, deconstruction is "the last, predictable stage in the suppression of reason and the denial of the possibility of truth in the name of philosophy" (p. 379). Bloom reports, furthermore, that in spite of its burgeoning American trendiness, postmodernism is already passe in Paris. Bloom is not alone in framing postmodernism as the "opiate of the intelligentsia" (Dowling, 1984:85).[15]

Surveying the reception of postmodernism in the academy, there are those who warn that postmodernism fosters nihilism, relativism and political irresponsibility (Habermas, 1987; Macdonell, 1986; Dews, 1987). Many fear that it is especially dangerous for the marginalized (Hartsock, 1987; Alcoff, 1987; Christian, 1987; West, 1987). Such a position urges caution that, at best, the deconstructive dismantling of Enlightenment myths such as a self-correcting science, the transcendental, humanist subject and the assumption of a teleological progress has both emancipatory and reactionary effects (McLaren, 1988). The debunking of foundational grounding, especially anything other than local, contingent theory, the insistence upon a fragmented, de-centered self, and the retreat from teleology via historical progress and human agency—these may be useful strategies "for the inheritor of the voice of the transcendental ego" (Hartsock, 1987:201), but they pose dangers for any appropriation of postmodernism on the part of the marginalized.

No few see postmodern theory as an outcome of capitalist decline and decadence, a new form of abstract, disengaged radical chic, of "nouveau smart" (Storr, 1987) theoreticism which marks the " 'betrayal of the intellectuals' " (Scott, quoted in Peller, 1987:30). Some few are unambiguously celebratory. Deleuze, for example, writes "It is as if, finally, something new were emerging in the wake of Marx" (1988:30). Many, myself included, remain ambivalent, attracted to some parts of postmodern thought and practice, repelled by others (Morris, 1988; Grossberg, 1988a,b; McLaren, 1988; Giroux, 1988).

Hutcheon recommends this ambivalence as a way "to interrogate the limits and powers of postmodern discourse" (1988b:8). Johnson (1987) and Spivak (1987) recommend moving back and forth among the various contestatory discourses of neo-Marxisms, feminisms, "minoritarianisms," and poststructuralisms in order to interrupt one another.[16] Aligning with this position, I have found especially helpful Foucault's (1984) essay, "What is Enlightenment?"

Grounded in Kant's 200-year-earlier analysis of the same question, Foucault distinguishes between both the Enlightenment and humanism and between archaeological and transcendental arguments. Salvaging the emancipatory project by displacing the universal, the necessary, the obligatory with the singular, the contingent, and the strategic, Foucault argues for "an attitude, an ethos, a philosophical life in which the critique of what we are is at one and the same time the historical analysis of the limits that are imposed on us and an experiment with the possibility of going beyond them" (p. 50).

"[T]his work done at the limits of ourselves" (p. 46) shifts the focus from a search for formal structures and universal values to how we are constituted as subjects of our own knowledge. This work done at the intersection of knowledge, power and ethics is neither "for" nor "against" the Enlightenment. It is, rather, against that which presents itself as finished and authoritarian, and for that which is "indispensable for the constitution of ourselves as autonomous subjects" (p. 43)—a permanent critique of ourselves, "always in the position of beginning again" (p. 47).

Those seeking to appropriate poststructuralism in the name of liberatory politics urge that we use the postmodern moment of the growing uncertainty within Western thought to think more about how we think (Flax, 1987:624). As such, postmodernism might be construed as a form of academic consciousness-raising that can lead to a more accurate self-understanding of the ambiguity of our position as "engaged intellectuals" (Rajchman, 1985) concerned with using our knowledge and engagement in potent ways.

Ashley writes: "I believe that the burgeoning interest in 'postmodernism' is a symptom of the anxieties contemporary elites are now experiencing with regard to the possible failure or collapse of those hegemonic modes of representation that have served them so well. As far as non-elites are concerned, there is both good and bad in this development" (forthcoming, b:1). What is "the good and the bad" in terms of the appropriation of postmodernism on the part of the marginalized?

In terms of the positive things that the ongoing construction of postmodernism offers to "non-elites," central is the possibility for less fixed and determined ways of looking. For example, a less puritanical feminism with room for play, desire, and fantasy might displace "the legion of feminist thought police" (Snitow, 1989:14) who dominate so much of feminism with the dead hand of ideological soundness and binary notions of "us" and "them." To keep feminism opening out, moving beyond its own boundaries, that is the challenge offered by postmodernism.

Postmodernism offers feminists ways to work within and yet challenge dominant discourses. Within postmodernist feminism, language moves from representational to constitutive; binary logic implodes, and debates about "the real" shift from a radical constructivism to a discursively reflexive position which recognizes how our knowledge is mediated by the concepts and categories of our understanding. Hegemonic forms of academic discourse are thoroughly challenged, including those at play in our intendedly counter-hegemonic work: "My point is not that everything is bad, but that everything is dangerous. . . ." (Foucault, quoted in Sawiki, 1988:189). As such, postmodernism offers feminism opportunities to avoid dogmatism and the reductionism of single-cause analysis, to produce knowledge from which to act, and to diffuse power as a means to take advantage of the range of mobile and transitory points of resistance inherent in the networks of power relations (Weedon, 1987:124).

The negatives of postmodernism for "non-elites" include the penchant for aesthetics over ethics, a kind of "languacentricity" that denies the growing global maldistribution of power and resources. For example, the distribution of private wealth in the U.S. now greatly exceeds the level of inequality that existed during Marx's time (Harvey, 1989:191).

Secondly, too often, positively valorized marginality deteriorates into first-world appropriation of third-world difference (Hutcheon, 1989:38). Bordo (1989) warns of a postmodern "voice from everywhere" displacing the detached "voice from nowhere" and thereby collapsing specificities into generalized otherness. And Spivak cautions against postcolonial writers packaging cultural differences "for transnational consumption" in ways that totalize and deny complexity (1989a:276).

In terms of acting in the world, the derision of metatheory and the lack of any effective theory of agency undercuts efforts toward reasoned action and community and/or collective purpose. Additionally, the ironically anti-totalizing totalizations of postmodern discourse often degenerate into a new "regime of truth," a telos, a closure where its willful compromise and ideological ambivalence are easily misread and/or subverted/coopted (Hutcheon, 1989).

Finally, there is the issue of access to the discourse. Bordo writes that "We deceive ourselves if we believe that postmodern theory is attending to the inclusion of 'Otherness' so long as so many concrete 'others' . . . are excluded from the conversation" (1989:140). Given the postmodern suspicion of what Spivak derides as "clear and rousing pieces, . . . lists of ingredients making like recipes" (1989:292), this issue, like so much of postmodernism, evokes a doubled strategy where one attempts "to seek accessibility, without surrendering its right to criticize the consequences of that access" (Hutcheon, 1989:119). Combining the verbal and the visual helps, as does drawing on popular culture, but, at present, much of postmodern discourse constructs a very specialized audience. Positioning educational interventions as powerful sites for working out the possibility of constructing new subject positions from which to resist hegemony, Lentricchia frames the issue thusly:

> If intellectuals have to talk to one another in specialized terms, so be it. The question becomes 'Does that get translated at some level into the classroom?' And if it *does,* then the barn door is open. Once you get into the undergraduate classroom successfully, then you're outside the ivory tower. You're into the culture. (*Rolling Stone,* March 23, 1989:146)

Lentricchia's pedagogical strategy uses poststructural analysis to help students create subject positions such as "a kind of new person who's not going to be satisfied with the usual canonical things" (ibid.:148). In doing so, he opens up the possibility of grounding an exploration of the politics of postmodernism by tracing how it is being inscribed in the discourses of emancipatory education.

The discourses of emancipatory education

In this section, I will first construct a necessarily partial "review of the literature" to provide an overview of the intersection of postmodernism and the discourses of emancipatory education. I will then explore that intersection via a reading of Ellsworth's 1989 "Why Doesn't This Feel Empowering? Working Through the Repressive Myths of Critical Pedagogy."

At one level, the problematic of postmodernism is to "make of our disorders new knowledge" (Hassan, 1987:81). What this might mean within the context of educational thought and practice is captured by Johnson's argument that the politics of undecidability, the unavoidable open-endedness and inherent perspectivity of knowledge, "become an access route to a whole rethinking of the educational enterprise" (1987:44). Some of this work is beginning regarding pedagogy. Much of the "deconstructivist pedagogy" literature comes from the area of literary criticism and cultural studies, but work located in educational studies is emerging.[17] Ellsworth's situated problematizing of the abstract prescriptions of critical pedagogies, to be dealt with later, is a highly visible example given its recent publication in a major educational journal and its targeting for commentary by some of the chief architects of "critical pedagogy" (Giroux, 1988; McLaren, 1988).

Britzman's (1989) exploration of a poststructural account of teacher identity brings issues of subjectivity, language and power to bear on teacher education, while the postmodern focus on what makes our knowledge both possible and problematic underscores the projects of Cherryholmes (1988), Wexler (1987), and Whitson (1988). Cherryholmes' book, the first in education to have "poststructural" in the title, is especially valuable in its effort to work at an introductory level. Arguing that "Much of the unfamiliarity and strangeness of poststructuralism recedes when applied to everyday life" (142), Cherryholmes describes educational reform as one structural invasion after another by looking at Bloom's taxonomy, Tyler's rationale, Schwab's "The Practical 4," the relationship between textbooks, standardized tests and teaching, empirical research, and critical "emancipatory" practice. Beyond an introductory level, he also looks at issues of theory and practice, construct validity and pragmatism within educational discourse/practices.[18]

In Britain, Stuart Hall and the cultural studies groups probe popular culture as a means to understand the formation of subjects in relations of power. A growing body of such work is also developing in the U.S. (e.g., Roman, 1988). Schooling is one of many sites looked at in the development of a non-dualistic theory of subjectivity that privileges neither the romanticized individual nor social, linguistic and cultural structures as determinants (Henriques et al., 1984). A discursive focus on networks of practices which constitute subjects in shifting, multiple, contradictory sites constructs a more complex understanding of identity and citizenship. Seen as effects of techniques of subjectification rather than as natural rights or as essences which the discourses of emancipation can unfurl (Donald, 1985), poststructural perspectives problematize received wisdom in social theory regarding identity, subjectivity and agency. Context and meaning in everyday life are posited as co-constructions, multiple, complex, open and changing, neither pre-given nor explainable by large-scale causal theories, but made and re-made across a multiplicity of minor scattered practices. Agency is re-conceptualized within the context of a fluid, changeable social setting, in motion via the interaction of a plurality of multiply-sited, diffused agents who create "always there and always fragile systems" (Bauman, 1989:51). Walkerdine has amassed a considerable body of work in this area: a deconstruction of Piaget and theories of developmental psychology (1984), the effects on girls of their contradictory positioning in primary classrooms in both dominant/subordinate and power/resistance discourse/practices (1985), and the discursive positioning of females as teachers and students in schools (1981, 1986).

A focus on the reception by students of curricular interventions done in the name of liberation is exemplified in Davies' (1989) work on preschool student responses to feminist fairy tales. By foregrounding the ambiguities of how texts make meaning, such a focus has great implications for curriculum. More abstract efforts to rethink curricular issues are Doll (1989), a forthcoming book, *Foucault and Education,* edited by Stephen Ball, and such work as Bowers (1988) and Green and Bigum (n.d.) on computers and the move away from text-based pedagogy. Finally, Henry Giroux has edited a 1988 special issue of the *Journal of Education,* "Schooling in the Postmodern Age."

To explore the problems and possibilities that this emerging body of work on postmodernism and education raises for emancipatory education, I turn to Ellsworth's implosion of the canons of critical pedagogy where she places the key discourses in the literature of critical pedagogy in relation to her interpretation of her experience of teaching a university level anti-racism course. Examining the discourses within which critical pedagogues are caught up, the concepts of empowerment, student voice, dialogue and the term "critical" itself are problematizied by asking "which interpretations and 'sense making' do these discourses facilitate, which do they silence and marginalize, and what interests do they appear to serve?" (1989:298).

Rooted in her own experience of the limits of the prescriptions of critical pedagogy, she suggests a movement from "dialogue" to "working together across differences" (p. 314), from a concept of an eventually unified dialogue to the construction of "strategies in context" (p. 317) for dealing with the unsaid and unsayable present within classrooms where "all voices . . . are not carrying and cannot carry equal legitimacy, safety, and power" given present social structures. As she notes, this problematizes the concept of "voice" so evident in liberatory discourse in education.[19] "Pluralizing the concept of 'voices' implies correction through addition. Such unproblematic pluralizing loses sight of the contradictory and partial nature of all voices" (p. 312):

> Conventional notions of dialogue and democracy assume rationalized, individualized subjects capable of agreeing on universalizable "fundamental moral principles" and "quality of human life" that become self-evident when subjects cease to be self-interested and particularistic about group rights. Yet social agents are not capable of being fully rational and disinterested; and they are subjects split between the conscious and unconscious and among multiple social positionings. (p. 316)

Especially interested in what she calls "the violence of rationalism against its Others" (p. 304), Ellsworth shifts the focus from the effort to create a dialogical community to an effort toward "sustained encounter with currently oppressive formations and power relations," an encounter "that owned up to my own implications in those formations and was capable of changing my own relation to and investments in those formations" (p. 308). Unsettling received definitions, multiplying subject positions, unlearning our own privileges, "profoundly contextual (historical) and interdependent (social)" (p. 323), such a pedagogy has no prescriptions. Moving out of the position of "master of truth and justice" (Foucault, 1977:12), Ellsworth conceptualizes her task as "the challenge of constructing classroom practices that engage with the discursive and material spaces that such a removal opens up" (Ellsworth, 1989:323).

In terms of exploring the construction of postmodernism in educational discourse, Ellsworth's essay and reactions to it exemplify the complexities of what it means to do praxis-oriented intellectual work in a post-foundational context. Are we talking about the end of liberatory struggle or a re-situating of it? Positioning modernist assumptions of truth, objectivity and "correct readings" as ensnared in phallocentric and logocentric rationalities, how can postmodernism begin to clear the ground and challenge the plethora of concepts that appear as givens in our debates about the possibilities and limits of emancipatory education? How can such self-reflexivity both render our basic assumptions problematic and provisional and yet still propel us to take a stand?

In raising such issues, postmodernism positions emancipatory reason as vulnerable to interrogation. Tracing the collusion of intellectuals with emancipatory desires in the very cultural dominants they are opposing via the intersection of liberatory intentions and the "will to power" that underscores the privileged positions of knowing and changing, the discourses of emancipation are located as much within Foucault's "regimes of truth" as not. Additionally, rather than separating the "true" from the "false," postmodernism destabilizes assumptions of interpretive validity and shifts emphasis to the contexts in which meanings are produced.

Any exploration of the conditions of receptivity within which an intervention such as Ellsworth's is situated grows out of the postmodern assumption that audiences are fragmented and multiple in their production of any meanings that a text might have. Given congested and conflicted semiotic environments and different positionalities in the "difference crisis" that repositions centers and margins in leftist discursive practices, multiple and contradictory readings are to be expected. As an example, I will read McLaren's (1988) and Giroux's (1988) readings of Ellsworth's text against mine.

McLaren, admittedly ambivalent about postmodernism, frames Ellsworth in a "post-critical" position of

> political inertia and moral cowardice where educators remain frozen in the zone of "dead" practice in which it is assumed

> that all voices are those which silence or which contain the "other" by a higher act of violence, and all passionate ethical stances are those built upon the edifices of some form of tyranny or another. Unable to speak with any certainty, or with an absolute assurance that his or her pedagogy is untainted by any form of domination, the "post-critical" educator refuses to speak at all. (pp. 71–72)

According to McLaren, Ellsworth's essay is, furthermore, an attempt to "discredit" selected critical educators via the assumedly inadequate "proof" of her account of her own teaching and the use of "decontextualized quotes" to represent theorists' positions, thereby "setting up critical pedagogy to fail from the very beginning." This "woeful misreading of the tradition she so cavalierly indicts" is full of "distortions, mystifications, and despair" based on her "self-professed lack of pedagogical success" and "her inability to move beyond her own self-doubt," thereby "hold[ing] her voice hostage" and "using theory as a scapegoat for failed practice" (p. 72).

Giroux positions Ellsworth's piece as "a liberal call to harmonize and resolve differences" (p. 170). Conversely, Giroux argues that Ellsworth's view of differences as "merely antagonistic" results in "separatism [a]s the only valid political option for any kind of pedagogical and political action, . . . a crippling form of political disengagement" (p. 177). An "attempt to delegitimate the work of other critical educators" (ibid.), he positions her as

> claiming rather self-righteously the primacy and singularity of her own ideological reading of what constitutes a political project, . . . degrad[ing] the rich complexity of theoretical and pedagogical processes that characterize the diverse discourses in the field of critical pedagogy. In doing so, she succumbs to the familiar academic strategy of dismissing others through the use of strawman tactics and excessive simplifications which undermine not only the strengths of her own work, but also the very nature of social criticism itself. This is "theorizing" as a form of "bad faith," a discourse imbued with the type of careerism that has become all too characteristic of many left academics. (p. 178)

Across McLaren and Giroux's readings, I present two of my own readings of Ellsworth. The first focuses on the textual practices that she uses to locate her intervention. The second reading offers a construction of both how her work evokes ways to work with rather than be paralyzed by the loss of Cartesian stability and unity (Weedon, 1987) and what the material consequences of her project might be. Foregrounding the reductiveness of the interpretive act, I propose my readings across these complex, shifting and polyvalent fields as neither "correct" nor final. Like Lanser (1989) in her reading of the political unconscious inscribed in white academic feminists' readings of Gilman's "The Yellow Wallpaper," I call on Adrienne Rich in order to frame my readings as evocations to look beyond old critical premises and toward continuing revision:

> How can I fail to love
> your clarity and fury
> how can I give you
> all your due
> take courage from your courage
> honor your exact
> legacy as it is
> recognizing
> as well
> that it is not enough?
> (Rich, in Lanser, 1989:436)

In terms of textual performativity in her essay, Ellsworth's move is to clear a space from which to articulate her own difference within a field of competing discourses. Using self-reflexive experience as a basis for knowing, she operates out of what Hutcheon calls "a very feminist awareness of the value of experience and the importance of its representation in the form of 'life-writing'—however difficult or even falsifying that process might turn out to be" (1989:167). Self-consciously positioning herself as an alternative to the presumed dominant, she sets herself both within and against the political terrain where Enlightenment discourses function and have their effectivity. Inserting herself into a largely unexplicated but privileged field of feminist pedagogy, she does battle with other texts according to her own ground rules, texts which precede and surround the "intertextual arena" that she creates (Collins, 1989). Intensifying differences as a way to clear such a space, she tends to "a counter-cultural Salvation Army beating its moral drum about the wickedness of the dominant" (Collins, 1989:122). Her seizing of a moral high-ground and her demonizing of critical pedagogy's "repressive myths" perpetuates monolithic categories of dominant/dominated, thereby intensifying the conflictive nature of the semiotic environment. A way out of this might have been to foreground how her construction of herself as a privileged alternative inscribes as well as subverts, in essence deconstructing her own strategies of self-legitimation. Such a move would have added another textual dimension to the Foucauldian suspicion of every operation that seeks to center a subject who is in a position to know, a suspicion that is at the heart of her project.

Shifting from textual practices to her inscribing of the realms of pedagogy and curriculum as powerful sites for liberatory interventions, Ellsworth's work displaces the totalizing desire to establish foundations with a move toward self-critique. This move is premised on her acknowledgment of the profound challenge that poststructural theories of language and subjectivity offer to our capacity to know the "real" via the mediations of critical pedagogy. Primary to this move is her decentering of the "transformative intellectual" (Aronowitz and Giroux, 1985) as the origin of what can be known and done. To multiply the ways in which we can interrupt the relations of dominance requires deconstructing such vanguardism. Britzman's questions evoke this reflexive process: "What kinds of practices are possible once vulnerability, ambiguity, and doubt are admitted? What kinds of power and authority are taken up and not admitted?" (1989:17). Deconstructing vanguardism means asking ourselves hard questions about how our interventionary moves render people passive, "positioned as potential recipients of predefined services rather than as agents involved in interpreting their needs and shaping their life-conditions" (Fraser, 1989:19).

To abandon crusading rhetoric and begin to think outside of a framework which sees the "Other" as the problem for which they are the solution is to shift the role of critical intellectuals from universalizing spokespersons to cultural workers who do what they can to lift the barriers which prevent people from speaking for themselves. Perhaps the subtext of what Foucault and Lyotard are saying about the end of the great narratives of emancipation and enlightenment is that *who speaks* is more important than *what is said* (Said, 1986:153, original emphasis). Their pronouncements may have more to do with the end of some speaking for others than the end of liberatory struggle.

Rather than attacking the work of others, Ellsworth's project can be read as an example of how deconstruction can serve to problematize critical pedagogy in ways that *resituate* our emancipatory work as opposed to destroy it. Making the workings of pedagogy more apparent,

Ellsworth's project demonstrates how deconstructing our own practices can animate and expand our sense of the structure of possibilities in regard to change-oriented practices. Ellsworth also begins to give a feel for the political possibilities of the multiply-sited subject of poststructuralist theory, a subject characterized by heterogeneity, irreducible particularities, and incalculable differences. Her focus on different differences or Derrida's differánce, the condition of differences *and* identity (Grosz, 1989:31), is radically other than the separatism of which Giroux accuses her. Rather than speaking to Ellsworth's intervention as "a crippling form of political disengagement" (p. 177), I read his accusation as saying more about his own continued investments in the liberal struggle for equality and identity politics via the mediations of critical pedagogy.

Against the inertia and moral cowardice that McLaren speaks of, I position Ellsworth's intervention as an act of courage in taking on such dominant architects of critical pedagogy. This is especially so given the vitriol she has evoked as illustrated by McLaren's reading of Ellsworth's openness and uncertainties regarding her pedagogical strategies as "a scapegoat for failed practice." Instead of "dead" or "failed" practice, I read her as positioning herself "always in the position of beginning again" (Foucault, 1984:47) within the context of both the foregrounding of limits that is postmodernism and the embodied reflexivity that characterizes feminist pedagogy. In regard to Giroux's pronouncements about the effects of her self-reflexive de-centering, I read his statements about "careerism" and the undermining of "the very nature of social criticism itself" (p. 178) as ironically repositioning himself and the other (largely male) architects of critical pedagogy at the center of her discourse. Disrupting any notion of a privileged, unproblematic position from which to speak, she seems to have unleashed "the virulence and the power invested in logocentric thought" (Grosz, 1989:34).

McLaren and Giroux worry much about the nihilism assumed to undergird postmodernism's suspicion of claims to truth, the will to knowledge and the primacy of reason. I share Derrida's suspicion of the nihilism charge often levelled against postmodernism as "not just a simplification; it is symptomatic of certain political and instrumental interests" (in Kearney, 1984:124). Ellsworth's project belies such charges of nihilism. Like most of the work mentioned in this section, it demonstrates how postmodernism has much to offer those of us who do our work in the name of emancipatory education as we construct the material for struggle present in the stuff of our daily lives to which we all have access.

Such a reading of the incursion of postmodernism into the discourses of liberatory education foregrounds my position that there is nothing in postmodernism that makes it intrinsically reactionary. The postmodern moment is an open-ended construction that is contested, incessantly perspectival and multiply-sited. Framing reactions to Ellsworth as disparate, full of unresolvable tensions, and necessarily partial, I have used what Collins terms "juxtaposition as interrogation" (1989:140) in order to foreground what is at stake in our interpretive practices. Such deconstructive textual strategy illustrates how postmodernism both imposes a severe re-examination on the thought of the Enlightenment and is being inscribed by those who want to critically preserve the emancipatory impulse within a framework sympathetic to postmodernism's resituating of that impulse (Peters, 1989).[20]

Conclusion

In this process of exploring the implications of postmodernism for our practices in the world, we need to be cautious that dissembling the master narratives, especially those of Marx and Freud, is not replaced by Foucault, Derrida, Baudrillard, Lacan, etc., as new master discourses. Flax (1987), for example, advises a "necessary ambivalence" on the part of feminists regarding the essentially male discourse of postmodernism. The same is certainly true of the stormy history of feminism and Marxism. My argument is in no way a collapsing of all these theoretical moments into some spurious synthesis. As we create "a weave of knowing and not-knowing which is what knowing is" (Spivak, 1987:78), I cannot but believe that it is in both our parallels and our differences across the various feminisms, Marxisms and post-structuralisms that we can begin to move toward a future that transcends our present limitations.

3

Research as Praxis

> The attempt to produce value-neutral social science is increasingly being abandoned as at best unrealizable, and at worst self-deceptive, and is being replaced by social sciences based on explicit ideologies. (Hesse, 1980:247)
>
> Since interest-free knowledge is logically impossible, we should feel free to substitute explicit interests for implicit ones. (Reinharz, 1985:17)

Fifty years ago, the Italian neo-Marxist Gramsci urged intellectuals to adhere to a "praxis of the present" by aiding "developing progressive groups" to become increasingly conscious of their own actions and situations in the world (quoted in Salamini, 1981:73). This chapter explores what it means to do empirical research in an unjust world. In it I discuss the implications of searching for an emancipatory approach to research in the human sciences. It is written from the perspective of one who believes that, just as there is no neutral education (Freire, 1973), there is no neutral research (Hall, 1975; Westkott, 1977; Reason and Rowan, 1981). Bearing in mind the words of Gramsci, my objective is to delineate the parameters of a "praxis of the present" within the context of empirical research in the human sciences.

I base my argument for a research approach openly committed to a more just social order on two assumptions. First, we are in a postpositivist period in the human sciences, a period marked by much methodological and epistemological ferment. There has been, however, little exploration of the methodological implications of the search for an emancipatory social science. Such a social science would allow us not only to understand the maldistribution of power and resources underlying our society but also to change that maldistribution in ways that help create a more equal world. My second argument is that research that is explicitly committed to critiquing the status quo and building a more just society—that is, research as praxis[1]—adds an important voice to that ferment.

My exploration of postpositivist, praxis-oriented research draws on three research programs—feminist research, neo-Marxist critical ethnography (Ogbu, 1981; Masemann, 1982), and Freirean "empowering" or participatory research (Hall, 1975, 1981; Maguire, 1987). Each of these research programs opposes prevailing scientific norms as inherently supporting of the status quo; each is premised upon a "transformative agenda" with respect to both social structure and methodological norms; each is, in other words, concerned with research as praxis (Rose, 1979:279). All three of these postpositivist research programs are examples of what Hesse, borrowing from Althusser,[2] terms the "epistemological break" (1980:196) of developing a critical social science with an openly emancipatory intent. After brief overviews of both praxis-oriented, critical research and recent efforts in radical educational theorizing to help create an empirically informed Marxist theory of schooling, this chapter focuses on the development of empowering approaches to generating knowledge.

The postpositivist era

Research approaches inherently reflect our beliefs about the world we live in and want to live in (Haberman, 1971; Bernstein, 1976; Fay, 1975; Hesse, 1980). Currently, we are in a period of dramatic shift in our understanding of scientific inquiry. Lecourt has termed this postpositivist era "the decline of the absolutes" (1975:49; see, also, Bernstein, 1983; Smith and Heshusius, 1986). No longer does following the correct method guarantee true results, rather, "method does not give truth; it corrects guesses" (Polkinghorne, 1983:249). It is increasingly recognized that the fact/value dichotomy simply drives values underground. Facts are never theory-independent (Hesse, 1980:172); they are as much social constructions as are theories and values. Whereas positivism insists that only one truth exists, Rich argues that, "There is no 'the truth,' 'a truth'—truth is not one thing, or even a system. It is an increasing complexity" (1979:187). Postpositivism has cleared methodology of prescribed rules and boundaries. The result is a constructive turmoil that allows a search for different possibilities of making sense of human life, for other ways of knowing which do justice to the complexity, tenuity, and indeterminancy of most of human experience (Mishler, 1979).

Broadly speaking, postpositivism is characterized by the methodological and epistemological refutation of positivism (Bernstein, 1976, 1983; Mitroff and Kilmann, 1978); much talk of paradigm shifts (Smith, 1983; Phillips, 1983; Eisner, 1983); and by an increased visibility for research designs that are interactive, contextualized, and humanly compelling because they invite joint participation in exploration of research issues (Reinharz, 1979, 1983; Reason and Rowan, 1981; Sabia and Wallulis, 1983). Postpositivism is marked by inquiry approaches which recognize that knowledge is "socially constituted, historically embedded, and valuationally based. Theory serves as agentic function, and research illustrates (vivifies) rather than provides a truth test" (Hendrick, 1983:506). What this means is that openly ideological,[3] advocacy-based research has arisen as a new contender for legitimacy.

Research programs that disclose their value-base have been typically discounted, however, as overly subjective and, hence, "non-scientific." Such views do not recognize that scientific neutrality is always problematic; they arise from an objectivism premised on the belief that scientific knowledge is free from social construction (Fox-Keller, 1985; Harding, 1986). Rather than the illusory "value-free" knowledge of the positivists, praxis-oriented inquirers seek emancipatory knowledge. Emancipatory knowledge increases awareness of the contradictions distorted or hidden by everyday understandings, and in doing so it directs attention to the possibilities for social transformation inherent in the present configuration of social processes. Admittedly, this approach faces the danger of a rampant subjectivity where one finds only what one is predisposed to look for, an outcome that parallels the "pointless precision" (Kaplan, 1964) of objectivism. Thus a central task for praxis-oriented researchers becomes the confrontation of issues of empirical accountability—the need to offer grounds for accepting a researcher's description and analysis—and the search for workable ways of establishing the trustworthiness of data in critical inquiry.

Research as praxis

The foundation of postpositivism is the cumulative, trenchant, and increasingly definitive critique of the inadequacies of positivist assumptions[4] in light of the complexities of human experience (Kaplan, 1964; Cronbach, 1975; Bernstein, 1976; Mishler, 1979; Giroux, 1981; Guba and Lincoln, 1981; Feinberg, 1983). Postpositivism argues that the present methodological orthodoxy in the human sciences is obsolete and that new visions for generating social knowledge are required (Rose, 1979; Schwartz and Ogilvy, 1979; Hesse, 1980; Reason and Rowan, 1981). Those committed to the development of a change enhancing, interactive, contextualized approach to knowledge-building have amassed a body of empirical work that is provocative in theory and, increasingly, method.

Several examples of this work are available. Consider Bullough and Gitlin's (1985) case study of one middle-school teacher, a study designed to encourage rethinking the meaning of resistance and its place in theories of cultural and economic reproduction within the context of teachers' work lives. Their research design included the teacher's written response to a preliminary interpretation of the data, which is an example of the most common form of an emancipatory approach to research—the submission of a preliminary description of the data to the scrutiny of the researched. In an earlier study, Willis (1977) focused on the school-to-work transition in the lives of twelve working-class British "lads." The most oft-cited example of neo-Marxist critical ethnography, Willis' work both identifies the area of resistance to authority as a fruitful corrective to the overly deterministic correspondence theories then popular in neo-Marxist circles (e.g., Bowles and Gintis, 1976; see Apple, 1980–81 for a critique), and builds into his research design an attempt to take the research findings back to the lads for further dialogue. McRobbie (1978) conducted a similar study with a focus on the role of socialization into femininity in the lives of working-class British females. Finally, a more praxis-oriented example is Mies's (1984) action research project in Germany designed to respond to violence against women in the family. A high visibility street action attracted people who were then interviewed regarding their experience with and views on wife beating. The resulting publicity led to the creation of a Women's House to aid victims of domestic abuse. A desire for transformative action and egalitarian participation guided consciousness-raising in considering the sociological and historical roots of male violence in the home through the development of life histories of the women who had been battered. The purpose was to empower the oppressed to come to understand and change their own oppressive realities. (Fur further examples, see Hall, 1981; Roberts, 1981; Berlak and Berlak, 1981; Anyon, 1980, 1982, 1983; Everhart, 1983; Tripp, 1984; McNeil, 1984; Miller, 1986).

Such examples are part of a rich ferment in contemporary discourse about empirical research in the human sciences, a discourse that spans epistemological, theoretical and, to a less developed degree, methodological issues. Within radical educational circles, for example, there have been several calls for an end to the dichotomy between empirical work and the construction of emancipatory theory (Wexler, 1982; Anyon, 1982; Ramsay, 1983). There are, however, few clear strategies for linking critical theory and empirical research.

This failure to probe the methodological implications of critical theory has led to a number of difficulties for praxis-oriented research. The abundance of theoretically guided empirical work affiliated with the "new sociology of education"[5] attests to both the conceptual vitality offered by postpositivist research programs and the dangers of conceptual overdeterminism. This nondialectical use of theory leads to a circle where theory is reinforced by experience conditioned by theory. Marxism's history of sectarianism and "theoretical imperialism" (Thompson, 1978; see, also, Bottomore, 1978) gives evidence of the need for open, flexible theory-building grounded in a body of empirical work ceaselessly confronted with, and respectful of, the experiences of people in their daily lives. Far too often, however, one is left with the impression that neo-Marxist empirical work is conducted to provide empirical specificities for a priori theory (Hargreaves, 1982; Lather, 1986b). Such work demonstrates the continued relevance of Thompson's (1978:13) assertion that too much of Marxist social theory is "an immaculate conception which requires no gross empirical impregnation"[6] (see, also, Kellner, 1975:149; Wright, 1978:10; Krueger, 1981:59; Comstock, 1982:371).

Additionally, too often, neo-Marxist empirical studies are characterized by an attitude toward the researched captured in the words of one research team: "We would not expect the teachers interviewed to either agree with or necessarily understand the inferences which were made from their responses" (Bullough, Goldstein and Holt, 1982:133). Given the all-male research team and the largely female teacher subjects, one could make much of the gender politics involved in such a statement. But the issue here is the implications of such a stance for the purposes of emancipatory knowledge-building and the empowerment of the researched.

The difficulties which continue to characterize critical inquiry raise central questions about the effort to develop a style of empirical research that advances emancipatory knowledge. First, what is the relationship between theory and data in emancipatory research? In grounded theory-building the relationship between data and theory, according to Glaser and Strauss (1967), is that theory follows from data rather than preceding it. Moreover, the result is a minimizing of researcher-imposed definitions of the situation, which is an essential element in generating grounded theory. Given the centrality of a priori theory in praxis-oriented research, it is evident that emancipatory theory-building is different from grounded theory-building. Understanding those differences requires a probing of the tensions involved in the use of a priori theory among researchers who are committed to open-ended, dialectical theory-building that aspires to focus on and resonate with lived experience and, at the same time, are convinced that lived experience in an unequal society too often lacks an awareness of the need to struggle against privilege. Second, growing out of the first question, how does one avoid reducing explanation to the intentions of social actors, by taking into account the deep structures—both psychological and structural, conscious and unconscious—that shape human experience and perceptions, without committing the sin of theoretical imposition? This question is tied to both the issue of false consciousness (defined later in this chapter) and the crucial role of the researcher vis-a-vis the researched in emancipatory inquiry. An exploration of both of these central questions comprises the remainder of this chapter.

For praxis to be possible, not only must theory illuminate the lived experience of progressive social groups; it must also be illuminated by their struggles. Theory adequate to the task of changing the world must be open-ended, nondogmatic, speaking to and grounded in the circumstances of everyday life. It must, moreover, be premised on a deep respect for the intellectual and political capacities of the dispossessed. This position has profound substantive and methodological implications for postpositivist, change-enhancing inquiry in the human sciences.

Empowering approaches to the generation of knowledge

> For persons, as autonomous beings, have a moral right to participate in decisions that claim to generate knowledge about them. Such a right . . . protects them . . . from being managed and manipulated. . . . [T]he moral principle of respect for

> persons is most fully honored when power is shared not only in the application . . . but also in the generation of knowledge. . . . [d]oing research on persons involves an important educational commitment: to provide conditions under which subjects can enhance their capacity for self-determination in acquiring knowledge about the human condition. (Heron, 1981:34–35)

Krueger notes, "There are hardly any attempts at the development of an alternative methodology in the sense of an 'emancipatory' social research to be explored and tested in substantive studies" (1981:59). Along these lines, Giddens (1979) suggests that the task of a critical social science is to explore the nature of the intersection between choice and constraint and to center on questions of power. Is this not equally true of the research situation itself? Insofar as we have come to see that evolving an empowering pedagogy is an essential step in social transformation, does not the same hold true for our research approaches?

I am arguing for an approach that goes well beyond the action research concept proposed over 30 years ago by Lewin, which has given rise to "a very active and lively field" in Britain, Australia and New Zealand over the past decade (Tripp, 1984:20; Lauder and Kahn, 1988). While Tripp (1984) and Grundy (1982) note the existence of some critical and emancipatory teacher-based action research, the vast majority of this work operates from an ahistorical, apolitical value system which lends itself to subversion by those "who are tempted to use merely the technical form as a means of engineering professional teacher development" (Tripp, 1984:20).

An emancipatory social research calls for empowering approaches to research where both researcher and researched become, in the words of feminist singer-poet, Cris Williamson, "the changer and the changed." For researchers with emancipatory aspirations, doing empirical work offers a powerful opportunity for praxis to the extent that it enables people to change by encouraging self-reflection and a deeper understanding of their particular situations. In an attempt to reveal the implications that the quest for empowerment holds for research design, I will focus on three interwoven issues: the need for reciprocity, the stance of dialectical theory-building versus theoretical imposition, and the question of validity in praxis-oriented research.

The need for reciprocity

> No intimacy without reciprocity (Oakley, 1981:49).

Reciprocity implies give and take, a mutual negotiation of meaning and power. It operates at two primary points in emancipatory empirical research: the junctures between researcher and researched and data and theory. The latter will be dealt with in the next section of this paper; I here address reciprocity between researcher and researched.

Reciprocity in research design is a matter of both intent and degree. Regarding intent, reciprocity has long been recognized as a valuable aspect of fieldwork, for it has been found to create conditions that will generate rich data (Wax, 1952). Everhart, for example, presents reciprocity as "an excellent data gathering technique" (1977:10) because the researcher moves from the status of stranger to friend and thus is able to gather personal knowledge from subjects more easily. He traces his evolution from detachment to involvement in a study of student life in a junior high school where he comes to recognize "the place of reciprocity in productive fieldwork" (p. 8). I argue that we must go beyond the concern for more and better data to a concern for research as praxis. What I suggest is that we consciously use our research to help participants understand and change their situations. I turn now to those who build varying degrees of reciprocity into their research design for purposes of empowering the researched.

Laslett and Rapoport (1975), who studied school dropouts in Britain, build a minimal degree of reciprocity into their research design. They term their approach "collaborative interviewing and interactive research." A central component of their strategy is to repeat interviews at least three times. The repetition is "essential to deal with the feelings roused, often covertly, in order to 'unlock' deeper levels of data content" (p. 973). Furthermore, they urge " 'giving back' " to respondents a picture of how the data are viewed, both to return something to research participants and to check descriptive and interpretive/analytical validity.

A Marxist survey researcher (Carr-Hill, 1984) expands the use of reciprocity to identify, through initial interviews, a group of twelve to fifteen people with whom the researcher engaged in a series of open discussions around the mismatch between formal education and the way people live their lives. This resulted in a collectively generated survey given to one hundred people, a survey couched in the language of respondents and "in terms of the social categories through which they perceive the world" (p. 281). Additionally, interested participants attended evaluation seminars where survey results stimulated respondents "to critically analyze their own educational history and its relation to their present life-styles" (Ibid., p. 281).

A maximal approach to reciprocity in research design can be found in the work of two evaluators involved in a four-year project to assess the curricular reform movements of the 1960s (Kushner and Norris, 1980–81). The goal of their research was to move people from articulating what they know to theorizing about what they know, a process the researchers term "collaborative theorizing" (p. 27). This methodology is characterized by negotiation: negotiation of description, interpretation and the principles used to organize the first draft report. While they admit that final drafts are usually the preserve of the researcher, Kushner and Norris suggest that the attractiveness of this approach is that all participants, within time constraints, are allowed a role in negotiating the final meanings of the research. Such collaboration, they contend, offers "an opportunity to extend the range of theories and meanings . . . to give participants the dignity of contributing to theorizing about their worlds . . . [and], through sharing meaning-production, . . . develop significant understandings of schooling and education" (p. 35).

A final example is demonstrated by Tripp (1983). He explores what it means for interviews to be co-authored and negotiated in a conscious effort to democratize the research situation. In his case studies in alienation and the school-to-work transition, Tripp held one-to-one and group discussions "as a means of developing participants' views" (p. 32). The resulting co-authored statements constituted an agreed-upon account of the views of the participants. Tripp cautions, however, that "the negotiation process must be clearly bounded" (p. 38) because participants often wish to "unsay" their words. In Tripp's view, "the right to negotiate [on the part of research participants] was replaced by the right to comment" (p. 39). Researchers are not so much owners of data as they are "majority shareholders" who must justify decisions and give participants a public forum for critique.

Tripp's research design, however, is not fully interactive. Reciprocity in the negotiation of meaning is limited to the early stages of investigation. No attempt is made to involve research participants in either the interpretation of the descriptive data or the construction of empirically grounded theory. The lack of involvement of research participants in these later stages of the research process makes possible a situation where the entire issue of false consciousness is skirted. False consciousness is the denial of how our common sense ways of looking at the world are permeated with meanings that sustain our disempowerment (Gamsci, 1971; Salamini, 1981; Bowers, 1984); it is a central issue in any maximal approach to reciprocity.

In order to address this issue, Fay (1977) argues that we must develop criteria/theory to distinguish between people's reasoned rejections of interpretations and theoretical arguments and false consciousness. Fay pinpoints what he considers a glaring omission, a black hole,[7] if you will, in critical theory: "the conditions that must be met if people are going to be in a position to actually consider it [critical theory] as a possible account of their lives" (p. 218). Fay is pointing out that the creation of emancipatory theory is a dialogic enterprise. Both the substance of emancipatory theory and the process by which that theory comes to "click" with people's sense of the contradictions in their lives are the products of dialectical rather than top-down impositional practices.

Dialectical practices require an interactive approach to research that invites reciprocal reflexivity and critique, both of which guard against the central dangers to praxis-oriented empirical work: imposition and reification on the part of the researcher. As Comstock argues, "dialogic education is integral to every research program which treats subjects as active agents instead of objectifying them and reifying their social conditions" (1982:386). Yet, notably more often than in either feminist or Freirean praxis-oriented research, the neo-Marxist researcher's self-perceived role is as "interpreter of the world" (Reynolds, 1980–81:87), exposer of false consciousness. This non-dialectical, non-reciprocal perception of the role of the researcher confounds neo-Marxist researchers' intent of demystifying the world for the dispossessed. Respondents become objects—targets of research—rather than active subjects empowered to understand and change their situations. As a result, neo-Marxist empirical work too often falls prey to what Fay notes as the irony of domination and repression inherent in most of our efforts to free one another (1977:209). In the name of emancipation, researchers impose meanings on situations rather than constructing meaning through negotiation with research participants.

There are at present few research designs which encourage negotiation of meaning beyond the descriptive level. The involvement of research participants in data interpretation as well as (to take one further step toward maximal reciprocity) theory-building remains largely "an attractive aspiration" (Kushner and Norris, 1980–81:35). But as Fay notes, feminist consciousness-raising groups provide a model for how to begin to flesh out the nature of maximal reciprocity, the involvement of research participants in the construction and validation of knowledge.

Throughout the late 1960s and 1970s, thousands of small grassroots groups formed to provide a way for women to exchange thoughts, experiences and feelings. From this movement emerged the feminist maxim: the personal is political. What were once thought to be individual problems were redefined as social problems that require political solutions. For Fay, the lesson from these groups is that:

> Coming to a radical new self-conception is hardly ever a process that occurs simply by reading some theoretical work; rather, it requires an environment of trust, openness, and support in which one's own perceptions and feelings can be made properly conscious to oneself, in which one can think through one's experiences in terms of a radically new vocabulary which expresses a fundamentally different conceptualization of the world, in which one can see the particular and concrete ways that one unwittingly collaborates in producing one's own misery, and in which one can gain the emotional strength to accept and act on one's new insights.
>
> The experience of the Women's Movement confirms that radical social change through rational enlightenment requires some mechanism for ensuring that those conditions necessary for such enlightenment will be established and maintained. (1977:232)

Following Fay, I propose that the goal of emancipatory research is to encourage self-reflection and deeper understanding on the part of the researched at least as much as it is to generate empirically grounded theoretical knowledge. To do this, research designs must have more than minimal reciprocity. The following is a summary of the procedures that move us toward full reciprocity in research:

—Interviews conducted in an interactive, dialogic manner that requires self-disclosure on the part of the researcher encourage reciprocity. An example of self-disclosure can be found in Oakley's (1981) research with women and their experience of motherhood. Arguing the need for interactive self-disclosure, Oakley emphasizes a collaborative, dialogic seeking for greater mutual understanding. This is opposed to mainstream interview norms where interview respondents' questions about the interviewer's own life are deflected (see, also, Acker, Barry and Esseveld, 1983; Hanmer and Saunders, 1984).

—Sequential interviews of both individuals and small groups to facilitate collaboration and a deeper probing of research issues work toward reciprocity.

—Negotiating meaning helps build reciprocity. At a minimum, this entails recycling description, emerging analysis and conclusions to at least a subsample of respondents. A more maximal approach to reciprocity would involve research participants in a collaborative effort to build empirically rooted theory.

—Discussion of false consciousness needs to go beyond simply dismissing resistance to Marxist interpretations as such. We need to discover the necessary conditions that free people to engage in ideology critique, given the psychological hold of illusion—"the things people cling to because they provide direction and meaning in their lives" (Fay, 1977:214). There is a dialectic between people's self-understandings and efforts to create an enabling context to question taken-for-granted beliefs and the authority culture has over us (Bowers, 1984). There, in the nexus of that dialectic, lies the opportunity to create reciprocal, dialogic research designs which both lead to self-reflection and provide a forum in which to test the usefulness, the resonance, of conceptual and theoretical formulations.

Dialectical theory-building versus theoretical imposition

> I do not believe that imposing Marxist rather than bourgeois categories is socialist practice (Carr-Hill, 1984:290).

The goal of theoretical guided empirical work is to create theory which possesses "evocative power" (Morgan, 1983:298). By resonating with people's lived concerns, fears and aspirations, emancipatory theory serves an energizing, catalytic role. It does this by increasing specificity at the contextual level in order to see how larger issues are embedded in the particulars of everyday life. The result is that theory becomes an expression and elaboration of progressive popular feelings rather than abstract frameworks imposed by intellectuals on the messy complexity of lived experience.

Building empirically grounded theory requires a reciprocal relationship between data and theory. Data must be allowed to generate propositions in a dialectical manner that permits use of a priori theoretical frameworks, but which keeps a particular framework from becoming the container into which the data must be poured. The search is for theory which grows out of context-embedded data, not in a way that automatically rejects a priori theory, but in a way that keeps preconceptions from distorting the logic of evidence. For example, Ramsay aptly criticizes Anyon's critical ethnographies which focus on the effects of class and gender on the structures of U.S. public school classrooms for telling us more about her predispositions than about the phenomena studied. Anyon's *certainty* and *clear-cutness* are particularly problematic, for as Ramsay notes, "While we would agree that there is no such thing as 'value-free' or objective research, we would argue that there is a need to keep as open a frame of reference as is possible to allow the data to generate the propositions" (1985:316).

Theory is too often used to protect us from the awesome complexity of the world. Yet, "the road to complexity is what we are on in our empirical efforts" (Clark, 1984:49). Moving beyond predisposition requires a set of procedures that illuminates the ways that investigators' values enter into research (Feinberg, 1983:159–160; Bredo and Feinberg, 1982:439). Anchoring theoretical formulations in data requires a critical stance that will reveal the inadequacies of our pet theory and be open to counter-interpretations. Apple (1980–81), in cautioning that conceptual validity precedes empirical accuracy, neglects the largely undialectical role that theory plays in most critical ethnography.[8] Empirical evidence must be viewed as a mediator for a constant self and theoretical interrogation between self and theory. Otherwise, neo-Marxist theory will fail to transcend "the hubris of the social sciences" (Moon, 1983:28) still present in the two emergent alternatives to positivist orthodoxy—the interpretive and critical paradigms. The struggle, of course, is to develop a "passionate scholarship" (Du Bois, 1983) which can lead us toward a self-reflexive research paradigm that no longer reduces issues of bias to a canonized methodology for establishing scientific knowledge (Goddard, 1973:18; Cronbach, 1980).

The search for ways to operationalize reflexivity in critical inquiry is a journey into uncharted territory. Sabia and Wallulis make clear the danger: too often critical self-awareness comes to mean "a negative attitude towards competing approaches instead of its own self-critical perspective" (1983:26). Guidelines for developing critical self-awareness , hence, are rare. Nevertheless, while the methodological implications of critical theory remain relatively unexplored (Bredo and Feinberg, 1982:281), the need for research which advances a more equal world is receiving some attention (Acker, Barry and Esseveld, 1983; Apple, 1982; Fay, 1975, 1977; Comstock, 1982). Various suggestions for operationalizing reflexivity in critical inquiry can be drawn from that small body of work.

First, critical inquiry is a response to the experiences, desires and needs of oppressed people (Fay, 1975). Its initial step is to develop an understanding of the world view of research participants. Central to establishing such understanding is a dialogic research design where respondents are actively involved in the construction and validation of meaning. The purpose of this phase of inquiry is to provide accounts that are a basis for further analysis and "a corrective to the investigator's preconceptions regarding the subjects' life-world and experiences" (Comstock, 1982:381).

Second, critical inquiry inspires and guides the dispossessed in the process of cultural transformation; a process Mao characterized as, "Teach[ing] the masses clearly what we have learned from them confusedly" (quoted in Freire, 1973:82). At the core of the transformation is "a reciprocal relationship in which every teacher is always a student and every pupil a teacher" (Gramsci quoted in Femia, 1975:41). Thus, critical inquiry is a fundamentally dialogic and mutually-educative enterprise. The present is cast against a historical background while at the same time the "naturalness" of social arrangements is challenged so that social actors can see both the constraints and the potential for change in their situations.

Third, critical inquiry focuses on fundamental contradictions which help dispossessed people see how poorly their "ideologically frozen understandings" (Comstock, 1982:384) serve their interests. This search for contradictions must proceed from progressive elements of participants' current understandings, what Willis (1977) refers to as "partial penetrations," the ability of people to pierce through cultural contradictions in incomplete ways that, nevertheless, provide entry points for the process of ideology critique.

Fourth, the validity of a critical account can be found, in part in the participants' responses. Fay writes: "One test of the truth of critical theory is the considered reaction by those for whom it is supposed to be emancipatory. . . . Not only must a particular theory be offered as the reason why people should change their self-understandings, *but this must be done in an environment in which these people can reject this reason* (Fay, 1977:218–219, original emphasis). The point is to provide an environment that invites participants' critical reactions to our accounts of their worlds. As such, dialogic research designs allow us both to begin to grasp the necessary conditions for people to engage in ideology critique and transformative social action and to distinguish between what Bernstein calls "enabling" versus "blinding" biases on the part of the researcher (1983:128).

Fifth, critical inquiry stimulates "a self-sustaining process of critical analysis and enlightened action" (Comstock, 1982:387). The researcher joins the participants in a theoretically-guided program of action over an extended period of time.

Earlier in this chapter, I argued for reciprocity as a means to empower the researched. Here reciprocity is employed to build more useful theory. Research designs can be more or less participatory, but some amount of dialogic encounter is required if we are to invoke the reflexivity needed to protect research from the researcher's own enthusiasms. Debriefing sessions with participants provide an opportunity to look for exceptions to emerging generalizations. Submitting concepts and explanations to the scrutiny of all those involved sets up the possibility for theoretical exchange, the collaborative theorizing at the heart of research which both advances emancipatory theory and empowers the researched.

A strictly interpretive, phenomenological paradigm is inadequate insofar as it is based upon an assumption of fully rational action.[9] Sole reliance on the participants' perceptions of their situation is misguided because, as neo-Marxists point out, false consciousness and ideological mystification may be present. A central challenge posed to the interpretive paradigm is the argument that reality is more than negotiated accounts—that we are both shaped by and shapers of our world. For those interested in the development of a praxis-oriented research paradigm, a key issue revolves around this central challenge: how to maximize self as mediator between people's self-understandings and the need for ideology critique and transformative social action *without becoming impositional*.

Comstock says that the critical researcher's task is to stimulate research participants into "a self-sustaining process of critical analysis and enlightened action" (1982:387). Doing such work in a non-elitist and non-manipulation manner means that, rather than a "one-way propagandist," one wants to be like the Cobbett written about by Thompson; Cobbett acknowledged "the aid which he is constantly deriving from those new thoughts which his thoughts produce in their minds." Thompson notes, "How moving is this insight into the dialectical nature of the very process by which his own ideas were formed! For Cobbett, thought was not a system but a relationship" (1963:758).

For theory to explain the structural contradictions at the heart of discontent, it must speak to the felt needs of a specific group in ordinary language (Fay, 1975:98). If it is to spur toward action, theory must be grounded in the self-understandings of the dispossessed even as it seeks to enable them to re-evaluate themselves and their situations. This is the central paradox of critical theory and provides its greatest challenge. The potential for creating reciprocal, dialogic research designs is rooted in the intersection between people's self-understandings and the researcher's efforts to provide a change-enhancing context. Such designs would both lead to self-refection and provide the forum Fay (1977) calls for whereby the people for whom the theory is supposed to be emancipatory can participate in its construction and validation.

In sum, the development of emancipatory social theory requires an empirical stance which is open-ended, dialogically reciprocal, grounded in respect to human capacity and, yet, profoundly skeptical of appearances and "common sense." Such an empirical stance is, furthermore, rooted in a commitment to the long-term, broad-based ideological struggle necessary to transform structural inequalities.

Issues of validity

> The job of validation is, not to support an interpretation, but to find out what might be wrong with it. . . . To call for value-free standards of validity is a contradiction in terms, a nostalgic longing for a world that never was. (Cronbach, 1980:103–105)

What does empirical rigor mean in a postpositivist context?[10] If validity criteria are the products of the paradigms which spawn them (Morgan,

1983), what validity criteria best serve praxis-oriented research programs? The need to systematize as much as possible the ambiguity of our enterprise does not mean, though, that we must deny the essential indeterminancy of human experiencing—"the crucial disparity between the being of the world and the knowledge that we might have of it" (White, 1973:32). My point is, rather, that if illuminating and resonant theory grounded in trustworthy data is desired, we must formulate self-corrective techniques that check the credibility of data and minimize the distorting effect of personal bias upon the logic of evidence (Kamarovsky, 1981).

Currently paradigmatic uncertainty in the human sciences is leading to the re-conceptualizing of validity. Past efforts to leave subjective, tacit knowledge out of the "context of verification" are seen by postpositivists as "naive empiricism." Inquiry is increasingly recognized as a process whereby tacit (subjective) and propositional (objective) knowledge are interwoven and mutually informing (Heron, 1981:32; Polanyi, 1967). The absence of formulas to guarantee valid social knowledge forces us to "operate simultaneously at epistemological, theoretical and empirical levels with self-awareness" (Sharp and Green, 1975:234). Our best tactic at present is to construct research designs that demand a vigorous self-reflexivity.

For praxis-oriented researchers, going beyond predisposition in our empirical efforts requires new techniques and concepts for obtaining and defining trustworthy data which avoid the pitfalls of orthodox notions of validity. The works of Reason and Rowan (1981) and Guba and Lincoln (1981) offer important suggestions in this regard. Reason and Rowan advise borrowing concepts of validity from traditional research but caution us to revise and expand those concepts in ways appropriate to "an interactive, dialogic logic" (1981:240). Their notion of validity is captured in the phrase "objectively subjective" inquiry (p. xiii). Guba and Lincoln argue for analogues to the major principles of orthodox rigor. They state that the minimum requirement for assessing validity in new paradigm research should enlist the techniques of triangulation, reflexivity and member checks (1981). Building on these, I offer a re-conceptualization of validity appropriate for research that is openly committed to a more just social order.

First, *triangulation* is critical in establishing data trustworthiness, a triangulation expanded beyond the psychometric definition of multiple measures to include multiple data sources, methods, and theoretical schemes. The researcher must consciously utilize designs which seek counter patterns as well as convergence if data are to be credible.

Second, *construct validity* must be dealt with in ways that recognize its roots in theory-construction (Cronbach and Meehl, 1955). Our empirical work must operate within a conscious context of theory-building. Where are the weak points of the theoretical tradition we are operating from within? Are we extending theory? Revising it? Testing it? Corroborating it? Determining that constructs are actually occurring rather than mere inventions of the researcher's perspective requires a self-critical attitude toward how one's own preconceptions affect the research. Building emancipatory social theory requires a ceaseless confrontation with and respect for the experiences of people in their daily lives to guard against theoretical imposition. A *systematized reflexivity* which reveals how a priori theory has been changed by the logic of the data seems essential in establishing construct validity in ways that will contribute to the growth of illuminating and change-enhancing social theory.

As an example, Acker, Barry and Esseveld, in a noteworthy effort to reconstruct "the social relations that produce the research itself" (1983:431), write, "Our commitment to bringing our subjects into the research as active participants influenced our rethinking of our original categories. . . . (p. 434). As part of their self-reflexive essay on research into the relation between changes in the structural situation of women and changes in consciousness, they explore the tension "between letting the data speak for itself and using abstracted categories." They ask, "How do we explain the lives of others without violating their reality?" (p. 429). Contrast this with Willis's (1977) classic ethnography where there is no clear sense of how researcher perspectives were altered by the logic of the data. With no account of this, one is left viewing the role of theory in this research (which is so strongly shaped by a priori conceptions) as being nondialectical, unidirectional, an imposition that disallows counter-patterns and alternative explanations (Lather, 1986b; see, also, Walker, 1985).

Third, *face validity* needs to be reconsidered. Kidder contends that although it has been treated lightly and dismissed, face validity is relatively complex and inextricably tied to construct validity: "Research with face validity provides a 'click of recognition' and a 'yes, of course,' instead of 'yes, but' experience" (1982:56). Face validity is operationalized by recycling description, emerging analysis, and conclusions back through at least a subsample of respondents: "good research at the non-alienating end of the spectrum . . . goes back to the subjects with the tentative results, and refines them in light of the subjects' reactions" (Reason and Rowan, 1981:248). The possibility of encountering false consciousness, however, creates a limit on how useful "member checks" (Guba and Lincoln, 1981) can be in establishing the trustworthiness of data. While false consciousness is an admittedly problematic phenomenon (Acker, Barry and Esseveld, 1983), for reasons much illuminated by Gramsci's (1971) theories of hegemony, most people to some extent identify with and/or accept ideologies which do not serve their best interests. Thus, an analysis which only takes account of actors' perceptions of their situations could result in research being wrongly termed invalid. The link between face and construct validity and the possible false consciousness of research participants is an area that very much needs empirical exploration. Perhaps the best that can be suggested at this point is that, just as reliability is necessary but not sufficient to establish validity within positivism, building face validity into our new paradigm research should become a necessary but not sufficient approach to establishing data credibility.

Fourth, given the emancipatory intent of praxis-oriented research, I propose the less well-known notion of *catalytic validity* (Reason and Rowan, 1981:240; Brown and Tandom, 1978). Catalytic validity represents the degree to which the research process re-orients, focuses and energizes participants toward knowing reality in order to transform it, a process Freire (1973) terms conscientization. Of the guidelines proposed here, this is by far the most unorthodox; it flies directly in the face of the positivist demand for researcher neutrality. The argument for catalytic validity lies not only within recognition of the reality-altering impact of the research process, but also in the desire to consciously channel this impact so that respondents gain self-understanding and, ultimately, self-determination through research participation.

Efforts to produce social knowledge useful in the struggle for a more equitable world must pursue rigor as well as relevance. By arguing for a more systematic approach to triangulation and reflexivity, a new emphasis for face validity, and inclusion of catalytic validity, I stand opposed to those who claim that empirical accountability is either impossible to achieve or able to be side stepped in praxis-oriented, advocacy research. Lack of concern for data credibility within praxis-oriented research programs will only decrease the legitimacy of the knowledge generated therein. Praxis-oriented research can only benefit from agreed-upon procedures which make empirical decision-making public, and hence subject to criticism. Most important, if we do not develop such procedures, our theory-building will suffer from a failure to protect our work from our own passions and limitations.

Conclusion

This chapter has one essential argument: a more collaborative approach to critical inquiry is needed to empower the researched, build emancipatory theory, and move toward the establishment of data credibility within praxis-oriented, advocacy research. The present turmoil in the human sciences frees us to construct new designs based on alternative tenets and epistemological commitments. My goal is to move research in many different and, indeed, contradictory directions in the hope that more interesting and useful ways of knowing will emerge. Rather than establish a new orthodoxy, we need to experiment, document and share our efforts toward emancipatory research. To quote Polkinghorne:

> What is needed most is for practitioners to experiment with the new designs and to submit their attempts and results to examination by other participants in the debate. The new historians of science have made it clear that methodological questions are decided in the practice of research by those committed to developing the best possible answers to their questions, not by armchair philosophers of research. (1983:xi)

Chapters 4 and 7 of this book exemplify my efforts to avoid becoming "am armchair philosopher of research" myself by exploring student resistance to liberatory curriculum in an introductory women's studies course. They are separated by two chapters which attempt to capture how the "deconstructive impulse" might play itself out in my empirical work. Beginning to raise such issues in the following chapter, it captures my movement between a rather unproblematized emancipatory impulse and the profound questions raised by postmodernism about such efforts.

4

Feminist Perspectives on Empowering Research Methodologies

> Perhaps this is the time to stress *technique* again? . . . A detour into *strategy, tactics, and practice* is called for, at least as long as it takes to gain vision, self-knowledge, self-possession, even in one's decenteredness. (Irigaray, 1985:136)

This chapter is an attempt to flesh out some of the methodological ideas of the previous chapter within the context of feminist efforts to create empowering and self-reflexive research designs. I will especially focus on my three-year empirical study of student resistance to liberatory curriculum in an introductory women's studies course.[1]

While feminist empirical efforts are by no means a monolith, with some operating out of a conventional, positivist paradigm and some out of an interpretive/phenomenological paradigm, an increasing amount operate out of a critical, praxis-oriented paradigm concerned with both producing emancipatory knowledge and empowering the researched. I turn now to feminist efforts to empower through empirical research designs which maximize a dialogic, dialectically educative encounter between researcher and researched.

Postpositivist feminist empirical practice

> This assertion of the priority of moral and political over scientific and epistemological theory and activity makes science and epistemology less important, less central, than they are

> within the Enlightenment world view. Here again, feminism makes its own important contribution to postmodernism—in this case, to our understanding that epistemology-centered philosophy—and, we may add, science-centered rationality—are only a three-century episode in the history of Western thinking.
>
> When we began theorizing our experiences during the second women's movement a mere decade and a half ago, we knew our task would be a difficult though exciting one. But I doubt that in our wildest dreams we ever imagined we would have to reinvent both science and theorizing itself in order to make sense of women's social experience. (Harding, 1986:251)

This chapter addresses three questions: What does it mean to do feminist research? What can be learned about research as praxis and practices of self-reflexivity from looking at feminist efforts to create empowering research designs? Finally, what are the challenges of postmodernism to feminist empirical work? I address the latter question via a self-reflexive critique of my research into student resistance to liberatory curriculum.

What is feminist research?

Very simply, to do feminist research is to put the social construction of gender at the center of one's inquiry. Whether looking at "math genes" (Sherman, 1983) or false dualisms in the patriarchal construction of "rationality" (Harding, 1982), feminist researchers see gender as a basic organizing principle which profoundly shapes/mediates the concrete conditions of our lives. Feminism is, among other things, "a form of attention, a lens that brings into focus particular questions" (Fox-Keller, 1985:6). Through the questions that feminism poses and the absences it locates, feminism argues the centrality of gender in the shaping of our consciousness, skills and institutions as well as in the distribution of power and privilege.

The overt ideological goal of feminist research in the human sciences is to correct both the *invisibility* and *distortion* of female experience in ways relevant to ending women's unequal social position. This entails the substantive task of making gender a fundamental category for our understanding of the social order, "to see the world from women's place in it" (Callaway, 1981:460). While the first wave of feminist research operated largely within the conventional paradigm (Westkott, 1979), the second wave is more self-consciously methodologically innovative (Eichler, 1980; Reinharz, 1983; Stanley and Wise, 1983; Bowles and Duelli-Klein, 1983). For many of those second wave feminist researchers, the methodological task has become generating and refining more interactive, contextualized methods in the search for pattern and meaning rather than for prediction and control (Reinharz, 1983; Acker, Barry and Esseveld, 1983).

Hence, feminist empirical work is multi-paradigmatic. Those who work within the positivist paradigm see their contribution as adhering to established canons in order to add to the body of cumulative knowledge which will eventually help to eliminate sex-based inequality. Some, like Carol Gilligan (1982), start out to address methodological problems within an essentially conventional paradigm and end with creating knowledge which profoundly challenges the substance and, to a less dramatic degree, the processes of mainstream knowledge production (Lather, 1986b).[2] But it is to those who maximize the research process as a change-enhancing, reciprocally educative encounter that I now turn.

Research as praxis

Research as praxis is a phrase designed to respond to Gramsci's call to intellectuals to develop a "praxis of the present" by aiding developing progressive groups to become increasingly conscious of their situations in the world (quoted in Salamini, 1981:73). At the center of an emancipatory social science is the dialectial, reciprocal shaping of both the practice of praxis-oriented research and the development of emancipatory theory. In praxis-oriented inquiry, reciprocally educative process is more important than product as empowering methods contribute to consciousness-raising and transformative social action. Through dialogue and reflexivity, design, data and theory emerge, with data being recognized as generated from people in a relationship.

In the preceding chapter, I looked at three interwoven issues in the quest for empowering approaches to inquiry: the need for reciprocity, dialectical theory-building versus theoretical imposition, and issues of validity in praxis-oriented, advocacy research. My task here is to look at some feminist efforts toward empowering research designs, focusing mostly on my own empirical efforts to study student resistance to liberatory curriculum, but briefly highlighting four other examples. Mies (1984) field-tested seven methodological guidelines for doing feminist research in an action research project in Cologne, Germany, desiged to respond to violence against women in the family. A high visibility street action drew people who were then interviewed regarding their experiences with and views on wife beating. The resulting publicity led to the creation of a Women's House to aid victims of domestic abuse. A desire for transformative action and egalitarian participation guided consciousness-raising in considering the sociological and historical roots of male violence in the home through the development of life histories of the battered women who came to the Women's House. The purpose was to empower the oppressed to come to understand and change their own oppressive realities.

Hanmer and Saunders studied the various forms of violence to women through community-based, at-home interviewing with the purpose of feeding the information gained back to the community in order to "develop new forms of self-help and mutual aid among women" (1984:14). Research involvement led to an attempt to form a support group for survivors of violence and make referrals to women's crisis and safety services. Like Oakley (1981) discovered in her interview study of the effects of motherhood on women's lives, Hanmer and Sauders found that, "Women interviewing women is a two-way process" (p. 20) as research participants insisted on interactive, reciprocal self-disclosure.

Acker, Barry and Essevold, in a laudatory effort to "not impose our definitions of reality on those researched" (1983:425), studied women entering the paid labor force after years in a homemaking role in order to shed light on the relationship between social structure and individual consciousness. A series of unstructured interviews began with sixty-five women and followed thirty for 5 years. Data was used as a filter through which the researchers engaged in

> an ongoing process of reformulating our ideas, examining the validity of our assumptions about the change process, about how to conceptualize consciousness, the connections between changing life circumstances and changing views of self, others and the larger world, and how to link analytically these

individual lives with the structure of industrial capitalism in the U.S.A. in the 1970s. (p. 427)

Like Hanmer and Saunders, their work notes the insistence of the researched on reciprocal dialogue and is especially noteworthy for its attention to methodological discussion. Both studies do what Polkinghorne says is so important: "for practitioners to experiment with the new designs and to submit their attempts and results to examination by other participants in the debate" (1983:xi). The methodological self-reflections of Acker et al. are especially provocative as they wrestle with issues of false consciousness versus researcher imposition: "The question becomes how to produce an analysis which goes beyond the experience of the researched while still granting them full subjectivity. How do we explain the lives of others without violating their reality?" (1983:429).

A final example before turning to my own work is that of a group called Women's Economic Development Project (WEDP), part of the Institute for Community Education and training in Hilton Head, South Carolina.[3] Funded by the Ford Foundation, low-income women were trained to research their own economic circumstances in order to understand and change them. The participatory research design involved eleven low-income and underemployed women working as community researchers on a one-year study of the economic circumstances of three thousand low-income women in thirteen South Carolina counties. Information was gathered to do the following:

1) raise the consciousness of women regarding the sources of their economic circumstances;
2) promote community-based leadership within the state;
3) set up an active network of rural low-income women in S.C.;
4) support new and pending state legislation centering on women and work, and on educational issues.

With the culmination of our research process, the mechanism to effect changes in the status of low-income women is in place. Women from across the state have come together through the project, and are stronger for it. The project, thus, has stimulated a process of consciousness-raising and action-taking that will continue to grow for a broad spectrum of S.C. low-income women in the years to come. (January, 1987, research update)

A conference held March 13–15, 1987, was the second in a series designed to network low-income women in South Carolina. The First Statewide Women's Symposium in March, 1985, drew 150 women from twenty of South Carolina's forty-six counties.

The project's success, of course, depends on the degree to which low-income and underemployed women are at the center of this process of identifying and acting upon issues. Thusfar, 150 of the women originally interviewed continue to participate in the project's ongoing efforts of "building self-confidence, developing a support network for getting and sharing information, and empowering underemployed women, . . . building a statewide coalition of low-income women," developing leadership training and funding sourcebooks, and planning annual Statewide Women's Symposiums (1987 project pamphlet). As an example of praxis-oriented research, this project illustrates the possibilities for what Comstock regards as the goal of emancipatory research: stimulating "a self-sustaining process of critical analysis and enlightened action" (1982:387) by participating with the researched in a theoretically guided program of action over an extended period of time. The WEDP is especially interesting for how the research process itself serves to engage people in the project's ongoing activities, activities designed to help people understand and change the material conditions of their lives.

These examples of feminist efforts toward empowering research designs help frame my own empirical efforts to study student resistance to liberatory curriculum in an introductory women's studies course. A few years ago I wrote of women's studies as counter-hegemonic work, work designed to create and sustain opposition to social inequities (Lather, 1983, 1984). Women's studies, I argued in that earlier work, creates spaces where debate over power and the production of knowledge could be held "through its cogent argument that the exclusion of women from the knowledge base brings into question that which has passed for wisdom" (Lather, 1984:54). C.A. Bowers terms such spaces "liminal cultural space that allows for the negotiation of new meanings" as traditional forms of cultural authority are relativized (1984:vii). He then clearly states my substantive focus in my research into student resistance to liberatory curriculum: that our challenge is to use such openings in a non-impositional way.

Bowers writes in his chapter, "Understanding the Power of the Teacher": Teachers need to problematize "areas of consensus belief, grounded in the habitual thinking of the past" (p. 58), but that the danger is substituting our own reifications for those of the dominant culture. This leaves the student without the conceptual tools necessary for genuine participation in the culture. Bowers goes on to argue that issues need to be explored in settings free of slogans and predetermined answers. Reproducing the conceptual map of the teacher in the mind of the student disempowers through reification and recipe approaches to knowledge. Unlike Freire, says Bowers, he does not believe that "the dialectical relationship of student to teacher can transcend the problem of cultural invasion" (p. 96). Issues of imposition, hence, become of prime importance in understanding what happens in our classrooms in the name of empowering, liberatory education.

Theoretically, my own empirical work is grounded in a desire to use and expand upon the concept of "resistance" as it has developed in recent neo-Marxist sociology of education[4] in order to learn lessons from student resistance in the building of what Giroux calls "a pedagogy of the opposition" (1983b). Rather than dismiss student resistance to our classroom practices as false consciousness, I want to explore what these resistances have to teach us about our own impositional tendencies. The theoretical objective is an understanding of resistance which honors the complexity of the interplay between the empowering and the impositional at work in the liberatory classroom. As a taste of where we're heading, one of my graduate students came up with our research team's working definition of resistance:

> a word for the fear, dislike, hesitance most people have about turning their entire lives upside down and watching everything they have ever learned disintegrate into lies. "Empowerment" may be liberating, but it is also a lot of hard work and new responsibility to sort through one's life and rebuild according to one's own values and choices. (Kathy Kea, Feminist Scholarship class, October, 1985)

This is far different from the standard usage: those acts of challenge that agents intentionally direct against power relations operating widely in society (Bernstein, 1977:62). There is something which tells me that the difference is rooted in what feminist and postmodern ways of knowing have to offer toward the development of a less patriarchal, dogmatic Marxism. But I jump ahead of myself. I want now to simply describe the research design that evolved throughout our three-year study of student resistance to liberatory curriculum.

In the fall of 1985, the study began with the intention of studying 20% of the 150 students who take our introduction to women's studies course each quarter. Within that approximately thirty students, I expected to find some who would not like the course. It is they I found of particular interest, given my theoretical concern with the processes of "ideological consent" (Kellner, 1978:46), especially the processes by which false consciousness is maintained. What I had not anticipated was the combination of generally positive student response to the course with the way the experience of participating in the research project shifted in a more positive direction the reactions of even the few who did develop a critical stance toward aspects of the course.

Working with the ten researchers-in-training from my Feminist Scholarship class, we interviewed twenty-two students three times, at the beginning, middle and end of the course, regarding their attitudes toward and knowledge gained from the course. The second interview included collaborative group work on designing a survey to eventually be used as a pre/post-measure for purposes of ongoing formative course evaluation. In groups of five or six, the students were first asked to articulate changes they perceived going on inside themselves as a result of the course and then asked to critique the questions the research team designed based on students' own words and sense of the issues. The third interview included collaborative group response to the preliminary report which summarized interviews one and two, the results of field-testing the survey, and findings from phone interviews with ten former students of the course. We also asked them to comment on what they saw as the impact of participating in the research process on their experience of the class.

So, what did I learn in a very hurried quarter of data gathering?

—Sequential interviews conducted in an interactive, dialogic manner that entails self-disclosure on the part of the researcher foster a sense of collaboration.

—Group interviews provide tremendous potential for deeper probing and reciprocally educative encounter.

—Negotiation of meaning did not play as large of a role as I anticipated. Students felt that the preliminary report accurately captured their sense of the situation. "Member checks" (Guba and Lincoln, 1981) seemed to have the major effect of contributing to a growing sense of collaboration as opposed to a negotiated validation of the descriptive level. Negotiation never even attempted either the collaborative validation of interpretation or, moving even closer to a fully participatory research design as delineated in the preceding chapter, the collective development of empirically grounded theory.

—Issues of false consciousness and the dangers of conceptual overdeterminism in theoretically guided empirical work are every bit as complex as I had anticipated. Regarding false consciousness, for example, as I look for how students incorporate new oppositional or alternative concepts[5] into old ideological formations, I do not see the distortion of evidence that contradicts prior belief for which social psychologists argue (Unger, in press). Instead, the overwhelming response is, "My eyes are opened"; "Why didn't I see that before?" "It's like I'm just waking up"; or, my favorite, "The point is, I didn't know I didn't know." All involved became much more sensitive to the "psychological vertigo" that occurs in many students as a result of the course. One, for example, said, "I'm highly impressionable as I search for meaning. Can you be a feminist and do what's right for yourself and still have a husband and family? I don't want to lose my family in the finding of myself." And one of my favorites: "When you asked us where we stood on feminism at mid-term, it was the first time I became upset in the class. I didn't feel it was right to let myself change so much in such a short time."

Regarding the dangers of imposing researcher definitions on the inquiry, I know I had a preconceived notion of a "resister": someone so saturated with false consciousness that she could not see the "light" being offered her in our classrooms. The work of Ann Berlak (1983) began to focus my attention on the sins of imposition we commit in the name of liberatory pedagogy. And an emergent focus began to take shape: to turn the definition of resistance inside out somehow so that it could be used to shed light on efforts toward praxis in the classrooms of those of us who do our teaching in the name of empowerment and emancipation. As I designed the continuation of research over the next two years, I focused increasingly on the conditions which enhance the likelihood that students will begin to look at their own knowledge problematically and those that limit this process (Berlak, 1986). I especially attempted to probe the enabling conditions which open people up to oppositional knowledge.

The survey was field-tested and then, beginning fall quarter, 1986, we began to collect survey data for each of the fifteen sections of the course taught yearly. The survey grew out of dialogue with students taking the course and was, hence, couched in their own language and understanding of key experiences in taking the course. My colleague, Dr. Janet Lee, has written abut the results of the survey data.[6]

In the fall of 1986, along with students in the Feminist Scholarship class, I worked with twenty of the students in the introductory course in a *participatory research design* to interview their peers regarding their reactions to course readings. We held non-structured interviews to co-develop the questions for the peer interviews. We then conducted group mini-training in interviewing skills prior to their interviewing four or five of their peers regarding their reactions to course readings. Finally, we held meetings with five or six student co-researchers where they reported their data and we began to wrestle with what the data meant.

In the fall of 1987, I and the Feminist Scholarship students interviewed twenty-two students who had taken the course 1–3 years ago in order to provide some grasp of the longitudinal effects of the course. Interviews were conducted in both structured and unstructured ways in an effort to ground the interview questions. Descriptive data was pulled together and mailed out to research participants for a "member check." Finally, throughout the years of this research, I have been collecting journal entries from the introductory students that address their reactions to the course.

By addressing a series of methodological questions raised by post-structualism in Chapter 7, I want to use the data amassed in this study to explore the parameters of what might be called deconstructivist empirical inquiry. As I work with the data, I feel keenly how empirical work is selective, partial, positioned (Roman, 1987). Self-reflexivity becomes increasingly central as I attempt to make sense of my interaction with the data and the politics of creating meaning.[7]

Practices of self-reflexivity

> Can an approach that is based on the critique of ideology itself become ideological? The answer is that of course it can. . . . What can save critical theory from being used in this way is the insistence on reflectivity, the insistence that this theory of knowledge be applied to those propounding or using the theory. (Bredo and Feinberg, 1982:439)

> A maximally objective science, natural or social, will be one that includes a self-conscious and critical examination of the relationship between the social experience of its creators and the kinds of cognitive structures favored in its inquiry. (Harding, 1986:250)

Bowers (1984) argues that *reflexivity* and *critique* are the two essential skills we want our students to develop in their journey toward cultural demystification. I argue that the same is true for those of us who teach and do scholarly work in the name of feminism. As feminist teachers and scholars, we have obviously developed critical skills as evidenced by a body of scholarship which critiques patriarchal mis-shapings in all areas of knowledge (e.g., Spender, 1981; Spanier, Bloom and Boroviak, 1984; Schmitz, 1985). But developing the skills of self-critique, of a reflexivity which will keep us from becoming impositional and reifiers ourselves remains to be done.

As Acker, Barry and Essevold so aptly state, "An emancipatory intent is no guarantee of an emancipatory outcome" (1983:431). Too often, we who do empirical research in the name of emancipatory politics fail to connect how we do research to our theoretical and political commitments. Yet if critical inquirers are to develop a "praxis of the present," we must practice in our empirical endeavors what we preach in our theoretical formulations. Research which encourages self and social understanding and change-enhancing action on the part of "developing progressive groups" requires research designs that allow us as researchers to reflect on how our value commitments insert themselves into our empirical work. Our own frameworks of understanding need to be critically examined as we look for the tensions and contradictions they might entail.

In my own research, the question that interests me most right now is the relationship of theory to data in praxis-oriented research programs. Gebhardt, for example, writes: "what we want to collect data *for* decides what data we collect; if we collect them under the hypothesis that a different reality is possible, we will focus on the changeable, marginal, deviant aspects—anything not integrated which might suggest fermentation, resistance, protest, alternatives—all the 'facts' unfit to fit" (1982:405). Given my combination of feminism and neo-Marxism (or

Neon-Marxist, as my students have christened me), I have some strong attachments to particular ways of looking at the world. The intersection of choice and constraint, for example, is of great interest to me, given Marx's dictum that people make their own history, yes, but not under conditions of their own choosing. Also, I see gender as a central explanatory concept everywhere I look, including why male neo-Marxists deny its centrality through what Mary O'brien (1984) terms the "commatization of women" phenomenon.[8] A question I want to explore in chapter 7 is how such *a priori* concepts shape the data I gather and the ways in which that data is interpreted.

The challenges of poststructuralism to feminist empirical work

> Translation was never possible.
> Instead there was always only
> conquest, the influx
> of the language of metal,
> the language of either/or,
> the one language that has eaten all the others.
> (Margaret Atwood, 1986)

> The demise of the Subject, of the Dialectic, and of Truth has left thinkers in modernity with a *void* which they are vaguely aware must be spoken differently and strangely. (Jardine, 1982:61)

The implications of postmodernism for the ways we go about doing emancipatory research and teaching is the focus of the remainder of this book. I want to conclude this chapter by briefly introducing some of the issues involved in doing research that takes the deconstructive impulse into account.

The fundamental tensions between the Enlightenment and postmodernist projects provide a fertile instability in the most foundational tenets of how we regard the processes of knowledge production and legitimation. And, as feminist philosopher of science Sandra Harding writes, "the categories of Western thought need destabilization" (1986:245). Harding's critique of feminist critiques of science explores "the problem of the problematic" (p. 238) as she opposes *objectifying* versus *relational* world views (p. 185) and argues that feminism must run counter to "the psychic motor of Western science—the longing for 'one true story' " (p. 193). To avoid the "master's position" of formulating a totalizing discourse, feminism must see itself as "permanently partial" (p. 193) but "less false" (p. 195) than androcentric, male-centered knowledge. Harding argues that we find ourselves in a puzzling situation where the search for a "successor science" "epistemologically robust and politically powerful enough to unseat the Enlightenment version" (p. 150) is in tension with a postmodernism which struggles against claims of totality, certainty, and methodological orthodoxy.

The chapters that follow explore both Harding's conundrum and the territory opened up by Irigaray's recommendation of a detour into *technique* as we struggle toward "vision, self-knowledge, self-possession, even in one's decenteredness" (1985:136). For the present, what it means to de-center the self within the context of a feminism devoted to women's self-knowledge and self-possession continues to confuse me. Although I understand Longino (1986) and Harding's (1986) caution against a "suspect universalization" produced by a failure to de-center the self, I stand suspicious of what Meese warns as "a premature de-privileging of women as the political or feminist force within feminist criticism itself" (1986:79). While postmodernism makes clear that the supplanting of androcentric with gynocentric arguments so typical of North American academic feminism is no longer sufficient, Derrida argues for a necessary stage of deconstructive reversal. "Affirmations of equality will not disrupt the hierarchy. Only if it includes an inversion or reversal does a deconstruction have a chance of dislocating the hierarchical structure" (Culler, 1982, quoted in Meese, 1986:85).

Exchanging positions, however, does not disrupt hierarchy and "What feminism and deconstruction call for is the displacement of hierarchicization as an ordering principle" (Meese, 1986:85). The goal is difference without opposition and a shift from a romantic view of the self as unchanging, authentic essence to a concept of "self" as a conjunction of diverse social practices produced and positioned socially, without an underlying essence. While all of this de-centering and de-stabilizing of fundamental categories gets dizzying, such a relational, non-reductionist way of making sense of the world asks us to "think constantly against [ourselves]" (Jardine, 1985:19) as we struggle toward ways of knowing which can move us beyond ourselves.

Notes toward a self-critique: student resistance to liberatory curriculum

What Baudrillard terms "the revolution of the object" (1981:185) displaces attention from the knower to the known, from the constructor's intentions to the construction of an object of investigation inscribed as an effect of power: the problem of the subject as object to be observed and explained. In this reversal/displacement which foregrounds the politics of knowing and being known, "our best examples must be ourselves" (Van Maanen, 1988:xv). To attempt to deconstruct one's own work is to risk buying into what Bowers (1984) points out as the extraordinary faith in the powers of critical reflection that places emancipatory efforts in such a contradictory position with the postmodern foregrounding of the limits of consciousness.[9] Johnson, too, draws attention to the inadequacies of immediacy, of belief in the self-presentation of meaning which "seems to guarantee the notions that in the spoken word we know what we mean, mean what we say, say what we mean, and know what we have said" (1981:viii). Rather than to take refuge in the futility of self-criticism, however, I want to attempt it as aware as possible of its inevitable shortcomings, all that which remains opaque to ourselves. There is much here I cannot reach, much that eludes the logic of the self-present subject. This excess demonstrates not the demise of meaning but its endless possibilities (Grosz, 1989:29).

To deconstruct is to demonstrate how a text works against itself; it is "writing turning back on itself to consider, questioningly, its beginning validity and principles" (Said, 1975:335). To deconstruct the desire that shapes a particular act of enframing is to probe the libidinal investment in form and content of the author-text relationship. It is to mark the belief that our discourse is the meaning of our longing. Deconstruction agitates "on behalf of the exhuberance of life against a too-avid fixing and freezing of things" (Cocks, 1989:222). As I look at my own empirical research into student resistance to liberatory curriculum, deconstruction helps me frame such questions as the following, many of which will be addressed in Chapter 7 where I deconstruct my study of student resistance to liberatory curriculum:

—Did I encourage ambivalence, ambiguity and multiplicity, or did I impose order and structure? What elements of legislation and prescription underly my efforts? How have I policed the boundaries of what can be imagined?

—What is most densely invested? What has been muted, repressed, unheard? How has what I've done shaped, subverted, complicated? Have I confronted my own evasions and raised doubts about any illusions of closure?

—Did I create a text that was multiple without being pluralistic, double without being paralyzed? Have I questioned the textual staging of knowledge in a way that keeps my own authority from being reified?

—Did I focus on the limits of my own conceptualizations?

—Who are my "Others"? What binaries structure my arguments? What hierarchies are at play? Have I imagined "a space that would contain only subjects: no more spectators, only actors, all similarly compromised, with no possible exceptions"? (Sollers, 1983:88).

—Did I make resistant discourses and subject positions more widely available? Did my work multiply political spaces and prevent the concentration of power in any one point? Perhaps most importantly, did it go beyond critique to help in producing pluralized and diverse spaces for the emergence of subjugated knowledges and for the organization of resistance?

—How was this work tied into what Van Maanen refers to as the by no means trivial "demands of contemporary academic careers" and disciplinary logics (1988:53)? What is this fierce interest in proving the relevance of intellectual work? To what extent is my work tied to "the pretensions of sociology toward politics"? (Riley, 1988:54).

Within my work, "the people," a somewhat undifferentiated mass, are foregrounded as capable of grasping a reality of domination, subordination and resistance, once engaged by "critical pedagogues." Enlightenment goals are unproblematized, especially the excessive faith in the powers of the reasoning mind. Subjects are theorized as unified and capable of full consciousness. Additionally, my text is a conventional univocal text, unless one counts what might be seen as excessive quoting to be an effort toward many-voiced discourse as opposed to exhortations of authority and a didactic mode of critique.

And yet, my work accepts the importance of specificity in critical practice. Situated in my own critical cultural practices, it probes my political conditions and circumstances in a way that refuses inside/outside dichotomies and the "demonologies of the Other" common to ideology critique. Ideology critique is a product of a binary logic in its moral denunciation of some "Other." In contrast, poststructuralists argue that there are no innocent positions, that one of the illusions fostered by emancipatory discourses is that there is some "outside" of ideology, some escape from our paradoxical incription in that which we hope to subvert (Hutcheon, 1989).

In addition to acknowledging my own inescapable complicity in practices of cultural production, my work also interrogates the notion of prescription and recognizes the contingency and indeterminacy of meaning (Solomon-Godeau, 1988:210). The impulse that guided my work was to disperse rather than to consolidate my own position with increasing authoritarianism and certainty. And all of this was done prior to my exposure to postmodern theory, grounded in experience of the introductory women's studies classroom as a Gramscian "historical laboratory" in which to "get smart" about the emancipatory convictions of what I now frame as my post-Marxist discourse on the Other.

Conclusion

> The most rigorous reading . . . is one that holds itself provisionally open to further deconstruction of its own operative concepts. (Norris, 1982:48)

In the quest for more empowering ways of knowing, the ideas presented in this chapter need to be viewed as pieces of a transitory epistemology which can, given broad self-reflexivity, help make Harding's hope come true: that "feminist empiricism has a radical future" (1986:162). Those of us interested in the development of a praxis-oriented approach to inquiry, however, need to wrestle with the postmodern questioning of the lust for authoritative accounts if we are not to remain as much a part of the problem as of the solution ourselves. The remainder of this book will explore what a postmodern praxis might look like within the context of emancipatory research and pedagogy, with the final chapter returning to my study of student resistance to liberatory curriculum.

5

Deconstructing/Deconstructive Inquiry: The Politics of Knowing and Being Known

Thou shalt not sit
With statisticians nor commit
A social science.
W.H. Auden (quoted in Van Maanen, 1988:13)

The relation of politics and social inquiry has taken an interesting turn of late. Academic journals are abuzz with talk of a fundamental turning point in social thought, an epochal shift marked by a thinking differently about the meaning of knowing. We seem somewhere in the midst of a shift away from the concept of a *found* world, "out there," objective, knowable, factual, and toward a concept of *constructed* worlds (Simon and Dippo, 1986). Here knowledge is construed as contested and partial, an "effect of power" (Foucault, 1980) shaped by the interplay of language, power and meaning. Within this context, the "politics of interpretation" (Mitchell, 1983), the politics of knowing and being known take on urgency in our discourse about what it means to do social inquiry.

Poststructural ethnographer, John van Maanen (1988), attributes this shift to the growing importance of European thought on American social sciences. Phenomenology, hermeneutics, semiotics, Frankfurt School Critical Theory, French poststructuralisms and feminisms, European neo-Marxism and British materialist feminism—all are intersecting with American empiricism and pragmatism in a time noted by Said (1989) as "the end of empire." Much of this has come to be coded with the term "postmodern" as, across the disciplines, profoundly unsettling questions challenge what we do in the name of the human sciences. Building on questions long-asked by feminist, neo-Marxist and minority criticisms, an objective scientific reason is being displaced by a consciously political and social reason.

In this chapter I explore the parameters of postmodern practice within the arena of empirical inquiry in the human sciences. After an overview of postmodernism and the politics of interpretation, I delineate the outlines of empirical work which takes the deconstructive impulse into account.

Modernity, postmodernity: the politics of interpretation

> The sciences of man [sic] are inseparable from the power relations which make them possible. . . . (Deleuze, 1988:74)

More properly pluralized in order to encompass the varied positions termed "postmodern," postmodernisms range across the neo-Freudianism of Lacan, the post-Marxism of Foucault and Baudrillard, the post-feminism of Kristeva, and the post-logocentrism of Derrida. Defining itself by what it comes after, postmodernism is a self-consciously transitional moment, "the boundary between the 'not yet' and the 'no longer' " (Blumenberg quoted in Jauss, 1988–89:35).

The "no longer" is modernity with its central assumption of human capacity to shape ourselves and our worlds. With roots into the Renaissance and, most clearly, from the French Revolution onward, eighteenth-century Enlightenment values have profoundly shaped Western intellectual and political projects. The Enlightenment project of secularized authority and redemption displaced theology with humanism, and tradition with a proliferation of possibilities. The character of Faust well represents the modernist assumption of the human potential for endless growth and power to change the world (Nelson, 1987; Berman, 1982). Modernity has been about "push[ing] ourselves and others as far as we can go" (Berman, 1982:50). The self-determining, unified, rational, sovereign subject of bourgeois expansionism was to wrest freedom from the feudal tyrannies of kings and priests.

The ground of postmodernity is the disappointed hopes engendered by optimistic confidence in the continuing progress and imminent triumph of Enlightenment reason, especially "the debacle of instrumental reason"

(Jauss, 1988–89:33). To position oneself in the twilight of modernity is to foreground the underside of its faith in rationality, science and the human will to change and master: Auschwitz, Hiroshima, My Lai, Three Mile Island, Chernobyl. It is not that the dreams of modernity are unworthy; it is what they render absent and their conflictual and confusing outcomes that underscore the limits of reason and the obsolescence of modernist categories and institutions.

Not only positivisms, but also existentialisms, phenomenologies, critical theories: all seem exhausted, rife with subject-object dualisms, teleological utopianisms, totalizing abstractions, the lust for certainty, and impositional tendencies tainted with colonialism and/or vanguard politics. All seem no longer capable of giving meaning and direction to current conditions, the bewildering new world space of multinational capital, a kind of "hypercapitalism" feeding and fed by an information explosion of global and frenzied proportions. Especially problematic is the search for a "master narrative" (Lyotard, 1984), a fixed point of reference, an archimedean standpoint outside of the flux of language and human interest, an innocent transcendental signified, a God's eye rationalist perspective, some non-contingent order of truth.

The exhaustion of the paradigms of modernity creates an affective space where we feel that we cannot continue as we are (Grossberg, 1988a). The modernist project of control through knowledge has imploded, collapsed inward, as the boundaries between ideology and science disintegrate. Political and social theory daily become less able to explain and offer useful solutions. It is the exclusions and oppressions of modernist excess that are at issue here, the failures of liberal humanism in the face of both mass consumer culture and the encroachment of what Foucault (1980) calls technologies of surveillance and normalization.

The meaning and value of postmodernity is a central concern of current academic theorizing. Hutcheon (1988b), for example, contrasts the "Neo-Nietzschean" strand of postmodernism with the marxist/feminist appropriations of it. In Hutcheon's typology, the former is concerned with what it sees as cultural degeneration into Baudrillardian "hyperreality" and "panic culture," the nihilistic destruction of the possibilities of meaning (e.g., Kroker and Cook, 1986). On the other hand, a politicized postmodernism shifts the debate to a questioning of what it means to know and be known, how and why discourse works to legitimize and contest power, and the limitations of totalizing systems and fixed boundaries. While dualistic and reductionistic, Hutcheon's categories delineate how critical appropriations of postmodernism focus on the regulatory functions of discourses that articulate and organize our everyday experiences of the world. Their "object" of inquiry is the power-saturated discourses that monitor and normalize our sense of who we are and what is possible.

While the critical theories of the various feminisms, neo-Marxisms and minority discourses have long asked questions about the way power shapes the generation and legitimation of knowledge, postmodernism foregrounds an awareness of our own structuring impulses and their relation to the social order. Within feminism, for example, recognition of the doubled movement of inscription and subversion presses one to acknowledge the ways in which feminism is both outside the discourse of the fathers and, simultaneously, inscribed in Western logocentrism, patriarchal rationality, and imperialistic practices. As an example, one has only to look at the hegemony of the Eurocentric academy over what is legitimated as "feminist theory" in women's studies (Lugones and Spelman, 1983).

It is this paradoxical "doubled movement" or "doubled consciousness" regarding both the contestatory and reproductive dimensions of our efforts to make meaning that is the hallmark of postmodernism (Johnson, 1987; Hutcheon, 1988b). To both confirm and complicate received codes is to see how language is inextricably bound to the social and ideological. This moves social inquiry to new grounds, the grounds of "discourse" where the ways we talk and write are situated within social practices, the historical conditions of meaning, the positions from which texts are both produced and received. Such a paradoxical doubledness can help us begin to sketch out what the "not yet" is in our movement away from the "no longer," some outside of both the logic of binary oppositions and the principle of non-contradiction where we can "reinscribe otherwise" while avoiding the fall into an infinite regress of demystification.

Hence, poststructuralism is not so much about a seismic cultural shift as it is about the Academy catching up with one. Poststructuralism is part of the Zeitgeist, the culture and ethics of its time (Gitlin, 1989). Its concerns tap into our preoccupation with the politics of knowing and being known which has been spurred by the multi-sited demise of positivism and the growing acknowledgment of the ways that values permeate what we do in the name of science. It is the discursive formations of inquiry, the system of norms or rules that govern a certain way of thinking and writing at a certain time and place upon which I turn my deconstructive gaze. My question is simple: What are the implications of deconstruction for the practices that we construct in the name of the human sciences?

Deconstructing/Deconstructive inquiry

> The time has come to envisage that science defined by Derrida as a "science of the possibility of science . . . science of the 'arbitrariness of the sign,' science of the unmotivated trace, science of writing before and in speech," which must lead us to the exploration of a nonlinear, multiple, and dissimulated space. . . . Thus we discover a science whose object is not "truth," but the constitution and annulment of its own text and the subject inscribed there. We can analyze this text as the *remainder* of an operation to be accomplished *again* (i.e., in "progress"). (Sollers, 1983:137 and 179)

While deconstructive methods are almost hegemonic in areas such as literature and art criticism, their implications for scientific ways of knowing are much less explored. A small body of literature, however, has begun to address postmodernism and science.[1] In this work, three shifts are especially noted. 1) The first is a shift from emphasis on general theorizing to problems of interpretation and description. Marcus and Fischer call this "the ethnographic moment," a "hunkering down on detail" (1986:118). 2) There is especially a deconstructive emphasis on writing, a focus on the textual staging of knowledge. 3) There is a focus on the social relations of the research act itself.

What follows will look at these three shifts more carefully and then draw upon some examples of deconstructivist empirical work in order to situate a postmodern philosophy of empirical inquiry in actual contexts of research. I conclude the chapter with a delineation of the parameters of deconstructive inquiry, a delineation intended to be evocative as opposed to prescriptive.

1. Problems of description and interpretation. Tyler (1985) refers to "the end of description" and argues that we do not so much *describe* as *inscribe* in discourse. Narrative realism, hence, is but one of many textual strategies with its assumption of the transparency of description; such realism is challenged by the crisis of representation which is, in essence, an uncertainty about what constitutes an adequate depiction of social reality. Nancy Zeller (1987), for example, argues that we actively select, transform and interpret "reality" in our inquiry, but that we usually conceal our structuring and shaping mechanisms behind masks of objectivity and fact. She goes on to argue that, as the filters through which experience is shaped and given meaning, we might find that fictive forms or strategies could enlarge the appeal, understandability and possibly even the authenticity of empirical work (p. 93).

Another problem in terms of description/interpretation is the foregrounding of one's own perspectivity. Can this be anything but an intrusive voice? How do we explore our own reasons for doing the research without putting ourselves back at the center? The writer is always in the text, "one among others creating meaning" (Gitlin et al., 198:26), but how does the writer speak from "a decentered position of acknowledged, vested interest" which strips the authority of one's own discourse in order to "interrupt dominant and alternative academic discourses that serve Eurocentric, sexist, racist, and classist power relations"?[2]

2. The textual staging of knowledge. To use language so that it gives the appearance of clear, referential meaning is to conceal the artifice that produces the appearance of objectivity. For example, in interview studies, dialogue is usually used "as a means of verisimilitude in the interest of empirical validation" (Tyler, 1985:93). Data might be better conceived as the material for telling a story where the challenge becomes to generate a polyvalent data base that is used to *vivify* interpretation as opposed to "support" or "prove."

Turning the text into a display and interaction among perspectives and presenting material rich enough to bear re-analysis in different ways bring the reader into the analysis via a dispersive impulse which fragments univocal authority. Such writing works against the tendency to become the locus of authority; it is writing that probes the blind spots of the interpretaters' own conceptualizations and attends to its own constitutive elements.

3. The social relations of the research act. All methods have a political moment which at a fundamental level expresses a relationship between people (Gitlin et al., 1988). Social relations mediate the construction of knowledge; who speaks for whom becomes a central question. Such a question de-centers what Dreyfus and Rabinow (1983) term the "Great

Interpreter" and Foucault calls the "master of truth and justice" (1977:12) whose self-appointed task is to uphold reason and reveal the truth to those unable to see or speak it. Conversely, a reciprocally educative focus breaks down the distinctions between emancipatory research and pedagogy by producing a collaborative analysis that doesn't impose the researcher's understanding of reality, that doesn't say what things mean via a privileged position and theoretical presuppositions (Gitlin et al., 1988:18). The following exemplars suggest ways that full attention to the research process itself can help develop forms of inquiry that are "interruptors" of the social relations of dominance. They are presented not as a cookbook or "the best of," but as concrete illustrations of a number of abstract qualities.

Exemplar 1

Mulkay (1985) has written a book, *The Word and the World: Explorations in the Form of Sociological Analysis,* where he implodes the boundaries of the sociological research monograph. The introduction presents a spirited dialogue between Author, Book and Reader. Mulkay then demonstrates the textual display of factuality by assembling ten letters exchanged between two biochemists involved in a technical debate, varied interviews, and documents which feature Nobel ceremony official records. Including a response of one of the scientists to Mulkay's analysis of the initial set of ten letters, Mulkay presents a form of "analytical collaboration" which "allows more than one voice, and more than one interpretative stance, into the analytical text on an equal footing" (p. 5).

As an effort to cope with "the potential multiplicity of varied accounts," Mulkay interweaves more conventional, univocal sociological discourse with "quasi-fictional text" (p. 5). In one part, Mulkay creates a play in which both researcher and researched take part as interpretative equals in a discussion of scientific replication. Interrupting the typical pattern of sociological discourse where the researcher claims interpretative dominance over participants (e.g., "false consciousness" judgments), Mulkay again moves into a quasi-fictional discourse. This time the topic is scientific discovery, and Mulkay creates an imaginary investigation into scientific fraud. In the final section, Mulkay creates an analytical parody of the Nobel ceremonies where textual agents from previous chapters as well as Nobel participants take part.

Mulkay's purpose is "to devise and try out new kinds of analysis which are more dialogic in form than conventional research texts" (p. 8). The contraints of orthodox form are broken and he creates a text that is non-linear, polyvocal, multi-leveled and open to multiple readings—all in an effort to capture the interpretive complexity of our lives. The distinction between fact and fiction is broken down as he demonstrates how both conventional and experimental forms of sociological discourse are "imaginative reconstructions of our world, in so far as that world is mediated through our own and other's interpretative work" (p. 11). In doing so, Mulkay enlarges our conception of what can be done with sociological data both in the analysis and in the writing-up.

Exemplar 2

As a literary critic, Patai's work on Brazilian women's life stories illustrates the "blurred genres" (Geertz, 1980) that so characterize post-modernism. The typical work of literary critics is "writing texts about written texts" (Patai, 1988:143); Patai moves from this to collecting, editing, and translating oral accounts of the lives of ordinary Brazilian women. Interviewing sixty women of different ages, races, and economic situations, Patai's focus on the circumstances and constraints that framed the interviews themselves yields the following insights and issues:

—"What might have been considered offensive personal curiosity" is transformed into something respectable, legitimated by "having a project,' " including the paraphernalia of tape recorders and notebooks (p. 144).

—Being a foreigner with language problems "help[ed] restore a needed balance between the researcher and the researched, especially in the case of poor and uneducated women" (p. 144).

—"The hope that the interviewer might solve a problem or know what to do" (p. 145) raised ethical issues. How do our research procedures and "limited sense of obligation" reproduce the structural inequalities involved when "*other* women serve as the subjects of *our* books" (p. 165).

—Patai's own interactive, dialogic role is probed although she warns that situating the researcher's experience at the center of the inquiry perpetuates the very dominance our liberatory intentions hope to fight (p. 147).

—"The authority and creativity of the speaker weaving her own text" (p. 147) is more about "how a person verbally constructs an image of her life, how she creates a character for herself, how she becomes the protagonist of her own story" (p. 150), than it is a capturing of some static sense of "reality."

—The texts constructed from interviews are not transparent; they are constructions which inherently distort due to the shift, in this case, from one language to another and, in all cases outside of co-writing, from words spoken by one person to words shaped into written form by another. Written texts, then, are "a point of intersection between two subjectivities" (p. 146) which could easily have produced a different story with different emphases given different interview conditions. Patai's response to this dilemma is to present the words of one woman, Marialice, a housecleaner, in the form of free verse where the broken lines indicate the pauses and reflections of the speaker's voice. Rather than the transparent slice of "reality" typical of interview write-ups, the words of Marialice become a poem of her struggle to make sense of her life through her actions and her representations of those actions via language (p. 163). Marialice uses the spoken word to diminish the hold of mere circumstances over the shaping of her life (p. 164).

Patai's aim was to use her skills "to work on the problem of invisible women, . . . to learn from these women how their lives appeared to them" (p. 143). Like Mulkay, she has exploded/imploded the idea of how a proper interview text should appear. Patai uses her text to make Marialice's self-representing expressions authoritative, thereby countering "the elite assumption of the unreflected silence of ordinary people" (Wexler et al., 1987:233). What Jane Marcus calls "the subjective authority of women's own experience" (1986:4) is presented in a relatively unmediated way. Through its prose poem format, Patai's text rejects the more typical formats, which produce interview texts of sociological verite, paraphrasing, or the self-centered reflexive style "where the people studied are treated as garnishes and condiments, tasty only in relation to the main course, the sociologist" (Richardson, 1988:205). Patai's revelations of the structuring of her own text and the problematics of her discipline as well as her bringing the reader into the inquiry as an analytic partner help move her text into a place where it serves the purposes of both demystification and social change.

Exemplars 3 and 4

As one of the more critical developments in the human sciences, feminism is in the forefront of developing less oppressive ways of knowing. Its claim that the choice of sociopolitically motivated goals and objects of research will affect our very methods is well illustrated by the following two examples of collective self-study.

Ellsworth, Larson and Selvin (1986) investigated the social construction of pleasure by interrogating their own reactions to MTV videos in order to challenge current theories of reception in media studies. By examining their own contradictory experiences of watching MTV, they were able to foreground and examine their own subjectivities as two white, middle-class women watching black women sing, and as a woman and a man watching a heterosexual man sing. Analysis was grounded in how their use, interpretation and pleasure of the videos was linked to their social history and power positionings via class, race, gender and sexual orientation. The text is constructed as a dialogue with each speaker's voice clearly identified. Through a not undifficult process, which to some degree problematized collaboration by surfacing hidden power imbalances, each reports the gain of new language and understanding of their own and one another's relations to MTV, gender differences, and the construction of multiple, varying and contradictory subjectivities. Within this study, self is both subject and object in a way that reveals the vulnerability of being an object of scientific scrutiny.[3]

A second example is the collective biography method developed by groups of German women over a two-year period (Haug, 1987). Taking their own bodies as objects of study, their goal was greater understanding of resistance to the dominant at the level of the individual as well as how we inscribe ourselves in dominant values. Their specific focus was women's processes of self-construction via the investment of parts of the body with a whole range of social and psychological significance. Subtitled "A Collective Work of Memory," the book presents a method that combines the consciousness-raising long central to feminist processes with an analysis of female sexualization through writing stories out of personal memories. Focusing on a particular body part, each woman wrote a story which was then analyzed collectively by tracing how initial opinions and judgments grew out of existent theories and popular knowledge, how, in essence, their reactions were colonized by dominant patterns of thought. Each woman then rewrote her story by "writing against the grain" (p. 60) of the way initial reactions were inscribed in dominant discourse. Writing became a process of active change, a "weapon of defense' against seeing themselves through the eyes of others.

By identifying a site and elaborating a practice for a critical cultural production of a usable theoretical language for themselves and their readers regarding how women insert themselves into the construction of female sexuality, this reflexive method spans the theory-practice gap. By requiring that the subject and object of the research be the same person and that everyone contribute to the writing, the method avoids both appropriation of the experience of the "Other" and the inherent disparity between the writer and the written about. As Sollers notes, "*Whoever does not write is written*" (1983:199, original emphasis). Hence, this method goes far toward achieving its goal as "an intervention into existing practices" (Haug, 1987:35) which is productive of new configurations of social relations rather than reproductive of the behaviors that instill dominant values in us.

By foregrounding how their inquiry process consolidates relations of power, how it is reproductive of the modes of domination, the method works deconstructively to help locate the exclusions, limitations, and constraints placed on practice (Sholle, 1988). As such, the method of collective biography where we "make ourselves the objects of our own research" (Haug, 1987:50) models a way of doing inquiry that promotes new forms of subjectivity via a refusal of individuality and a diffusion of the sites and practices from which dominance can be challenged.

Exemplars 5 and 6

Like all of the human sciences, educational research is thusfar not much touched by the issues raised by poststructuralism. The two exemplars that follow give some feel for the possibilities; they were chosen for their full attention to the research process itself. The first is a self-critique of past research, and both are from projects very much in process.

Gitlin, Siegel and Boru (1988) challenge both the passive, non-interventionist stance of interpretive ethnography[4] and the rhetorical and ideological innocence of methods assumed by radical sociologists of education. Their goal is to displace "trickle down" change strategies with dialogic understanding and reciprocal change models that foreground how social relations mediate the construction of knowledge. Organized around much commentary on the need for dialogic textual production, reflexive versus realist ethnographic tale-telling, and the politics of who speaks for whom, the authors deconstruct their own approaches to inquiry.

Subsuming their three voices into one third-person omniscent narrative voice, Gitlin's earlier realist approach to ethnography in curriculum studies is termed "fieldwork as television watching" (p. 18). In this "spectator" approach to inquiry, his own privileged position and theoretical assumptions were used "to say what things mean." In his more recent work, a shift in focus is noted from "reporting the facts" to reporting the struggle to create a dialogical community with a group of teachers in a way that brings the author into the text. Using a peer evaluation model, teachers chose and framed classroom problems to study. Gitlin acted as "consultant and trouble shooter"; teacher teams collaboratively wrote reports.

The same third-person omniscent voice focuses on Siegel's work with a sixth-grade teacher who invited her to collaborate in the development of an alternative literacy curriculum. Using the "authoring curriculum" (Harste, Woodward and Burke, 1984), Siegel, the teacher and a graduate student conducted a one-year collaborative ethnography of this attempt to use an alternative to skills-based literacy programs. In addition to shared time in the classroom, weekly dialogic meetings were held to establish a process that brought teaching and research into a productive cycle where the boundaries were blurred between "insiders" and "outsiders," "teachers" and "researchers," "knowing" and "doing."

In a second exemplar rooted in educational practice, Johnston (1990) details a self-termed deconstructive project where her purpose is to demystify and democratize research. Critiquing her four-year effort to construct collaborative inquiry with classroom teachers, she reflects on how the first phase imposed a research design that was too neat and tidy to be anything other than minimally collaborative. As the project emerged, "Intrigue with openendedness eventually replaced worries about predictability" (p. 175); "Our talks began to feel more like conversations than interviews . . ." (p. 176). The biggest shift was in the writing of the text. Early reports had included teachers in a "member check" where they responded to what the researchers had written. In spite of such member checks, "Clearly our voice was the dominant one" (p. 177). Later, the teachers began to write into the text, elaborating, extending, contradicting, "co-laboring" (p. 176). There was also a shift in the object of the gaze, from them to herself (p. 181). But Johnston did not discuss her own changing attitudes with the teachers: "I didn't know how to do it nor even how to talk about it very clearly" (p. 176). Making explicit her own doubts and concerns is a focus of her ongoing work with this project.

Both exemplars struggled with the differences in role expectations, especially the need to de-center the "expert" role of the university-based researcher. Johnston calls for "genuine dialogue about differences" (p. 179) and new language and writing forms (p. 19): "There was a haunting sense that I was burying my point of view in objective language in order to avoid upsetting the personal sensibilities of the teacher" (p. 20). Her words were echoed in Gitlin, Siegel and Boru's recommendations that prejudgments about collaboration be brought out into the open, the social relations of the project be assessed regularly, and there be some historicizing of personal and institutional lives in order to explore how the past affects beliefs and actions. Such work can lay the groundwork for understanding differences by seeking out investments of privilege and struggle early on via foregrounding the motivations, histories and stakes of the individuals involved.

While each of the exemplars attempts to disrupt conventions and to intervene in ways productive of new configurations, the first has some tendencies toward policing knowledge and appropriating the experience of the "Other." As a movement that inscribes more than it contests boundaries, Gitlin, Siegel and Boru's call for "a regulatory ideal for emancipatory research" (p. 29) is in stark contrast to McCloskey's (1983) argument that the business of those engaged in experiments at the limits of their disciplines is to resist the ridigity and pretention of rules, to interrupt received categories and procedures. In terms of the politics of the gaze, while it is somewhat unclear, it seems that Siegel's teaching of the alternative curriculum was as much an object of investigation as was the "teacher's." In Gitlin's case, however, not including his own teaching as an object of study and defining his role as "consultant and trouble-shooter" is reproductive of the very "cult of expertise" they wanted to de-center. So, too, is the third-person omniscent voice that narrates this tale of an attempt to do otherwise in the search for practices of educational research that transform the relations of dominance. The latter point was much discussed amongst the research team, demonstrating the gulf between what is possible to be communicated in making public one's in-process efforts to do research more democratically and the finitude of what is actually spoken or written.[5]

The Habermasian assumptions about "consensus" and "rationality" that permeate this piece and Johnston's call for a "genuine dialogue about differences" are problematized by Ellsworth's (1989) arguments regarding rationalism and "dialogue" as discussed in Chapter 2. To take unequal, muliply-sited and conflicting subject positions into account is to foreground the unsaid and unthought, the partial and open-ended nature of our efforts to create more democratic ways of knowing. Partaking in such a continual contesting of the dangers and normalizing tendencies in our own liberatory discourses is to participate in the radical unsettling that is postmodernism.

The parameters of deconstructivist inquiry

What can such exemplars teach us about the parameters of deconstructive inquiry? Mulkay suggests incorporating more voices, more interpretative stances into the analytical text in ways that use the writer's authority to disperse authority and reveal the text's own construction of meaning. The political moment inherent in all method and all formulations of understanding is made explicit and maximized (Gitlin et al., 1988) via collaborative analysis and, especially, Mulkay's interruption of orthodox conceptions of factuality. By foregrounding the fuzzy boundaries between "fact" and "fiction," he demonstrates that the facts of knowledge, like truth, objectivity and reason, are *the effects of power*. They are textual and social constructions created by us in our efforts to understand our situations.[6]

Patai stresses the centrality of asking what right we have to intrude into the lives of others and the inequalities attendant upon relationships of researcher/researched and writer/written about. Emphasizing what Foucault terms "the indignity of speaking for others" (quoted in Kritzman, 1988:xviii), she also cautions against putting the researcher at the center of the inquiry as she shows how a focus on the excluded and marginalized functions both as intrusive surveillance and examination and as counter-disciplinary practice.

Ellsworth, Larson and Selvin and Haug's self-studies implicitly ask what it means for our lives to become "data" to be manipulated in the interest of better theory. Both studies raise many questions about the constitution of the gazer and the gazed upon, the knower and the known. Such questions suggest that we may have to move to a more coeval terrain in order to break the methodological intrusiveness inherent in the disciplinary powers which constitute the human as knowable object and upon which the technologies of dominance are based. The collective biography method is especially a model of minimizing the researcher's ability to police knowledge. The analysis grows out of collaborative assessment of participants' judgments via egalitarian discourse which extends the role of the researched much beyond merely "being understood" (Gitlin et al., 1988:14). Such a method diversifies the possibilities of struggle, especially diffused and dispersed struggles, and models the self-reflexivity that is "the new canon" of deconstructivist work (Rajchman, 1985).

Finally, the exemplars more overtly rooted in educational practice demonstrate how our efforts to generate less oppressive ways of knowing are *both* reproductive and transformative. While the never-ending self-critique called for by Foucault can be paralyzing, it also offers the hope of developing more effective social change practices.

More emergent than codified and more experimental than standardized, these exemplars are well aware of the inescapable incursion of politics, desires, belief into social inquiry. Each thinks beyond received habits of thought and practice, outside the range of the permissable bounds of science as usually conceived. As such, they demonstrate how postmodern thought and practice open up new avenues for recognizing the workings of power in the ways we construct our world and its possibilities.

Conclusion

> The problem is not one of changing people's "consciousness" or what's in their heads; but the political, economic, institutional regime of the production of truth. (Foucault, 1977:14)

These words I trace across the science and philosophy of my time feel both here, now, and as yet to find a future in a movement into something embryonic, liminal, not yet in place. In terms of the human sciences, the shift is away from cognitive, rule-based, behaviorally focused empirical work and toward more reflexive, language-based, interpretive practices. In this endeavor to "do science otherwise," it behooves us, I believe, to be cautious regarding how the new openness to interpretive ways of knowing might well be premised on their being a more "with it" version of the intrusive surveillance and examination that undergirds the increasingly invasive apparatuses of power of multinational "hypercapitalism." Additionally, we need to be cautious that our praxis-oriented work not be a pressured and coercive part of the "technologies of normalization."

A science capable of grasping the continual interplay of agency, structure and context requires a "becoming space" (Derrida, 1981:27) where we can think and act with one another into the future in ways that both mark and loosen limits. The deconstructive empirical work dealt with in this chapter lays the groundwork for such generative movement. After a chapter which reinscribes science differently, the final chapter of this book will attempt to build on this movement.

6

Reinscribing Otherwise: Postmodernism and the Human Sciences

> [Is it possible for social science] to be different, that is, to forget itself and to become something else . . . [or must it] remain as a partner in domination and hegemony? (Said, 1989:225)

> In these anti-foundationalist times, in which seemingly the ground is being swept from under our feet, perhaps it is timely for beings with legs to talk about how it is possible to take a stand—and whether it is impossible not to. (Yeo, 1989:10)

These are the days of disenchantment, of questions that cut to the bone about what it means to do empirical work in the human sciences. The erosion of the assumptions that support social inquiry is part of the relentless undermining of the Enlightenment code of values which increasingly appears the key Western intellectual project of the late twentieth century. Those choosing to encourage rather than resist this movement are using it to stretch the boundaries that currently define what we do in the name of science. A behavioral science governed by adherence to methods and standards developed in the natural sciences is being displaced by what Harland calls "a science for philosophers" (1987:92). A "narrative, semiotic, particularist, self-aware" science is emerging from those who work "to reorient and redirect theoretical, methodological and empirical aims and practices" across the human sciences (Van Maanen, 1988:125). Turning away from the enormous pretentions of positivism, their project is the development of a human science much more varied and reflexive about its limitations.

Rooted in such work, this chapter interrogates the values underlying the cultural practices we construct in the name of the human sciences. I begin by playing with the question, what is science? Next, I construct three possible framings of research in the human sciences in terms of ideology and methodological attitude. I then look at two key issues in what it means to reinscribe science, to do science in a post-foundational context: the issue of relativism, and the continued lack of an adequate poststructuralist theory of the subject. Both are surveyed by probing the varied moves in feminist receptions of postmodernism.

What is science?

> The sciences of man [sic] . . . which have so delighted our "humanity" for over a century, have their technical matrix in the petty, malicious minutiae of the disciplines and their investigations. These investigations are perhaps to psychology, psychiatry, pedagogy, criminology, and so many other strange sciences, what the terrible power of investigation was to the calm knowledge of the animals, the plants or the earth. Another power, another knowledge. . . . (Foucault, 1979:226)

> . . . the world that made science, and that science made, has disappeared, and scientific thought is now an archaic mode of consciousness surviving for awhile yet in degraded form. . . . (Tyler, 1987:200)

> Ethnology almost met a paradoxical death that day in 1971 when the Phillipine government decided to return to their primitive state the few dozen Tasaday discovered deep in the jungle, where they had lived for eight centuries undisturbed by the rest of mankind, out of reach of colonists, tourists, and ethnologists. This was at the initiative of the anthropologists themselves, who saw the natives decompose immediately on contact, like a mummy in the open air.
>
> For ethnology to live, its object must die. But the latter revenges itself by dying for having been "discovered," and

defies by its death the science that wants to take hold of it. (Baudrillard, 1984:257)

These passages from poststructuralist discourse evoke my puzzlement regarding how far to go with the anti-science position so evident in Foucault and Tyler's words. And what is one to make of Baudrillard, the "wild man" of postmodernism whose "hyper-deconstructions" of the basic premises of Western thought map hysterical forms of "panic" analysis as a strategy for unseating logocentrism? As Nelson points out, one does not need to accept *all* of what they say in order to learn from them (1987:10). My present position is neither an anti-science nor a post-science one. By deconstructing assumptions of a knowing subject, a known object, and an unambiguous, complete knowledge outside of the unsaid and unsayable, the embedded fore-structures of understanding, I will present science as one among many truth games. Rather than Althusser's movement from ideology to science, my argument is part of Foucault's movement of a succession of different ideologies, some of which consider themselves "scientific" (Harland, 1987:102). In this movement, truth is viewed as at least as rhetorical as it is procedural (Nelson et al., 1987), and science is, according to my present favorite definition, a much contested cultural space, a site of the surfacing of what it has historically repressed (Hutcheon, 1988a:74).

Legitimating itself in opposition to theology and aristocracy, science's claim to authority has been premised on its appeal to experience mediated by a purportedly value-neutral, logical-empirical method which promised the growth of rational control over our selves and our worlds (Popkewitz, 1984). In this postpositivist era, it is easy to not see that what Comte termed "positivism" was part of the liberatory impetus of the Enlightenment project. This was recently underscored for me by learning that it was British feminist, Harriet Martineau, who, in 1853, translated Comte's first lectures on the possibilities of a positive social science capable of leading the way to social betterment (Riley, 1988:49).

But the intentions of science to liberate reason from the dictates of kings and priests were inscribed into practices of control and prediction. These practices were rooted in a binary logic of hermetic subjects and objects and a linear, teleological rationality; the innocence of both observable facts and transparent language were assumed. Quantum physics has problematized such concepts in the natural sciences and it, along with the human sciences, is still reeling from the after-shocks. Binary either/or positions are being replaced by a both/and logic that deconstructs the ground of both reductionist objectivism and transcendental dialectics (Derrida, 1978). Linearity and teleology are being supplanted by chaos models of non-linearity (Gleick, 1987) and an emphasis on historical contingency (Foucault, 1980). Power is assumed to permeate all aspects of our efforts to know (Habermas, 1971; Nicholson, 1989), and language is theorized as constitutive rather than representational, a matrix of enabling and constraining boundaries rather than a mirror (Rorty, 1979; Tyler, 1987).

Within this poststructural context, the value-neutral claim at the heart of positivist authority is untenable. Foregrounded as an ideological ruse, the claim to value-neutrality is held to delimit our concept of science and obscure and occlude its own particularity and interest. Truth, objectivity and reason are reinscribed as what Foucault calls "effects of power," and the subject-object opposition implodes. Transhistorical assertions of value are seen as based not on an innocent reason or logic but on an alliance with power. Objectivity "creates its object to be objective about" (Harland, 1987:104). Facts are not given but constructed by the questions we ask of events. All researchers construct their object of inquiry out of the materials their culture provides, and values play a central role in this linguistically, ideologically, and historically embedded project that we call science.

Contesting the suppression of values in the production and legitimation of knowledge has been led by the "ex-centrics" (Hutcheon, 1988a) who, in turn, have had their way paved by the sociology of knowledge, broad intellectual traditions in social theory (e.g., Marx, Nietzsche, Freud), and attention to the actual practices of science itself. While the critique of scientism ante-dates Kuhn, he was the first to show historically how infused with the social and the arbitrary were the allegedly neutral and empirical observations of science. Such work has propelled the surge away from positivism and toward an interpretive, value-searching conception of the human sciences (Inglis, 1988). Neutrality, objectivity, observable facts, transparent description, clean separation of the interpreter and the interpreted—all of these concepts basic to positivist ways of knowing are called into question. Science as codified by conventional methods which marginalize value issues is being reformulated in a way that foregrounds science as a value-constituted and constituting enterprise, no more outside the power/knowledge nexus than any other human enterprise.

Ideology and methodological attitude

Frame 1: the discourse of paradigm shifts

> Scientists firmly believe that as long as they are not *conscious* of any bias or political agenda, they are neutral and objective, when in fact they are only unconscious. (Namenwirth, 1986:29)

Thomas Kuhn's 1962 *The Structure of Scientific Revolutions* has been appropriated by postpositivist philosophers of science as a canonical text. The concept of paradigm shift has permeated discourse across the disciplines now for over two decades. With positivist hegemony broken, many see this as a time for exploring ways of knowing more appropriate for a complex world of interacting, reflexive subjects rather than for the mute objects upon which is turned the gaze of methods developed in the natural sciences (Bakhtin, 1981). Kuhn wrote: "Rather than a single group conversion, what occurs [with a paradigm shift] is an increasing shift in the distribution of professional allegiances" as practitioners of the new paradigm "improve it, explore its possibilities, and show what it would be like to belong to the community guided by it" (1970:157–158).

Kuhn's model of scientific change is rooted in the history of the natural sciences. In his view, the social sciences are a pre-paradigmatic hodgepodge of techniques largely borrowed from the natural sciences, too unformed to support productive normal sciences (1970:160). This aspect of Kuhn's thought has not been much noted, however, by those in the human sciences who have appropriated his language of successive paradigms, anomalies, revolutions, and competing modes of scientific activity.

Within Kuhnian arguments, the central tension that causes a paradigm shift is internal to the discipline, technical breakdown brought on by the inability of the dominant paradigm to explain empirical anomalies: "Change comes from within and is formed by the limitations of what is already known. It is a closed system, constrained by the limited knowledge of the trained practitioners who are admitted to the club" (Gonzalvez, 1986:9). The interspersal of periods of normal and revolutionary science is assumed via an orderly succession of paradigmatic shifts.

Within such frameworks, method serves to provide some standards of logic and evidence and is seen as emergent but capable of increasing systematization (e.g.,Lincoln and Guba, 1985; Bogdan and Biklen, 1982; Miles and Huberman, 1984). Methodological variety is presented as assumedly politically neutral choices, all of which seek to capture, via language, the closest possible representation of what is "really going on." Ideology is framed either as a de-politicized sort of world view that shapes paradigmatic choice, or as bias to be controlled in the name of objectivity. The descriptive adequacy of language as a transparent representation of the world is assumed.

By assuming the descriptive adequacy of language as a mirror of the world, such work remains positioned in a representational logic. Seeking to capture the object of our investigation as it "really" is, independent of our representational apparatus, such logic denies the productivity of language in the construction of the objects of investigation. Additionally, by de-emphasizing the political content of theories and methodologies, Kuhnian work sidesteps how politics pervades science. As Cherryholmes points out: "Policing some methodological rules to the exclusion of other sets of rules is a political as well as scientific activity. . . ." (1988:182; see, also, Eisner, 1988). "Truth" is still procedural, methods still objectifying, values still to be controlled and minimized in the effort toward precise, unbiased results.

In terms of the relationship between researcher and researched, what Dreyfus and Rabinow term, "The Great Interpreter who has privileged access to meaning" (1983:180) plays the role of adjudicator of what is "really" going on, while insisting that the truths uncovered lie outside of the sphere of power. Willis terms this claim of privileged externality, this assumedly politically neutral position, a "covert positivism" (1980:90) in its tendencies toward objectification, unitary analysis and distanced relationships between subject and object. In Foucault's words, "Knowable man [becomes] the object-effect of this analytic-investment, of this domination-observation" (quoted in Dreyfus and Rabinow, 1983:160).

Kuhnian frameworks de-emphasize the political content of theories and methodologies and deny the dissolving of the world as structured by referential notions of language. They also diminish the play of multiple emergent knowledges vying for legitimacy.[1] Caught up in a representational logic, they search for codifications and standards instead of asking if something more fundamental than a "paradigm shift" in the academy might be going on.

Caputo's term, "the post-paradigmatic diaspora" (1987:262), problematizes the concept of paradigm shift so central to contemporary discourse in the human sciences. The central argument is that "paradigm" may be a useful transitional concept to help us move toward a more adequate human science, but that, "To still pose one paradigm against the other is to miss the essential character of the moment as an exhaustion with a paradigmatic style of discourse altogether" (Marcus and Fischer, 1986:233). Atkinson et al. outline "the dangers of paradigms," "the dangers of Kuhnian rhetoric": the presentation of ideas as novel and distinctive that are better framed as historically rooted and relationally shaped by concepts that precede and parallel as well as interrupt them. They also note the "intolerance, fruitless polemic, and hypercriticism" that accompany paradigmatic allegiances (1988:233).

Caputo's Feyerabendian[2] "post-paradigmatic diaspora" creates a liminal moment in the human sciences that escapes, excedes and complicates Kuhnian structures. While we need conceptual frames for purposes of understanding, "classifying research and researchers into neatly segregated 'paradigms' or 'traditions' does not reflect the untidy realities of real scholars . . . and may become an end in itself. . . . 'Traditions' must be treated not as clearly defined, real entities but only as loose framewords for dividing research . . ." (Atkinson et al., 1988:243).

I will deal later with the poststructuralist argument that we must abandon efforts to represent the object of our investigation as it "really" is, independent of our representational apparatus, for a reflexive focus on how we construct that which we are investigating. I turn now to those concerned with the ways in which ideas about science serve particular political or economic interests, the discourse of feminists and neo-Marxists who raise the question, "in whose interest, by sex, race and class, has knowledge been generated?" (Gonzalvez, 1986:16).

Frame 2: discourse toward a critical social science

> What counts is the further scientific development at such a theoretical and methodological level, and in terms of such problem constellations, that the distance of science from

> politics becomes unacceptable by its own standards. (Dubiel, 1985:187)
>
> There is no social practice outside of ideology. (Hall, 1985:103)

Efforts toward a critical social science raise questions about the political nature of social research, about what it means to do empirical inquiry in an unjust world. Based on Habermas' (1971) thesis in *Knowledge and Human Interests* that claims to value-free knowledge obscure the human interests inherent in all knowledge, critical theorists hold that there is no end to ideology, no part of culture where ideology does not permeate. This most certainly includes the university and the production of social knowledge. Grounded in the re-emergence of the Frankfurt School and its concern with questions of domination and resistance at the level of subjectivity, "Action science as a form of praxis" aspires to paradigmatic status as a major alternative to other forms of social research (Peters and Robinson, 1984). A primary concern of discourse toward critical social science is how to generate knowledge in ways that turn critical thought into emancipatory action.

As part of the post-Althusserean rejection of economism and determinism, consciousness and subjectivity rise to the fore in critical inquiry as the juncture between human agency and structural constraint takes on theoretical urgency. The goal is a critical social science which alleviates oppression by spurring "the emergence of people who know who they are and are conscious of themselves as active and deciding beings, who bear responsibility for their choices and who are able to explain them in terms of their own freely adopted purposes and ideals" (Fay, 1987:74).

The subject of such a science is theorized as living in a crisis of legitimacy (Habermas, 1975); this crisis provides a material base for the hope that subordinated groups will arise to construct more democratic social forms. The ability of the oppressed to comprehend a reality that is "out there" waiting for representation by social inquirers is assumed (Flax, 1987; Fay, 1987), as is the central role to be played by "transformative intellectuals" (Aronowitz and Giroux, 1985), who will serve as catalysts for the necessary empowering dialogue. Much of this goes on under the rubric of "critical ethnography" (Simon and Dippo, 1986) where neo-Marxist ideology critique (e.g., Repo, 1987) is being supplanted by more linguistically informed ethnography. This emergent body of work combines phenomenology and semiotics to focus on the relationship between the conscious and unconscious dynamics embedded in social relations and cultural forms (e.g., Simon, 1987).[3]

Within the context of a critical social science, methodology is viewed as inherently political, as inescapably tied to issues of power and legitimacy. Methods are assumed to be permeated with what Gouldner terms "ideologically resonant assumptions about what the social world is, who the sociologist is, and what the nature of the relation between them is" (1970:51). Methods, then, are politically charged "as they define, control, evaluate, manipulate and report" (ibid.:50). The point is that "the role of ideology does not diminish as rigor increases and error is dissipated" (LeCourt, 1975:200). Such a stance provides the grounds for an "openly ideological" approach to critical inquiry (Lather, 1986b) where the central issue is how to bring together scholarship and advocacy in order to generate new ways of knowing that interrupt power imbalances. The line between emancipatory inquiry and pedagogy blurs as critical researchers focus on developing interactive approaches to research. In addition, there is growing concern regarding the dangers of researchers with liberatory intentions imposing meanings on situations, rather than constructing meaning through negotiation with research participants (e.g., Acker, Barry and Esseveld, 1983; Berlak, 1986; Miller, 1987).

Science could develop into a progressive moment within the consciousness of the society it both studies and shapes, but it is not enough to be oriented toward the interests of underprivileged social groups. An emancipatory, critical social science will develop out of the social relations of the research process itself, out of the enactment of what in the Frankfurt School was only incipient: implementation in research praxis (Dubiel, 1985:185). Fay argues that such a critical social science must be limited in aspiration and see itself as a way that intellectual effort might help improve the political situation, as opposed to seeing itself as "the key to redeeming our social and political life" (1987:ix).

As we shall see in the next section, however, poststructuralism argues that no discourse is innocent of the Nietzschean will to power. Spivak cautions, "the desire to 'understand' and 'change' are as much symptomatic as they are revolutionary" (1987:88). Whether the goal of one's work is prediction, understanding or emancipation, all are, for Foucault, ways of "disciplining the body, normalizing behavior, administering the life of populations" (Rajchman, 1985:82). All are forms of knowledge and discourse that we have invented about ourselves; all define, categorize and classify us. All elicit the Foucauldian question: How do practices to discover the truth about ourselves impact on our lives?

Frame 3: poststructuralism: discourse on discourse

> A good proportion of our intellectual effort now consists in casting suspicion on any statement by trying to uncover the disposition of its different levels. That disposition is infinite, and the abyss that we try to open up in every word, this madness of language [is an] abyss that has to be opened up first, and for tactical reasons: in order to break down the self-infatuation in our statements and to destroy the arrogance of our sciences. (Barthes, 1975, quoted in Smith, 1988:99)

The recent linguistic turn in social theory focuses on the power of language to organize our thought and experience. Language is seen as both carrier and creator of a culture's epistemological codes. The ways we speak and write are held to influence our conceptual boundaries and to create areas of silence as language organizes meaning in terms of pre-established categories. Poststructuralism displaces both the post-Kuhnian view of language as transparent, and critical theorists' view of language as ideological struggle waged on the playing field of dialectics. Raising both the dangers of objectification and the inadequacies of dialectics, poststructuralism demands radical reflection on our interpretive frames as we enter the Foucauldian shift from *paradigm* to *discourse,* from a focus on researcher ontology and epistemology in the shaping of paradigmatic choice, to a focus on the productivity of language in the construction of the objects of investigation.

Poststructuralism holds that there is no final knowledge; "the contingency and historical moment of all readings" means that, whatever the object of our gaze, it "is contested, temporal and emergent" (Clifford and Marcus, 1986:18–19). Whether the reign of paradigms is over or merely suspended for a time, the argument is that "the play of ideas free of authoritative paradigms" (Marcus and Fischer, 1986:80–81) will move us further into some new way of producing and legitimating knowledge. Van Maanen cautions: "Confident possession of some grail-like paradigm is at best a passing fancy or at worst a power play," but "the paradigm myth . . . dies more slowly than the post-paradigm reality" (1988:xiv).

From a poststructuralist perspective, ideology remains a much disputed term. While orthodox Marxists define it as false consciousness and oppose it to the "true" knowledge of scientific Marxism, Foucault argues for the concept of power/knowledge to replace the reductionist Marxian usage of ideology, finding it too embedded in assumptions of "false consciousness" and a human essence awaiting freedom from constraints (Sholle, 1988). Others view ideology as a constitutive component of reality: "the production of meaning, the positioning of the subject, and the manufacture of desire" (McLaren, 1987:303). Within this neo-Gramscian view, there is no meaning-making outside of ideology. There is no false consciousness, for such a concept assumes a true consciousness accessible via "correct" theory and practice (Hall, 1985). Postmodern feminist cultural critic Teresa Ebert defines ideology as follows:

> not false consciousness or distorted perception [but rather] the organization of material signifying practices that constitute subjectivities and produce the lived relations by which subjects are connected—whether in hegemonic or oppositional ways—to the dominant relations of production and distribution of power . . . in a specific social formation at a given historical moment. (1988:23)

Poststructuralism views research as an enactment of power relations; the focus is on the development of a mutual, dialogic production of a multivoice, multi-centered discourse. Research practices are viewed as much more inscriptions of legitimation than procedures that help us get closer to some "truth" capturable via language (Cherryholmes, 1988). Attention turns away from efforts to represent what is "really" there and shifts, instead, toward the productivity of language within what Bakhtin has termed "the framing authorial context" (1981:358). Objectivity, for example, is seen as a textual construction more fruitfully displaced by a deconstructive emphasis on writing as an enactment of the social relations that produce the research itself. Rather than "objectivity," questions such as the following rise to the fore:

—How do we address questions of narrative authority raised by poststructuralism in our empirical work?

—How do we *frame* meaning possibilities rather than *close* them in working with empirical data?

—How do we create multi-voiced, multi-centered texts from such data?

—How do we deconstruct the ways our own desires as emancipatory inquirers shape the texts we create?

—Why do we do our research? To use our privileges as academics to give voice to what Foucault terms "subjugated knowledges"? As another version of writing the self?

—What are the race, class and gender relations that produce the research itself?[4]

Within poststructuralism, a relational focus on how method patterns findings replaces the objectifying and dialectical methods of post-Kuhnian and critical approaches. For example, the following deconstructs what an interview is:

> As a mode of knowing, the interview technique is an exemplary strategy of traditional humanism since such a device inscribes fundamental humanist values (that is, liberal pluralism, unmediated knowledge, participatory democracy, consensus among free subjects) in the very practices it claims to be studying. . . . The focus of the interviews (unitary, sovereign subjects) reaffirmed the belief that people contain knowledge (they are self-present subjects) and all that one has to do to have access to that knowledge is to engage in "free" and "unconstrained" discussions. . . . The interview technique is, of course, an exemplary instance of what Derrida has called the desire for presence, which is an effect of the dominant logocentrism in the academy. (Zavarzadeh and Morton, 1986–87:16)

What is sought is a reflexive process that focuses on our too easy use of "imposed and provided forms" (Corrigan, 1987:33) and that might lead us toward a science capable of continually demystifying the realities it serves to create.

To conclude this section on reinscribing otherwise the cultural practices we call science, what we are talking about in Yvonna Lincoln's (1990) wonderful word play, "is NOT your father's paradigm." It is an altogether different approach to doing empirical inquiry. This approach, paradoxically, both calls into question "the dream of scientificity" (Barthes, quoted in Merquior, 1986:148) and advocates the creation of a "more hesitant and partial scholarship" capable of helping us "to tell a better story" (Grossberg, 1988a:147) in a world marked by the elusiveness with which it greets our efforts to know it.

Just say No to nihilism: relativism as a God trick

> Feminist theory is neither subjective nor objective, neither relativist nor absolutist: it occupies the *middle ground* excluded by oppositional categories. . . . Absolutism and relativism both ignore the concrete functioning of power relations and the necessity of occupying a position. . . . (Grosz, 1988:100)

> No more certainties, no more continuities. We hear that energy, as well as matter, is a discontinuous structure of points: punctum, quantum. Question: could the only certainty be the point? (Tschumi, 1989:263)

Postmodern theories of language, subjectivity and power profoundly challenge the discourses of emancipation on several fronts. The assumption of a potentially fully conscious human agent will be dealt with later in this chapter. What I want to address here are the contradictions involved in post-foundational intellectual work committed to social justice. I will focus specifically on the age-old issue of relativism as foregrounded in Bernstein's (1983) question: Does the move away from foundationalist or absolutist epistemologies entail embracing "the spectre of relativism" as our inevitable companion?

Postmodernism evokes criticism from all sites in the political spectrum. Both "neo-conservatives" and "progressives" reject the postmodern questioning of the "grand narratives of legitimation" (Lyotard, 1984) as a "French fad" which, by advocating the loss of foundational standards, propels us into irrationalism. Some lament the loss of "classical" standards and fear anarchy and cultural disintegration (e.g., Bloom,

1987). Others see a slide into relativism that is dangerous for the dispossessed in its undercutting of the grounds for social justice struggle and its feeding of nihilism and quietude (West, 1987; Dews, 1987; Hartsock, 1987). Nancy Hartsock (1987), for example, joins race, class and sex into a deconstruction of the intellectual moves that shape how postmodern issues get framed. Attempting to come to grips with the social and historical changes of the middle to late twentieth century, postmodern theorizers have "set the rules of the discussion in a way inappropriate to those of us who have been marginalized" (p. 200).

Hartsock's concerns are echoed in Longino's (1988) worries that a denial of objective value takes away the ground of feminist claims. Like Grosz's words which began this section by positioning concerns with relativism as within a binary logic, feminist philosopher of science, Sandra Harding, turns such fears of relativism upside down by arguing that we must "relativize relativism itself":

> Historically, relativism appears as an intellectual possibility, and as a "problem," only for dominating groups at the point where the hegemony of their views is being challenged. . . . The point here is that relativism is not a problem originating in, or justifiable in terms of, women's experiences or feminist agendas. It is fundamentally a sexist response that attempts to preserve the legitimacy of androcentric claims in the face of contrary evidence. (1987:10)

Caputo asks, "How many of our questions arise from foundational compulsions, Cartesian anxieties?" (1987:262). To see relativism as a Cartesian obsession is to argue that it is an issue only within the context of foundationalist epistemologies which search for a privileged standpoint as the guarantee of certainty. Regardless of political positioning, the concept of relativism assumes a foundational structure, an archimedean standpoint outside of flux and human interest. In Cherryholmes' words:

> Relativism is an issue for structuralists because they propose structures that set standards. Relativism is an issue if a foundational structure *exists* that is ignored. . . . A Derridean might argue, however, that the issue is *differance,* where meanings are dispersed and deferred. If dispersion and deferral are the order of the day, what is relative under structuralism is

> differance under deconstruction. If there is a foundation, there is something to be relative to; but if there is no foundation, there is no structure against which other positions can be "objectively" judged. (1988:185)

If the focus is on the procedures which take us as objects and involve us in systems of categories and procedures of self-construction, relativism becomes a non-issue. If the focus is on how power relations shape knowledge production and legitimation, relativism is a concept from another discourse, a discourse of foundations that posits grounds for certainty outside of context, some neutral, disinterested, stable point of reference. "Relativism is the perfect mirror twin of totalization in the ideologies of objectivity; both deny the stakes in location, embodiment, and partial perspective; both make it impossible to see well" (Haraway, 1988:584).

All thought is not equally arbitrary, Bakhtin (1984) argued over 50 years ago; positionality weighs heavily in what knowledge comes to count as legitimate in historically specific times and places. The world is spoken from many sites which are differentially positioned regarding access to power and resources. Relativism foregrounds the shifting sands of context, but occludes the play of power in the shaping of changing structures and circumstances. As such, it is what Haraway calls "a god trick . . . a way of being nowhere while claiming to be everywhere equally" (1988:584). In sum, fears of relativism and its seeming attendant, nihilism or Nietzschean anger, seem to me an implosion of Western, white male, class-privileged arrogance—if we cannot know everything, then we can know nothing.

Relativistic assumptions of a free play of meaning that denies power relations are of little use for those struggling to free themselves from normalizing boundaries and categories. Fraser and Nicholson point out the practical political interests of feminism that have saved it from some of the hand-wringing of other leftists: "women whose theorizing was to serve the struggle against sexism were not about to abandon powerful political tools merely as a result of intramural debates in professional philosophy" (1988:92). The point is that while oppositional, critical work remains to be developed in the wake of postmodernism, "In periods when fields are without secure foundations, practice becomes the engine of innovation" (Marcus and Fischer, 1986:166).

With practice as a privileged site for working out what it means to do emancipatory work within a post-foundational context, "The alternative to relativism is partial, locatable, critical knowledges . . ." (Haraway, 1988:584). Legitimacy is plural, local and context-specific: "instead of hovering above, legitimacy descends to the level of practice and becomes immanant in it" (Fraser and Nicholson, 1988:87). Interventions are situationally and participatorily defined. Cultural work becomes "a battle for the signified—a struggle to fix meaning temporarily on behalf of particular power relations and social interests" (Weedon, 1987:98). Ellsworth, for example, asks "How have we closed down the process of analysis and self-reflection long enough to take a stand, and what or who have we had to put on hold or bracket in order to do that?" (1987:14).

As Fekete notes, it is "strategically desirable to move people to think about life beyond the horizons of the more nihilistic and paralyzing aspects of postmodernism" (1987:acknowledgments). Fears of relativism are displaced by explicit interventions that collapse the boundaries between science and politics and make relativism less formidable by undercutting the usual ground taken up by critics (Alcoff, 1989:98). Absolute knowledge was never possible, anyway. Archimedean standpoints have always been shaped in the crucible of the power/knowledge nexus. We just thought otherwise, believing in gods and kings and, more recently, the "objectivity" of scientists.

The objective, the apolitical and the value-neutral have been foundational in scientific claims to authority. Relativity has been put forth as the great bugbear against which we must commit to some foundational absolute if anarchy and chaos are not to descend upon us. It has been the primary intent of this section to argue that such claims are cultural dominants which masquerade as natural, rational, necessary, but which are less a fact of nature than of human production. They are, in spite of their denial, embedded in what Foucault (1980) terms "regimes of truth," the power/knowledge nexus which provides the constraints and possibilities of discourse.

Subject-ed subjects[5] and identity politics

Fictions of the subject

A post-humanist theory of the subject combines Derrida's critique of the metaphysics of presence with a post-Althusserean focus on human agency. The result is a shift in cultural theory to seeing subjectivity as both socially produced in language, at conscious and unconscious levels, and as a site of struggle and potential change. In poststructuralist theories of the subject, identity does not follow unproblematically from experience. We are seen to live in webs of multiple representations of class, race, gender, language and social relations; meanings vary even within one individual.[6] Self-identity "is constituted and reconstituted relationally, its boundaries repeatedly remapped and renegotiated" (Scott, 1987:17). This focus on the fundamentally relational nature of identity results in the historically constituted and shifting self versus the static and essentialized self inherent in the concept of the free and self-determining individual.

Identities are continually displaced/replaced. The subject is neither unified nor fixed. We occupy conflicting subject positions where language is understood as competing discourses. Poststructuralism theorizes the subject "as a site of disarray and conflict, central to the process of political change and to preserving the status quo" (Weedon, 1987:21). In the discursive struggle for our subjectivity, we are "active but not sovereign" (Ibid.:41). Within this de-centering of the subject, the key Enlightenment equation of knowing, naming and emancipation becomes problematic. The self becomes an "empirical contingency" (Flax, 1987:626), both site and subject, produced by diffuse forms of power. The subject is constantly figured and refigured within a context of bombardment by conflicting messages, a "semiotic glut" (Collins, 1987:25), spawned by the intensified sign production of consumer society.

Johnson's "post-post-structuralist account of subjectivity" (1986–87:69) and Grossberg's rejection of postmodernism's tendency to reify a fractured, fragmented, schizoid subject (1987:39) illustrate the continued lack of an adequate poststructuralist theory of subjectivity. While we are not the authors of the ways we understand our lives, while we are subjected to regimes of meaning, we are involved in discursive self-production where we attempt to produce some coherence and continuity. We need a theory of the subject that recognizes both of these moments, a theory grounded in the "hunkering down on detail" (p. 118) so important in what Marcus and Fischer (1986) note as "the ethnographic task" of reconstructing dominant macroframeworks "from the bottom up, from the problem of description . . . back to general theory which has grown out of touch with the world on which it seeks to comment" (p. 118).

The subject of fictions

At the center of deconstruction is the fiction of the self-determining subject of modern political, legal, social and aesthetic discourse. Neither feminist nor neo-Marxist theorizing has escaped what Fay calls "a metaphysics of human agency" (1987:26), "an inflated conception of the powers of human reason and will" (p. 9). While competing conceptions of the subject have long haunted Marxism and forced it to re-examine its notion of the revolutionary subject, the subjects of critical activity have never been properly identified.[7] Marxism's premise of the constructedness of human nature has, however, saved it from some of the essentialism that reveals how much of feminist thought is embedded in the very assumptions it is critiquing. Postmodernism provides a critical analysis of the very discourse of liberation and revolution, of both the "ideological self-righteousness of the marxist critic" (Rajchman, 1985:80) and the essentialism that haunts contemporary feminist theory (Eisenstein, 1983; Harding, 1986; Haraway, 1985).

While we cannot but be engulfed by the categories of our times, self-reflexivity teaches that our discourse is the meaning of our longing. Derrida's "the always already" means that how we speak and write tells us more about our own inscribed selves, about the way that language writes us, than about the "object" of our gaze. The trick is to see the will to power in our work as clearly as we see the will to truth.

One example of a key concept that needs to be deconstructed is that of false consciousness. In trouble since Althusser, the concept of false consciousness "is a moment of extreme ideological closure" (Hall, 1985:105) which frames the issue in terms of a true consciousness, a totality. Given that "there is no experiencing *outside* of the categories of representation or ideology" (p. 105), understanding people's complicity in their own oppression becomes a matter of developing a non-reductive problematic that focuses on the relationship between conscious understanding and the unconscious dynamics embedded in social relations and cultural forms. This requires a poststructuralist theory of subjectivity where ideology is seen not as false consciousness but as an effort to make sense in a world of contradictory information, radical contingency and indeterminancies, "a way of holding at bay a randomness incongruent with consciousness" (Spivak, 1987:78). From this perspective, ideology becomes a strategy of containment for beings who, in spite of David Byrne's advice, cannot "Stop Making Sense."[8]

Identity politics

> My project . . . is an attempt to dis-cern the "subject," and to argue that the human agent exceeds the "subject" as it is constructed in and by much poststructuralist theory as well as by those discourses against which poststructuralist theory claims to pose itself. (Smith, 1988:xxx)

Marxism's long-running search for the revolutionary subject has focused much attention on the "death of the subject" supposedly promulgated by postmodernism. What has "died" is the unified, monolithic, reified, essentialized subject capable of fully conscious, fully rational action, a subject assumed in most liberal and emancipatory discourse. Such a subject is replaced by a provisional, contingent, strategic, constructed subject which, while not essentialized, *must* be engaged in processes of meaning-making given the bombardment by conflicting messages. To quote Foster:

> Here, then, we begin to see what is at stake in this so-called dispersal of the subject. For what is this subject that, threatened by loss, is so bemoaned? Bourgeois perhaps, but patriarchal and phallocentric certainly. For some, for many, this may indeed be a great loss, a loss which leads to narcissistic laments and hysterical disavowals of the end of art, of culture, of the west. But for others, precisely for Others, it is no great loss at all. (1985:136)

Shifting from an essentialized "artifice of 'identity' " to "the analytic of desire" (Bhabha, 1989:138), the sense-making activity of subjects is as important as how they are acted upon. Hence, de-centering is not so much the elimination of the subject as it is the multi-centeredness of action, a re-conceptualization of agency from *subject-centered agency* to *the plurality and agency of meaning*. The demise of foundationalist philosophy, the epistemological subject, and the traditional objectivist ideas of knowledge and truth create many problems for the emancipatory convictions of post-Marxist discourse on the Other. Ross asks in whose interest it is to abandon universals and answers that the very idea of interests must be problematized, as interests can no longer be universalized and identities are not already *there* (1988:xvii).

For example, Hall (1985) writes of how his sense of racial identity, his "blackness," has shifted over time and place. Pratt (1984) explores the same ground of meaning as the locus of action, but from the perspective of white privilege. Additionally, while class and gendered self-conceptions seem widely variable across and within individual biographies, sexual orientation seems especially shifting in terms of identity politics. While Lugones celebrates that ". . . the construction of 'lesbian' is purposefully and healthily still up in the air, in the process of becoming" (1987:10), Lerner (1987) raises cautions regarding how we treat our historical foremothers in terms of interpreting their sexuality. As Weedon writes, "the meaning of lesbianism changes with historical shifts in the discursive construction of female sexuality" (1987:159).

What all of this means strategically, how one builds a politics on a postmodern questioning of the unified, stable subject is only beginning to be articulated (Laclau and Mouffe, 1985; Weedon, 1987; Penley, 1986:142–144; Harasym, 1988; Smith, 1988; Epstein, 1987). I find Riley (1988) and Ellsworth (1989) especially evocative on this rethinking of agency within a context of the unknowable. Both stress West's point that in contemporary identity politics, totalizing categories like "women" and "blacks" and "third-world women" are most usefully conceptualized as heuristic rather than ontological categories (interview with Stephanson, 1988:270). To quote Riley: "Of course this means that feminism must 'speak women,' while at the same time, an acute awareness of its vagaries is imperative. . . . [W]hile it's impossible to thoroughly be a woman, it's also impossible never to be one. On such shifting sands feminism must stand and sway" (1988:113–114).

Conclusion

Preceded, paralleled and interrupted by critical "ex-centric" discourses and global struggles for social justice, postmodernism is a process of re-theorizing the objects and experiences of everyday life in the twilight of modernity, an epochal turning point in how the world and the possibilities of human agency are conceived. It is a shift from the conjunction of liberal humanism with positivistic science to a conjunction of de-centered subjectivity and multi-sited agency within a post-paradigmatic diaspora.

The resultant opening up of ways to produce and legitimate knowledge has profound implications for research and pedagogy aimed at interrupting relations of dominance. The last chapter of this book is an effort to give form to these philosophical wrestlings by way of an empirical study of student resistance to liberatory curriculum in an introductory women's studies course.

7

Staying Dumb? Student Resistance to Liberatory Curriculum

> To understand just one life, you have to swallow the world. I told you that. (Rushdie, *Midnight's Children,* 1982:126)

> What is known is always in excess of knowledge. Knowledge is never adequate to its object. (Spivak with Rooney, 1989b:133)

This chapter explores what it means to write science differently. It attempts to enact rather than simply state the upheavals produced as deconstruction circulates across recent critical social theory. My keenest sense in the writing of this chapter is the many different directions I could have gone with it, the gulf between the totality of possible statements and the finitude of what is actually written or spoken. The structuring impulse I have settled on is to craft four narrative vignettes, to tell four different "stories" about my data.

My data base is interviews, research reports, journal entries, and my own insights/musings collected over the course of a three-year inquiry (1985–1988) into student resistance to liberatory curriculum in an introductory women's studies course, introduced to you in Chapter 4. This data was collected by a team that shifted from year to year as students took the Feminist Scholarship class with me. Begun in 1985, the study has taken place over a long enough period of time that my theoretical vantage point keeps reshaping. I began by situating this empirical work within neo-Marxist studies of resistance (Giroux, 1983) and feminist efforts to explore empowering research approaches (Lather, 1988). I have grown increasingly intrigued with all the talk about "the crisis of representation" and "postmodern writing strategies," such as "multi-voicedness' and texts which interrupt themselves and foreground their own constructedness. The data sits there, "sprawling, diffuse, undefined, and diverse" (Lofland, quoted in Van Maanen, 1988:24), seemingly stable, waiting for me to figure out how to use it,which means figuring out what my purposes in all of this are.

Like Patai (1988), I am interested in how to put to work my skills and privileges in the service of contributing to the making of a space from which the unvoiced/unheeded can be said/heard. My goal here also is to move outside the domain of conventional textual practices, outside the restricted repertoire of rhetorical devices usually attendent upon "scientific" writing (Bazerman, 1987). In that space of the conventional writing of science, empirical work is concerned with portraying findings as factual and well founded in ways that are, often, in Van Maanen's characterization, "as if to satisfy some fetish of documentation or legitimation" (1988:23).

Instead, I want to attend to the textual operations of my own production and organization of meaning, to write in a way that foregrounds the performativity of language. Especially, I want to attend to the textual production of a certain appearance of transparency where a found world is assumed, communicable in a "clear" style in which there is no intrusion by language or an embodied researcher. I want to problematize conceptions of "the non-discursive 'real' or empirically discoverable world" (Sheridan, 1988:2), without falling into languacentricity, the collapse of the real into language. The ground I explore is that of a relentlessly heterogeneous reality, the irreducible particularies of which do not take well to dualistic categories. Such exploration is based in a politics that wants other than to marginalize that which does not fit categorical unities that order and classify. Additionally, rather than the erasure under which the "researcher" typically operates, I assume myself to be a social subject in relation with others. My specificity is assumed to profoundly shape the process and product of inquiry, not the least being my own particular interests in the discourses of emancipation and the methodologies of the human sciences.

As I wrestle with what it means to "do" critical, emancipatory science in a post-foundational context, the following questions become key. What is the special status of scientific knowledge? What work do we want inquiry to do? To what extent does method privilege findings? What is the place of procedures in the claim to validity? What does it mean to recognize the limits of exactitude and certainty, but still to have respect for the empirical world and its relation to how we formulate and assess theory?

Foucault's method of archaeology looks at discarded systems of linguistic and institutional artifacts left behind by successive generations as each took up anew the task of creating categories to explain its perception of the human condition (Martin et al., 1988). Such a method foregrounds that to put into categories is an act of power. The category systems we devise to "explain" empirical "findings" are re-inscribed by poststructuralism as strategies of legitimacy where exactitude and certainty deny the unthought in any thought, the shadow, supplement, alterity, the structuring absence inherent in any concept. Conceiving useful categorical schemes as provisional constructions rather than as systematic formulations, focus shifts to how data escape, excede and complicate rather than how to impose a specific direction of meaning on the unfolding of the narrative. And we stand poised in some movement into an altogether different approach to inquiry. From the use of interview data to construct a prose poem (Patai, 1988) to the "dada data" invoked by Clifford (1988:149), new practices are emerging which reshape our sense of the possibilities for what we do in the name of the human sciences.

This chapter explores not only what to do with "data" but also how to see one's own teaching as a situated discourse. With all of this in mind, I turn to pedagogy.

Situated pedagogies: Between limits & transgressions

> Pedagogy must itself be a text. (Ulmer, 1985:52)

> Pedagogy should be construed less as an interesting application of theory and more as a means for reconstructing the arena for intellectual debate. (Hariman, 1989:226)

Pedagogy is fruitful ground to help us address questions of how our very efforts to liberate perpetuate the relations of dominance at the micro level of local resistances. As Atkins and Johnson (1985) note, however, the powerful resources of deconstruction are not much focused on pedagogy. While much of the small body of literature that does exist is abstract theorizing, a few more situated presentations have emerged. Zavarzadeh and Morton (1986–87), for example, situate themselves within the debates about humanities curriculum reform. Ellsworth (1989) deconstructs the prescriptions of critical pedagogy within the context of her teaching of a university anti-racism course. In this emerging tradition of situated, embodied deconstructive discourse on pedagogy, I want to focus on the situated pedagogy with which I am most familiar, the introductory women's studies class.

Mankato State University teaches approximately 600 students a year in such a class, multiple sections of which are limited to thirty-five and taught by teams of faculty and teaching assistants, upper level undergraduates and master's students who have taken a course in feminist pedagogy. The course is an elective that counts for general education credit, one reason for the swelling numbers which result in most sections of the class closing early in the registration process.

Based on our survey of 546 students who took the course in 1987, students are primarily entry level undergraduates ranging in age from 18 to 70. Seventy-four percent are under 23. Twenty-six percent are 23 or over. The latter is due largely to the course being a popular draw for the university's Friday College Program which is aimed at "the returning woman student." Approximately 5% of those who take the course are male. Most of the students are first generation college goers. Most are working part-time. Many of those in the evening classes work full-time and are raising families. Three percent of the students at the university are minority, mostly Asian and Afro-American; 12% of the students in the introductory women's studies class are minority. The university's Alternative Lifestyles office recommends the course to lesbian and gay students; many of the community's feminist therapists do likewise. Scholarship programs are set up to enable women from the battered women's shelter, organizations working with impoverished women, and minority studies students to take the class. Students enter the course from a variety of backgrounds in terms of feminism. Many regard it as "lesbian man-hating." Many have mothers who are self-described feminists. A few describe themselves as feminists (19% from 1987 data), but many do not, with most being "uncertain" (50%).[1]

While each teaching team designs its own course, curricular coordination occurs via staff meetings and departmental curriculum guidelines. A review of the syllabi used from 1985–1988 reveals an issues approach to the course, with topics ranging across cultural images of women, violence against women and feminist responses, women in history, literature and the arts, the social construction of gender and sexuality, and the feminist movement, with the focus on the making of woman-centered culture. While each teaching team decides whether or not to use exams or a contract grading system, all use the weekly journal as a primary means of course evaluation.

The following chart grew out of my teaching of the course and was discussed at a staff meeting as an effort to use the topical focus of the course to help students begin to construct a sense of the politics of knowledge. Presented at mid-term, students are asked to respond to the chart in both class discussion and their journal writing. The mid-term discussion of what they resist and what they have opened up to is most illuminating for all concerned and evidences that, while most are more open to feminist perspectives, such openness is uneven. Most importantly, discussing the chart creates a space to name our variety, our differences in reaction to the class. A modified version of the chart is again presented at the end of the class to enable further reflection on the variations of our experiences of the class.

Stages of Feminist Consciousness-Raising

Patti Lather, 1986

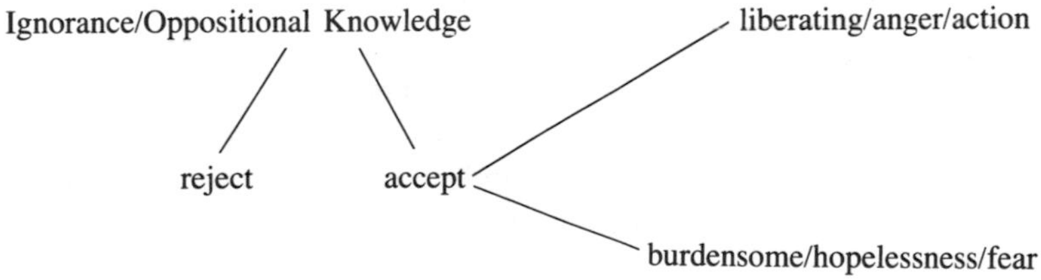

1. Who's to blame for our ignorance?
2. Not a linear process: one moves back and forth over this chart throughout one's life, often being in contradictory locations simultaneously.
3. What are some examples of knowledge claims advanced in this course that you have rejected? accepted?
4. In terms of this chart, where do you presently locate yourself?

In a paper prepared for presentation as part of a panel at the annual meeting of the 1987 National Women's Studies Association, Joycechild comments:

> We feel helping students name this process that many of them undergo, this alteration of consciousness, early on in the course in an on-going way, enhances their experiences of the course for a few reasons. *The first* is that, as instructors, since we are familiar with this process and observe it regularly in our teaching, there seems to be no need to keep it a secret. Why not name it upfront, the way we name, upfront, the fact that, as feminists, we are biased? *Second* is that it seems helpful to let students know they're not the only ones, or the first ones, to undergo a psychological upheaval (to whatever degree) as a result of participating in the course, and that their range of reactions—excitement, empowerment, feeling they've been duped/ignorant because they never had this knowledge before, resistance, disbelief, frustration, anger, burn-out, wanting to act but wondering how, feeling as though their worlds have been shaken up, getting hostile/resistant reactions from family and significant others—is "normal." It may still seem like wandering unchartered territory, but at least they can be aware there are co-wanderers. *Third,* the students in the study reported overwhelmingly that participating in the research gave them a fuller experience of the course. The opportunity to reflect on their experiences of the course, to name and shape their reactions in words with an attentive audience, and being able to learn their co-researchers' reactions, were all useful. *Fourth,* having a framework with pegs on which to hang strands of reaction and thought is useful in processing information and thinking critically.[2]

Each of the four tales I shall spin will be grounded in words generated via journals and interviews from students across varied sections of this introductory women's studies class. Borrowing loosely from Van Maanen (1988), I call these a realist tale, a critical tale, a deconstructivist tale, and a reflexive tale. By "realist," I mean those stories which assume a found world, an empirical world knowable through adequate method and theory. By "critical," I mean those stories which assume underlying determining structures for how power shapes the social world. Such structures are posited as largely invisible to common sense ways of making meaning but visible to those who probe below hegemonic meaning systems to produce counter-hegemonic knowledge, knowledge intended to challenge dominant meaning systems. By "deconstructivist," I mean stories that foreground the unsaid in our saying, "the elisions, blind-spots, loci of the *unsayable* within texts" (Grosz, 1989:184). Deconstruction moves against stories that appear to tell themselves. It creates stories that disclose their constructed nature. And, finally, by "reflexive," I mean those stories which bring the teller of the tale back into the narrative, embodied, desiring, invested in a variety of often contradictory privileges and struggles.

A realist tale

During the fall of 1985, I composed an eleven person research team out of the graduate and undergraduate students in my Feminist Scholarship class to do a sequential interview study of 10% of the 200 students who take the introductory women's studies course each quarter at Mankato State University in Minnesota. Additionally, one of the students collected interview and survey data for her thesis from six returning women students regarding their experiences of and attitudes toward women's studies (Anderson, 1986). In the fall of 1986, a second research team, comprised of twelve persons, collected data from 50% of the introductory students regarding their reactions to required reading for the course by using a participatory research design where students interviewed their peers. Throughout part of 1986 and all of 1987, pre/post-survey data were collected from 890 students regarding empowerment, critical thinking skills, and attitudes toward feminism (Lee, 1988). The survey grew out of dialogue with students enrolled in the course and is, hence, couched in their own language and understanding of key experiences in taking the course. As such, it exemplifies a *grounded* (Glaser and Strauss, 1967) approach to survey construction. In the fall of 1987, a third research team, numbering ten, interviewed nineteen students who had taken the course 1–3 years in the past.

Over this time span, a pool of qualitative and quantitative data was amassed. Its richness was recently underscored for me as four doctoral students worked with parts of the journal data and found it "compelling," "engulfing," "so mesmerizing" that it was "difficult to maintain a clear perspective."[3] What follows is a first-level analysis of that journal data, a section of a larger preliminary report that was written up and mailed out by the research team as a "member check" to the twenty-two students in the introductory course who had been interviewed and worked with us on the construction of the survey. The entire November, 1985, preliminary report is nineteen pages long and includes data summaries from three rounds of interviews, journals, a field test of the survey, and telephone interviews with ten students who had taken the course in the past. Following is a piece of that 1985 report, the data summary from journals written across six sections of the introductory women's studies courses.

> From our extremely erratic data base–journal entries selected by instructors—it is difficult to make any broad generalizations. Although our information is largely decontextualized, some strong threads run through even the rather haphazard collection of journal pages to which we have had access.
>
> One question we asked the journal writings was, "What topics opened students up to a more critical perspective on society?" Almost every topic covered was mentioned as being especially thought-provoking to someone: economic realities for women, the human cost of sex role socialization and stereotyping, anorexia, sexism in language, the history of both misogyny and the "struggles, hardships and suppressed lives of early women that were not in my history books—how long the struggle has been." Two noted the realization of "the way everything is connected, e.g., the oppression of Third World women affects everyone." The use of women in advertising "caused my first feeling of being discriminated against." The subject that elicited the most mixed feelings was that of welfare. For example, "I didn't realize how little these people get." But later in the same entry: "I think there are a lot of hidden issues that weren't discussed. We took the person's side but all the others were left out."
>
> One pattern was the realization of naivete and being "saddened by my ignorance." With the anti-pornography material: "I feel like my stomache is still tied in knots." "The subjects we discuss are very interesting and controversial and shocking due to the fact they exist without us even realizing it or how severe they are in society. . . . The topics arouse my

inner thoughts." "I'm really struck by the subtle ways women are discounted. It's no wonder I've felt disregarded a lot of my life."

A second pattern was contrasting new knowledge presented in the class with what had been previously learned. In regard to the standard portrayal of the Temperence Movement, "I never thought to question it." One student noted the huge difference in the way genital mutilation was presented in a psychology course versus her women's studies course.

A final pattern was a sense of exposure to topics which encourages further learning and action. After dealing with lesbian issues: "There is so much searching to do in this." "Some of the issues get me so riled up inside I can hardly stand it. But being so riled gives me the ambition to want to work harder for what I want."

A second question we asked the journals was, "What effect does the class have on the day-to-day lives of students?" Some students tell stories of taking action in some way regarding issues raised in class:

____was down watching a "skin flick" with some other guys. I asked him if he liked that kind of stuff. He said—"I don't know—it's alright." I told him that I can't really stand it.

I have no way of stopping the sexism in these textbooks but my mother is an elementary school teacher and I will talk to her about this problem.

In class today was the first time I had told straight people and people that I don't know very well that I'm a homosexual. I said, "Are you surprised?" . . . All of the women in our group gave me support.

I asked him how he would feel if he lived in a culture where every single day of your life someone is telling you how worthless you are. He told me I was exaggerating. Then I pointed out that practically every T.V. commercial is saying that. Simple, subtle put downs.

Some write of re-seeing past experience:

One of my brothers was particularly mean. If we didn't do as he said, we were in trouble. When I look back at this, I see it as battering and abuse.

I remember that ____ and I went to the Adult Book Store. . . . I know that now that I realize what happens in that building, I will never return, not even for a joke."
It is never good for one's "image" to be seen with someone of another race or lower class. That is sad and I need to work hard to refrain from being so discriminatory.

And some write of the effects of taking the course on the lives of those around them: "Because of worrying that someone will think I'm gay for taking this class, my boyfriend told me not to tell anyone that I'm taking this class."

A third question we asked the journals was, "Where is there evidence of student struggles with the course?" Reasons that emerged for having a difficult time with particular material presented in class ranged from conflict with religious beliefs, to a feeling that material was presented in a one-sided manner, to a feeling that the perspective presented in class invalidates one's own life: "I am happy, proud and fulfilled to be a wife and mother." Anti-feminist beliefs were challenged: "I was taught to think that feminists went too far. I am disoriented because I have begun to agree with so many of the points I disagreed with for so long. I never wanted the ERA to pass and women's libbers were always 'stupid radicals.' " A final pattern in terms of student struggles with the class was a not wanting to know: "This class has been hard for me, as I'm sure it has for others. If we don't see it, hear it and feel it, we won't know it exists." "This class makes me angry. I don't like to feel this way and avoid it whenever possible." "I don't want to believe the terrible things I am learning." "What good is knowing about this if I can't do anything about it?"

A final question we asked the journals was, "What made students feel empowered?" It became evident that there is a painful first step which we call "reality shock." Students enter the classroom at varying stages of feminist awareness and those from the most sheltered lives seem to suffer the most "reality shock." "At this time I feel disoriented, alienated, hopeless and angry. I feel somewhat like the floor has been pulled out from underneath me." These feelings were often expressed in a two-part journal entry which began on a "hopeless" note but ended with strength. For instance:

I am glad I took this class even though it has caused me confusion, alienation and fights with my boyfriend and I wish it was a requirement for everyone.
In this women's studies course I've gone from ignorance to being educated. I've felt the oppositional knowledge; indeed there are some days I wish I didn't have to deal with women's issues—but the wonderful hours come when I feel liberated, not angry, but full of love for sisterhood.

Many of the entries expressed simply an appreciation of the course and feelings of new-found power. "I feel informed when I stand up for my rights." "I've had tremendous growth in my awareness of women's issues in the past three months. So many things make sense to me now." "I want to be a conscious woman growing stronger and more confident in my mind, body and spirit." "This course keeps me aware of my options, supports me in directions I want to explore and provides me with information and experiences I don't always have first-hand." "I'm not the same person that went into this class. I've grown and become better from it." "We came away richer, having learned from one another."

One entry summed up what most students feel about the 210 class: "I will never be the same. What else can I say? This class makes me feel angry, happy, sad, numb, sick, wonderful, intelligent, dumb, responsible and most of all *aware!*"

After students had a chance to read the preliminary report, group meetings of four to six were held to discuss their reactions to the report. Members of the research team asked students to assess our efforts in the report to adequately represent both their experience and the diversity of student experiences of the class and the usefulness to them of participating in such a study. The nineteen students who took part in this "member check" wanted few changes and expressed an enhancement of their experience of the class due to participation in the research process, a position summed up with "Made 210 more meaningful to me" (Joycechild, 1987).

In writing of the realist tale, Van Maanan notes the convention of interpretive omniscence, the imperialism of rendering the "object" passive, the orchestration of quotes and footnotes, and the banishing of self-criticism and doubt on the part of an author who "disappears into the described world after a brief, perfunctory, but mandatory appearance in a method footnote tucked away from the text" (1988:64). In "Doing realism" (p. 67), "[a]uthority rests largely on the unexplicated experience of the author" (p. 64) who is "The Distant One" (p. 67) guided by the "Doctrine of Immaculate Perception" (p. 73).

This study was from the beginning not situated in claims of omniscience and desires to foster passivity. Its desire is otherwise, situated as it is in a space of "research as praxis" (Lather, 1986). Quotes are used to authorize, both in the sense of "I, the researcher was there, in the field," and to say, "Someone really said this exactly this way and this can be documented." Quotes are also used to provide a profuse and diverse specificity, a kind of "dialogical dynamism" beyond mere heterogeneity where "voices are juxtaposed and counterposed so as to generate something beyond themselves" (Stam, 1988:129). Self-criticism is evident in the opening focus on a "decontextualized," "erratic" "haphazard" data base. Authority comes not from adherence to "objective" method, but from engagement and the willingness to be self-reflexive. For example, the question "Where is there evidence of student struggles with the course?" began, "Where do you find resistance?" It was changed by a member of the research team. She writes,

> "Reasons for resistance" implied that we are right and had an elitist, dogmatic ring to it. "Sources for struggle" is also more descriptive of a process I found throughout in which students began with one line of thinking, but by the end of the journal entry or by the next entry seem to have come full circle or at least to have done some questioning of currently held beliefs (Luedke, 1985, Feminist Scholarship class).

When framed as "the questions we asked of the journals," the structuring elements of the text work to disperse the authority of specific, embodied knowers by foregrounding the ambiguity inherent in constructed versus found worlds. As such, this text works to deflate rather than inflate "the enormous pretensions of the realist enterprise" (Van Maanen, 1988:57). As a realist text, it assumes there is a world out there, that some things are knowable and that "we know that we know them" (Simmons, 1989:8). Nevertheless, its elements of legislation and prescription are few; its policing of the boundaries of legitimate practice moves against an alternative canon characterized by totality, closure and coherence. Rather, its move is toward the ambivalence and open-endedness characteristic of non-dominating, non-coercive knowledges which are located, partial, embodied (Haraway, 1988).

A critical tale

My exploration of what it means to tell a critical tale will be grounded in the following words from an extended journal entry submitted early in the quarter by a 21-year-old black women who was the first in her family to attend college:

> The film, *Killing Us Softly,* and the discussion were interesting and informational to me. They brought out many of the abusive behaviors and gestures that some commercials direct towards women.
>
> The movie was at first really funny to me and I didn't think much about the ads except that they were funny and somewhat entertaining. Then when we started to discuss the topic in class, I realized not everyone thought as I did. I was thinking what's wrong with what the movie was saying? It's always been that way, hasn't it? But listening to other students' reactions started me to thinking more closely about it. As I did, I became more and more upset. The movie actually showed me how TV exploits women. Sex is used so much in commercials and television programs. I never really thought about how the commercials and television programs portrayed us women. It really makes us look like slabs of meat and sluts.
>
> As the discussion proceeded on, students were talking of guilt, anger and shame. I was surprised. I didn't feel this way at all. I thought the commercials were naturally always like that.
>
> I left the class last Monday wondering why certain people got all upset over some commercials when they have always been that way, it was a fact of life.
>
> During the week as I watched television, I started to pay more attention to commercials and television programs. I started not to like what I saw. Everything was exploiting women with sex. I started to categorize programs from good to bad. I ended up not finding too many good programs that

> depicted women as intelligent individuals. By the middle of the week, I was highly upset at myself for not giving more thought to the discussion on Monday. I felt angry and ashamed. Angry at the people who make the commercials and television programs and ashamed at all the people including myself who don't even think about it and let it go on.
>
> The movie and discussion now make more sense to me. They have made me more aware of how women are misused and treated by society. I find myself now wondering what can I do to make a difference, if anything. Things will probably always be the same.

What does it mean to make meaning out of this journal entry as "data"? I present two readings, the first using hegemony theory, the second drawing from deconstruction, in order to juxtapose alternative representations and foreground the very constructed nature of our knowing.

Reading 1. The student has watched a film that is essentially a feminist ideology critique of the advertising industry. She positions herself as initially outside of what she constructs as the general class movement of sympathy, even illumination by the movie. Her journal entry presents a picture of every critical pedagogue's dream-come-true: the mystified student who undergoes "a sea change in received interpretations" (Cocks, 1989:191), a shake-up of her common sense conceptions, via a cognitive process of classroom exposure to and week-long wrestling with methods of analysis which enable her to see her real situation as woman in a patriarchal world. Additionally, her early-in-the-course identification of the agency/paralysis issue, as read in the four times repeated "but it's always been that way," and her marginalization by race and class as well as sex, position her as outsider and, perhaps, open to radicalization and activism. Her reaction to the film demonstrates both the value of "radical information" in changing attitudes and hope in the maturation of people's consciousness and commitment to social activism.

The hegemony model assumes elites who, through the agency of ideological state apparatuses, impose their meanings and agendas on subordinate groups, in this case, the film's construction of a patriarchal conspiracy regarding advertising's images of women. The "oppressed," unaware of alternatives, consent to the elites' definitions, despite the contradictions such definitions pose to their own experiences. The hegemonic relation " 'locks' the consciousness of the oppressed into interpreting their experiences in the categories, terms and values of the dominant ideology" (Winter, 1989:6), acquiescing to an encoding of the social world which acts against their own interests. Caught in false consciousness and mistaken about the real nature of the relations and ideas shaping their world, subjects are theorized via what Kipnis calls, "discursively tying the people into a radical political logic" (1988:151), capable of grasping a reality of domination, subordination and resistance, once engaged by "critical pedagogues."

In exploring the limits and possibilities of reading data through the prism of critical theory, hegemonic theories have much to teach about how structural forces work. Such theories, however, assume an excessive faith in the powers of the reasoning mind on the part of subjects theorized as unified and capable of full consciousness. Furthermore, they position the "oppressed" as the unfortunately deluded, and critical pedagogues as "transformative intellectuals" (Aronowitz and Giroux, 1985) with privileged knowledge free of false logic and beliefs. Such a bald statement points out the profound dangers in attempting to speak for others, to say what others want or need, of performing as the Grand Theorist, the "master of truth and justice" (Foucault, 1977:12).

Much of Marxism is "a veritable rationalist mystique" (Baudrillard, 1981:134) in its assumption that once the subjugated grasp the "true" nature of social reality, via the theoretical tools of the Marxist intellectual, they will then be free to remake the world in their own likeness. How do we use our position as teachers to breach the univocality of the "message," to restore the ambivalence of meaning and demolish the agency of the code (Ibid.:179), to break the pattern of yet another controlling schema of interpretation, even if offered in the name of liberation?

This is a central question in rethinking the role of teachers with liberatory intentions. How can we position ourselves as less masters of truth and justice and more as creators of a space where those directly involved can act and speak on their own behalf? How do we do so without romanticizing the subject and experience-based knowledge? Windschuttle, for example, writes:

> The idea . . . that working people are ignorant of the realities of the institution that most shapes their lives, the workplace, deserves to be rejected. Exploitation and inequality are widely recognized and injustices and contradictions are experienced every day. Indeed, major social institutions, including the trade

> unions and the labour parties, have been established by the working class to redress these very features of society. Any account of culture or ideology must start from this. (quoted in Winter, 1989)

Yet many do remain ensnared in and constituting of disempowering frameworks of meaning. The best solution I have been able to come up with is to position intellectuals as other than the origin of what can be known and done, some positioning of ourselves elsewhere than where the "Other" is the problem for which we are the solution. Such a "solution" accepts the importance of specificity in critical practice. Situated in locatable, embodied critical cultural practices, it probes political conditions and circumstances in a way other than ideology critique. Ideology critique views ideology as a property of the text, a cognitive lack/distortion, rather than as a process of production between text and audience. In contrast to this binary logic which demonizes the "Other" and positions itself as innocent, poststructuralists argue that "There are no social positions exempt from becoming oppressive to others. . . . [A]ny group—any position—can move into the oppressor role.' . . . '[E]veryone is someone else's 'Other' " (Minh-ha and Gentile, respectively, quoted in Ellsworth, 1989:322).

Reading 2. A deconstructive reading attempts to use this student's words differently than as "The 'we' who know better (who have somehow got science and can write the theory of their naive narratives) . . . where 'we' are the privileged subjects of knowledge and science" (Bennington, 1987:24). Rather than positioning her to read against the ideology of the advertisements, their effort to produce a particular kind of consciousness, deconstruction makes her production of meaning the object of the curriculum. The complexity of her response to both the movie and the analytical methods introduced by the teacher, methods positioned as not neutral but as "methods of analysis designed to reveal and to command assent to these answers" (Buckingham, 1986:93) encourage her to formulate her responses and then re-think her formulations.

Such an approach asks, as she watches the television that week, does she define herself against the advertisements as ideologically suspicious texts, or does she probe the complexity of the contradictory meanings and pleasures she derives from the media? As a movie, *Killing Us Softly* does not validate or investigate the production of differential readings. It produces, engineers a consensus reading. Its task is to make ideology visible, to reveal the suppressed ideological function of advertisements, to unmask and expose underlying values. It positions itself as demystifying and reduces the complexities of ideology and subjectivity to false consciousness which correct information can overcome, information disseminated in classrooms such as this one by a vanguard which leads, shapes, urges (Buckingham, 1986). What is her reaction to methods of analysis designed to reveal and to command assent to those revelations?

Not necessarily consciously, although the game of producing what the teacher wants to hear cannot be overlooked, students in women's studies classrooms learn to produce "correct" answers, to follow a kind of "group think" that respositions them within a "sisterhood" of oppressed women unified in their newly discovered outrage at "the patriarchy." There is pleasure in this way of transcending the competitive individualism that permeates western culture.[4] But there is, also, a suspiciously blanket rejection of popular forms here (Buckingham, 1986). She says a lot of ideologically correct things, with no foregrounding of the advertisements themselves as either contradictory or eliciting contradictory responses from her, pleasure as well as outrage. Informed by deconstruction, this is a suspicious reading which looks at both the production and investment of desire on the part of the "liberatory pedagogue" and the taboos, the lacunae, of critical theory.

There is a multiplicity of interpretations that could be made of this journal entry. Each reading would reflect Bordo's words: "We always 'see' from points of view that are invested with our social, political and personal interests, inescapably 'centric' in one way or another, even in the desire to do justice to heterogeneity" (1989:140). Hence, I end this deconstructive reading by foregrounding what there is here that is explicitly heterogeneous and discontinuous, what escapes, is Other and opaque, what refuses to be totalized. This is far different from a reading informed by hegemony theory where one's narrative tracks are covered in the construction of an analysis designed to oppose a "correct" reading against a "mystified" one.

A deconstructive tale

My focus in this deconstructive tale is on the ways an intendedly liberatory pedagogy might function as part of the technology of surveillance and normalization. Three questions will be addressed: 1) How do we constitute the object of emancipatory pedagogy? 2) How do we attend to the social relations of the emancipatory classroom? 3) What practices might help us deconstruct authority in the liberatory classroom? My exploration of these questions will be grounded in the following words from students as elicited by interviews and journals:

> I feel like they were telling me I'm wrong to feel the way I feel.
>
> There are a lot of outside things trying to force us to become one way or another. Feminism should free us to become what we are. We need to be careful feminism doesn't become part of the problem.
>
> Take what you want and use it should be the message of the course. [The] message I'm now getting: active involvement in feminism is being pushed. I don't want to become a radical. . . . I want to go through the course and be able to decide what's good for me without anyone being judgmental.
>
> I know I'm oppressed but I don't feel as oppressed/ discriminated against as this class makes me feel I should feel.
>
> [My] world is shaken up. I feel I am living in constant crisis.
>
> I can see that as each class goes by I am going to be less sure about things and more confused about what I probably should think and feel.
>
> In response to the question, "Who's to blame for our ignorance?": I think everyone is partly to blame for their own ignorance, yet I also think that society has an equal blame for making the lacked knowledge so meaningless to persons. [Written in response to being asked her views on the importance of "herstory."]
>
> I guess I'm a bit different from the majority of our class. My reason being is in this class everyone is always saying what's wrong with everything. I certainly realize that women only making 59 cents on the dollar is really unreal, but it's a lot better than 29 cents or 39 cents! I would love it if we made $1.00 on the dollar, but we don't. This class often dwells on the very negative side of every issue.

Each quote was selected from material elicited by a memo to course instructors (seven, myself included) asking for access to journal entries "that capture the struggle involved in learning the 're-seeing the world' that is the hallmark of Women's Studies." The students' words are presented in a deliberately fragmented, de-contextualized manner in order to fight the desire "to restore transparency by means of a great deal of information" (Baudrillard, 1981:201). Class, race, age, sexual orientation etc. are unmarked, erased.

Constituting the object of emancipatory pedagogy

The project of liberatory pedagogy requires a subject who is an object of our emancipatory desires. Who is this student? Rather than her demographics, let us focus on the desire that shapes her. My reading of the literature foregrounds three primary characteristics of the object of emancipatory pedagogy: she is both victimized and capable of agency; while she has something approximating false consciousness, that consciousness is unified and capable of Freirean conscientization, knowing the world in order to set herself free from it. Finally, a basic assumption in the construction of this subject is that it is knowledge that will set her free. I will deconstruct each of these primary characteristics of the object of emancipatory pedagogy.

In foregrounding assumptions regarding agency, false consciousness and empowering knowledge, it is important to take into account Foucault's warning of "the violence of a position that sides against those who are happy in their ignorance, against the effective illusions by which humanity protects itself' (1977:162). How do we minimize such violence by focusing less on disturbing cultural self-satisfaction and more on enhancing already there penetrations and frustrations? How can we use the contradictory consciousness endemic to the proliferation of discourses that characterizes this era of electronic media and micro-electronic communication to minimize such violence? Lewis, for example, argues that many women

> Both wish to appropriate and yet resist feminist theoretical and political positions. . . . We need to . . . consider the substance of why women may wish genuinely to turn away from the possibilities it offers. . . . We cannot continue to accept simple

> notions of false consciousness which buries the complexity of human choices in a too unproblematized notion of self-interest. . . . Rather than displace this young woman's terror into the safe ideological category of the falsely conscious . . . [we must take into account] the negotiations required to secure one's survival. (1989:9–11)

To avoid the "master's position" of formulating a totalizing discourse requires more self-consciousness about the particularity and provisionality of our sense-making efforts, more awareness of the multiplicity and fluidity of the objects of our knowing. An example of this is the evolution of the question mark in the title of this chapter. It was in the course of the inquiry and via the less neo-Marxist saturated theoretical vantage points of the student co-researchers who worked with me that the concepts of false consciousness and resistance began to be problematized. Resistance became

> a word for the fear, dislike, hesitance most people have about turning their entire lives upside down and watching everything they have ever learned disintegrate into lies. "Empowerment" may be liberating, but it is also a lot of hard work and new responsibility to sort through one's life and rebuild according to one's own values and choices. (Kathy Kea, Feminist Scholarship class, October, 1985)

In terms of false consciousness, while a January 19, 1986, research memo written by myself makes clear that "I want no predetermined definitions of consciousness. This will be emergent knowledge coming out of the research process," it also displays an unproblematic conception of the "processes by which false consciousness is maintained." By the following year, the question mark was added to the title of the study, marking movement in the research team's conceptions of the object of our inquiry. This is exemplified in Joycechild's (1988) movement "from their resistance to mine" where the object of her inquiry shifted from student resistance to liberatory pedagogy to her own resistance to the assumption that "their problem" was not buying into "our" version of reality.

The object of emancipatory pedagogy might more usefully be conceptualized as the power-saturated discourses that monitor and normalize our sense of who we are and what is possible. Ellsworth writes, "I am trying to unsettle received definitions of pedagogy by multiplying the ways in which I am able to act on and in the University both as the Inappropriate/d Other and as the privileged speaking/making subject trying to unlearn that privilege" (1989:323). And pedagogy becomes a site *not* for working through more effective transmission strategies but for helping us learn to analyze the discourses available to us, which ones we are invested in, how we are inscribed by the dominant, how we are outside of, other than the dominant, consciously/unconsciously, always partially, contradictorily.

Attending to the social relations of the emancipatory classroom

In developing a deconstructive pedagogy, our search is not to designate an object or describe a content but to foreground a relation between knower and known, teacher and taught, from an embodied perspective. Giroux and Simon quote Hebdige's reporting from a young male member of a subculture he was studying: "You really hate an adult to understand you. That's the only thing you've got over them, the fact that you can mystify and worry them.' Contemporary youth have cause to be wary of giving up their anonymity, of making their private and lived voices the object of public and pedagogical scrutiny" (1988:20). To what extent is the pedagogy we construct in the name of liberation intrusive, invasive, pressured?

Many of these quotes speak of the kind of "politically correct" thinking that can become operative in an intendedly liberatory classroom. Many speak of the "shoulds" that add another coercive discourse to their lives, a discourse designed to shake up their worlds but which often loses touch with what that shaken up experience feels like. The 29 cents quote presents a student who doesn't go along with such pressure, who resists both the "group think" in the classroom and the course's stress on women's negative social positioning, a stress designed to overcome the tendency of younger "post-feminist" women to see feminism as a dinosaur, no longer necessary, the enabling fiction of another generation.

U.S. feminism historically has valorized coercion as the truth of oppression (victimization theories) over *consent* as a political factor (Kipnis, 1988:151). Yet, what I heard the students in this study wanting to know/tell had something to do with resisting victimization and passivity. How an individual sustains a society's givens (Patai, 1988:143), how we are inscribed by dominant discourses (Haug, 1987), how we can come to understand our own collusion—this was the information they found most powerful. To begin to understand how we are caught up in power situations of which we are, ourselves, the bearers is to foreground the limits of our lives and what we can do within those boundaries. It is to begin to see the organization of knowledge and the production of ignorance in the curriculum in ways that valorize neither subjective agency nor objective determination.

The task is to construct classroom relations that engender fresh confrontation with value and meaning—not to demonstrate to students their ignorance in what Freire (1973) terms the "banking concept of education" where authoritarian talk shuts down communication, even if done in the name of liberation (Berlak, 1986, 1989). To challenge the unequal distribution of power in the classroom is to ask, Who speaks? For what and to whom? Who listens? Who is confident and comfortable and who isn't? (Orner and Brennan, 1989:18). It is, also, to probe the many reasons for silence (Lewis and Simon, 1986; Lewis, 1988) and to heed Joycechild's caution:

> The shoulds operating in the classroom, which students could feel after a few short weeks, need addressing. We need to learn more ways of hearing students' own voices, as we need to learn more ways of hearing one another's own voices, as different kinds of feminists in the movement. We need to unlearn political correctness, and move away from an oversimplified, monolithic, there's-one-best-way mode of presentation. We have a tendency to deny our own impositional "stuff" in the name of liberation. I don't think the importance of this can be overestimated (from document prepared for presentation to the 1987 National Women's Studies Association annual convention).

Deconstructing authority

To deconstruct authority is not to do away with it but to learn to trace its effects, to see how authority is constituted and constituting. A pedagogy to take us beyond ourselves would privilege helping us become aware and critical of how the social forces of authority affect us as we form and re-form our thinking (Naidus, 1987). For example, in dealing with media fed and video schooled students, Ulmer recommends focusing on media studies, especially its enframing processes: "It is not technology itself, but this blindness to its enframing, that must be confronted" (1985:15). In doing so, teachers become providers of language codes of varying complexities as they create pedagogical spaces where students can enter a world of oppositional knowledges and negotiate definitions and ways of perceiving (Bowers, 1987). Our pedagogic responsibility then becomes to nurture this space where students can come to see ambivalence and differences not as an obstacles, but as the very richness of meaning-making and the hope of whatever justice we might work toward.

Instead of commenting on a text or practice in ways that define it, a deconstructive approach links our "reading" to ourselves as socially situated spectators. It draws attention to the variety of readings, the partiality of any one view and our implications in historical social relations. This works against naturalizing, essentializing and foregrounds positionalities.[5]

Deconstructive pedagogy encourages a multiplicity of readings by demonstrating how we cannot exhaust the meaning of the text, how a text can participate in multiple meanings without being reduced to any one, and how our different positionalities affect our reading of it. Johnson's questions can help us learn to link our comments to ourselves as socially situated spectators: Why am I reading *this* text? What kind of act was the writing of it? What question about it does it itself NOT raise? What am I participating in when I read it? (1987:4). Van Maanen (1988) adds, Why am I reading this way and what produces this reading?, questions echoed by Fuss: "[W]hat are the various positions a reading subject may occupy? How are these positions constructed? Are there possible distributions of subject-positions located in the text itself? Does the text construct the reading subject or does the reading subject construct the text?" (1989:86). Johnston adds that we might replace questions like "What does it mean?" and "What does the author intend?" with "What does it work in conjunction with?" and "What new intensities does it produce?" (1990:91). These questions can be used to begin to critically interrogate our own unexamined techniques of sense-making. Hence, our reading of the text becomes the curriculum, a curriculum designed not so much to oppose a counter-hegemonic meaning system against a dominant one as to ask us to insert ourselves into the discourses that envelop us. Here, we deconstructively explore the relation between ourselves and how we negotiate the search for meaning in a world of contradictory information.

Such a pedagogy has no prescriptions:

> The terms in which I can and will assert and unsettle "difference" and unlearn my positions of privilege in future classroom practices are wholly dependent on the Others/others whose presence—with their concrete experiences of privileges and oppressions, and subjugated or oppressive knowledges—I am responding to and acting with in any given classroom. My moving about between the positions of privileged speaking subject and Inappropriate/d Other cannot be predicted, prescribed, or understood beforehand by any theoretical framework or methodological practice. It is in this sense that a practice grounded in the unknowable is profoundly contextual (historical) and interdependent (social). (Ellsworth, 1989:323)

Ellsworth's study of critical pedagogy within the context of her own teaching of a university level anti-racism course and my similar efforts in this chapter turn away from a focus on dominant power to a focus on our own discourses of criticism and resistance. Such a movement both creates complicating fragmentations and provides a richer understanding of the situations in which we do our oppositional work. In such a framework, women's studies provides both critique and alternative practices, and serves as a Gramscian "historical laboratory" for developing oppositional theory and practice.

A self-reflexive tale: the knowers and the known

The following is a "playlet" constructed out of the words of four doctoral students who worked with parts of the journal data on an assignment for a class in analyzing qualitative data in the spring of 1989. Their words come from their class writings and a tape recording of a meeting where the four of them compared and contrasted their approaches to analyzing the data.

Michel: I got my data from Patti today. . . . I'm really excited about these journals and interested in seeing how much of them I can relate to. I've been so nervous and depressed lately that I'm looking forward to reading about movement in people's thinking and the many feminist encounters of my life, while frustrating at times, have always lifted my spirits and moved me from my stance as a logical negativist! . . .

I have been working on the data for Patti's women's studies journals and I must say that this has been fascinating. This is my first attempt at actual coding . . . for qualitative analysis. I LOVE it, hard as it is. I feel like I am in this data—in my coding but also in these women's stories and reflections. The data is so rich . . . and the opportunities for direction are seemingly endless.

Dan: I became totally just engulfed, immersed in the entries. . . . [T]he stories were so compelling. It's our own personal perspective that came into play with the data. Even though we were doing it as "Patti's data," we were also looking at it as data that had personal meaning for us: one of us focused on social issues raised in the class, one on anger, one on labels people put on one another, one on what I as a curriculum leader in a school system can do to get more focus on women in the curriculum.

Myrna: My personal notes physically interrupt the text. My own feelings that came up—this text is so powerful to me. When I first [started putting in my reactions] I was compelled to do it. I turned it into Patti, making no judgments about it. She encouraged me to continue this. . . . I think this data has lots of stories to tell. It was personally validating for me to see women feeling free to express their feelings because mine had been suppressed for so long. So there was sort of an unconscious celebration of that, I think, that was very personal.

Ken: One interesting area was the instances of males being marginalized by this women's studies class. Being a white, Anglo-Saxon, protestant, colonial, semi-thin, tall, upper-middle class [I could go on] male, I have been aware of this marginalization within our class. It has not been in terms of deed, but in terms of this ever present list that seems to be in most every article of this sort. I am puzzled as to how to react to it. My first reaction is to say that it is OK because my accidental positionality has been privileged for so long that this marginalization is a small price for me to pay for my continuing privilege. My second reaction is to say this reverse discrimination is just as bad as the first and discrimination should not be tolerated by anyone. It should not be tolerated because it is *accidental* that I'm positioned within this group, and it is hard for me to support any act that distracts with people dealing with me as *me,* not just a member of some group. It is a rough dilemma.

Myrna: This stuff is so rich.

Michel: Oh, I thought so too.

Myrna: I just pray that my dissertation data is as rich; it'll be easy to do if it is. I just keep *wanting* to work on this.

Dan: The words, there was a jargon and allusions that I didn't understand. She had them thinking in a certain way.

Myrna: My experience with therapy and Michel's with taking an introductory women's studies course, a lot of these issues we've given voice to, so our experience [of the data] will be different.

Ken: Many students were kind of trying on voices. One was really mixed. She started talking about homosexuals and you heard the feminist or very liberal voice on how to treat homosexuals. Then all of a sudden she starts bringing the bible in and the old stuff came back in. This was a very interesting passage and I think it may prove to be an interesting place to "massage" [the data] more.

Michel: I like what you said, I like calling it trying on voices.

Myrna: Yeah, that's a neat idea. That would be a *really* interesting thing to use as a study with this material.

Michel: It doesn't sound like we're saying anything that different, which is validating for me.

Myrna: It's like layering our experiences with this data.

Patti's reflections: Having the doctoral student analyze this data grew in such unexpected directions. I didn't expect it to move my own work forward, to bring what I had come to call my "dead data" alive. Begun as a last-minute effort to get data in their hands, it grew into another layer of this inquiry which shed much light on the "black hole" of qualitative inquiry: data analysis. They came to the data without the theoretical baggage that I had. What struck me most was how much of themselves they brought to the analysis, how their wrestling to make sense of the data evoked their own investments of privilege and struggle, e.g., Ken's focus on "the lists of the demonized/privileged Other" used by feminists: the litany of the white, middle-class, heterosexual male and how that silences/marginalizes/paralyzes.

Listening to the tape especially put me in touch with how it feels to have your teaching and researching scrutinized—for example, their concern with whether I was imposing my own "regime of truth" in terms of, "She had them thinking a certain way." More uncomfortable was their concern regard-

> ing confidentiality issues. While I made clear that students had signed permission slips regarding use of their journal entries in possible publications, in photocopying journal entries for the doctoral students to work with, I did not take off some names. The tape of their meeting included a discussion of the ethics of this.

In the "reflexive tale," I use a narrative versus an argumentative rationality. The latter creates winners and losers while the former works to "illustrate rather than claim" (Van Maanen, 1988:122). The text is used to display rather than to analyze. Data are used differently; rather than to support an analysis, they are used demonstrably, performatively. Data are used to condense, exemplify, evoke, to embellish theoretical argument rather than to collapse it into an empirical instance where data function as a "certificate of presence" (Hutcheon, quoting Barthes, 1989:91), a buttressing facticity. Like each of the preceding tales, the words of diverse others come first in order to frame the theoretical discourse, to be relatively unmediated, heterogeneous, unmarked.[6]

Across the tales, I have presented alternative, conflicting representations, juxtaposed disparate textual styles and foregrounded the unresolvable tensions between them in order to understand what is at stake in creating meaning out of "data." With the realist and critical tales, I inscribe the conventions, induce conditioned responses and then subvert those responses by bringing to the fore the politics of how these codes operate (Hutcheon, 1989). Such simultaneous inscription and subversion of the codes by which we make meaning creates the doubly coded narrative that characterizes poststructural textuality.

Spanos writes that the most useful work in the present crisis of representation "is that which uses form to disrupt received forms and undermines an objective, disinterested stance" (1987:271). Van Maanen urges movement toward unmasking fieldwork by breaking methodological silences and inventing forms of textual self-consciousness. While he cautions that such self-reflexivity can become "vanity ethnography" (1988:93), he welcomes the more experimental forms of ethnographic writing. There, knower and known are brought together in representational form such as dramatic vignettes that startle complacent comfort with older forms. While anything short of full collaboration cannot avoid some degree of objectification and speaking for others, we can aim toward an introspection/objectification balance. The methodological self-reflection engendered by such experimental forms of textual construction is based on the realization that the so-called facts that one "discovers" are already the product of many levels of interpretation. As Hutcheon notes, "facts are events to which we have given meaning" (1989:57).

To work toward what it means to do empirical work in a post-foundational context is to move into the space of deconstructing/deconstructive inquiry, to tell stories that end in neither comprehended knowledge nor in incapacitating textual undecidabilty (Spanos, 1987:275). Disallowing claims to certainty, totality and archimedean standpoints outside of flux and human interest, it is to tell "a story that retrieves inquiry as a 'way' that is always already beginning, always already 'on the way,' " a different story "that makes a critical difference not only at the site of thought but also at the site of sociopolitical praxis" (Ibid.:276).

Conclusion

Out of all the stories that could be told about the multiplicity of influences on an inquiry, this essay is a "tale of the field" (Van Mannen, 1988), a self-reflexive pondering on the politics of our research and teaching practices. Rooted in the specificity of a particular, situated inquiry into the processes by which students may accept, integrate and/or reject oppositional knowledge, I have explored the parameters of deconstructivist empirical work. Those parameters blur genres, unsettle received definitions, and create a space from which to do otherwise in the name of the human sciences. With such parameters well evoked in a stanza from A. R. Ammon's "Corson's Inlet," it is with poetry that I leave you:

I allow myself eddies of meaning:
yield to a direction of significance
running
like a stream through the geography of my work:
you can find
in my sayings
swerves of action
like the inlet's cutting edge:
there are dunes of motion,
organizations of grass, white sandy paths of remembrance
in the overall wandering of mirroring mind:

but the Overall is beyond me: is the sum of these events
I cannot draw, the ledger I cannot keep, the accounting
beyond the accounts.

in nature there are few sharp lines: there are areas of
primrose
        more or less dispersed;
disorderly orders of bayberry; between the rows
of dunes,
irregular swamps of reeds,
though not reeds alone, but grass, bayberry, yarrow, all . . .
predominantly reeds.

I have reached no conclusions, have created no boundaries,
shutting out and shutting in separating inside
from outside: I have
drawn no line:
as

manifold events of sand
change the dune's shape that will not be the same
        shape
tomorrow,

so I am willing to go along, to accept
the becoming
thought, to stake off no beginnings or ends,
                                                establish
        no walls: . . .

(quoted in Spanos, 1987:236–37).

Postscript

> A good book, like a good girl, spells out the implications at the end, so that there is nothing left to do but close the book and buy another. (Kappeler, 1986:220)

Attempting to create a text that transgresses and subverts in ways that work against being recodified into new norms, there is much in me that wanted to end with the preceding poem. The above quote, however, was too good to not use and so has inspired me to attempt to restate some of the basic themes I have played with in these pages. I will do so using Kappeler's (1986) format of multiple endings.

This book is an effort to exceed the socially tolerable boundaries of representation in terms of empirical work in the human sciences. Its goal is to ease the hold of scientificity over the terrain of research and pedagogy done in the name of liberation, so that different representations may be possible. It offers no synthesis, no teleological conclusion, as its vision is somewhere other than progressively perfectable systems. Situated within the interstices of the various critical theories, it is an internal critique attempting to move research and pedagogy done in the name of liberation beyond the contemporary horizons of representation. Like Irigaray, its aim is to overburden existing forms of dominant discourses with their own ambiguities in order to create a space in which it is possible to do otherwise (Grosz, 1989).

With many disciplinary knowledges brought to an impasse of epistemological skepticism, science is in search of itself. A science wholly determined by empirical fact and rational cognitive structure is clearly not adequate to our present conjunction where social intelligence is outrun by our technical prowess. The fact/value dichotomy is part of this dangerous situation and new normative-factual interactions are in movement everywhere within science (Hooker, 1982). The nature and ramifications of this are too new to know, but the contemporary deconstruction of science is symptomatic of a fundamental crisis of Western culture, "a prophetic and ethical cry" (Levinas, referred to by Kearney in an interview with Derrida, 1984:118), "symptoms of a deep mutation in our search for meaning which deconstruction attempts to register" (Derrida, in Kearney, 1984:121).

What difference to the world does our theory try to make? A text that might help enable movement beyond received habits of thought and practice is a form of political intervention, even given the (largely unknowable) limits of discursive challenges. In the desire to move discourse/practices in the human sciences outside the range of the permissable, I have located my intervention at the site of emancipatory research and teaching. Research and pedagogy are sites where we can address change at the micro-level of local resistances versus the macro-level of dominating forces posited as centrally unified, for example, the concept of "patriarchy" which suggests a monolithic intentionality (Cocks, 1989). Deconstructing the work we do in the name of such liberatory efforts, this is a resituating of emancipatory work so that it might "appear to itself as other than itself, so that it can interrogate and reflect upon itself in an original manner" (Derrida, in Kearney, 1984:108).

How do we distinguish between thought that has been determined by power and thought that manages to see that determination (Cocks, 1989)? Such a distinction has been lost to structuralism with its privileging of social, linguistic and cultural structures as determinants. Unable to explain change, structuralism reached its apogee in Althusser's "process without a subject," a neo-Hegelian "solution" which only foregrounded the need for the question of the subject to be reopened (Benton, 1984). While Marxist materialism displaced the Hegelian idea with Capital as the motor force of history, the irreducibly necessary subject remained occluded (Spivak, 1987b). Structuralism displaced the agency of the idea with the agency of the material—but what organizes consciousness and the practices of historical agents that is the alterity, the Other, to structural determinants? That is the territory that poststructuralism attempts to map with its thesis that the map precedes the territory, its foregrounding of the constitutive effects of our uses of language, its efforts to enable another logic in which structure and agency are not either-or but both-and and, simultaneously, neither-nor.

"What is this 'man' who 'makes' history?" Althusser asked in his gender inscribed de-centering of the humanist subject as the "motor force" of history (1976:46). Phenomenology with its assumptions of the subject as master of meaning and source of knowledge was interrupted by rationalist, mechanistic, and formalist structural theories which privileged material determinants in explaining the play of power in how meaning is made. Such theories are now interrupted by poststructuralism. The critical cultural practices of Marxism and feminism have intersected with the post-Enlightenment projects of Derrida, Lacan and Foucault to aggravate the crisis of Enlightenment rationality that they themselves are part of: "The Enlightenment we seek to dismantle in the name of our political values is precisely a major source of such values" (Moi, 1988:17).

Poststructuralism foregrounds both the limits of consciousness and intentionality and the will to power inscribed in sense-making efforts which aspire to universal, totalizing explanatory frameworks. Such frameworks are promised as avenues by which "the oppressed" can grasp the underlying structures of reality as formulated by "universal intellectuals" who assume the role of "the master of truth and justice upholding reason and revealing the truth to those unable to see or speak it" (Smart, 1986:165). Premised otherwise on a profoundly unsettling critique of the primacy of consciousness and the politics implicit in the critical practices of those who propose to speak for or on behalf of others, deconstructive strategies are not instruments for mastery of self and/or others but an exploratory tool for how we might move beyond our present positions.

The politics of social transformation is adrift in a sea of profound cultural and no-growth economics which has helped the New Right seize the moment. Existing critical approaches have become trapped in their own limitations. For example, Bromley (1989) notes that the Marxist project in American education has been largely ineffective, devastated by theoretic shortcomings, too disembodied and abstract to be useful as an organizing tool. Shapiro suggests that it is continuing attachment to Enlightenment rationalism that has led to the lack of a Left political agenda for education that is popularly resonant due to Marxist "embarrassment at a discourse that achieves political mobilization through an explicit appeal to moral traditions and aspirations" (1989:95). Even feminist theory evokes "an urgent desire to keep feminist theory from stiffening into orthodox positions" (Sheridan, 1988:4), in spite of its more embodied grounding in the politicization of personal experience.

Poststructuralism refuses both individual/social dualisms and reductionist views of causality in the social. Addressing the impasse between idealist voluntarism and structuralist fatalism, it serves as a theoretical tool to help analyze mechanisms of power locally. Focusing on contextualized notions of power-in-use, it enables us to explore the meanings of difference and the possibilities for struggling against multiple oppressive formations simultaneously: first by naming the micro-dispersal of power, second by exploring the contradictions involved in inhabiting multiple and simultaneous privileges and oppressions, and thirdly by tracking our own implications in multiple oppressive formations and knowledges (Ellsworth, 1989).

Within such a context, poststructuralism helps us ask questions about what we have not thought to think, about what is most densely invested in our discourse/practices, about what has been muted, repressed, unheard in our liberatory efforts. It helps us to both define the politics implicit in our critical practices and move toward understanding the shortcomings of theories of political transformation.

Epilogue

> I'm just glad feminist master-thinkers have matched wits with the old boys, wrestled with them on their own terms and brought them down. Somebody had to do it. (Kendall, 1990:16)

> This is an old and primary tool of all oppressors to keep the oppressed occupied with the master's concerns. (Lorde, 1984:113)

A book such as this raises questions about the relations that feminist intellectuals have to male-dominated knowledges. Grosz (1989) insists that we must engage phallocentrism on its own grounds, as opposed to Lorde's (1984), "The master's tools will never dismantle the master's house." Grosz writes, "women must become familiar with the patriarchal discourses, knowledges and social practices which define and constrain them: these provide the only sources and tools against patriarchy. Only through its own techniques can patriarchy be challenged and displaced" (1989:133).

And yet, clearly, the many different discourse/practices of feminist struggle need not all engage in metatheoretical wrangling with male pantheons. While "the practice of the production of meanings, discourses and knowledges" (Grosz, 1989:234) is an important aspect of feminism, much of this goes on outside of the academy and outside of male framed discursive fields. This is to be celebrated. This is what escapes, excedes, and complicates that feminist work which does situate itself at the site of metatheory, theory about theory, a discourse formulated largely by white, class privileged male theorists.

At a 1989 conference on "Alternative Paradigms for Inquiry," I spoke metatheoretically, at great length. Asking for response, one woman expressed her dismay at having sought out a feminist space she assumed would be speaking otherwise to the male discourse which she had begun to feel battered by at the conference. While my desire may be "to speak with meanings that resonate, that are tactile and corporeal as well as conceptual, that reverberate in their plurality and polyvocity" (Grosz, 1989:132), such commentary indicates that my discourse is very much inside logocentrism. I take such concerns to heart, playing with possibilities for future writing, forms less alienated to lived experience. But something there is in me that sees, also, the need to take on male discourse at its own site and to attempt to "speak otherwise" within its parameters.

Feminism is often placed as the "hysterical other to the cool of marxist reason" (Campioni and Gross, 1983:118). While full of contradictory tendencies, with languages of subversion and languages of order circulating and repositioning, feminism's tendencies toward a sort of "proto-postmodernism" might very well help it serve as the "quantum physics of postmodernism" (Kroker and Cook, 1986). As argued in Chapter 2, this means both that critical appropriations of poststructuralism cannot afford to ignore feminist discourse/practices and that feminist efforts toward a world in which we all can flourish must be both within and without that discourse. To repeat a line from Chapter 2, "The issue is not so much where poststructuralism comes from, but what it will be."

Afterword

> I do not really wish to conclude and sum up, rounding off the argument so as to dump it in a nutshell on the reader. A lot more could be said about any of the topics I have touched upon. . . . I have meant to ask the questions, to break out of the frame. . . . The point is not a set of answers, but making possible a different practice. . . . (Kappeler, 1986:212)

As used in this book, postmodernism/poststructuralism is the code name for the crisis of confidence in Western conceptual systems. It is borne out of the uprising of the ex-centrics, the revolution in communication technology, the fissures of a global multinational hyper-capitalism, and our sense of the limits of Enlightenment rationality, all creating a conjunction that shifts our sense of who we are and what is possible.

The following chart attempts, absurdly, to grasp all of this on a single page. Multiple caveat's are in order: its system of analytic "cells" reproduces the very binary logic poststructuralism attempts to unthink; its movement from "premodern" to "modern" to "postmodern" is teleological linearity at its most bare-faced; its division of postmodernisms into "neo-Nietzschean schizocynicism" and "critical appropriations" (Hutcheon, 1986b) is reductionist and dualistic; its central categories are reifications that are represented as pure breaks with the past, unfolding under my very explications. I could go on and invite you to do so.

But I have found the chart a useful pedagogical tool. I have worked through it in anywhere from 15 minutes to 4 hours. It has been much refined via presentations in various incarnations to groups in education, women's studies and social science research from North Dakota to New Zealand. Reactions to it from those groups regarding its usefulness have impelled me to include it here in spite of all its limitations.

	Pre Modern	Modern	Postmodern "the as-yet unnameable which begins to proclaim itself" (Derrida)	
form of authority, legitimate knowledge	the sacred:church/state theocracy, divinely sanctioned consensus. Few alternative codifications of knowledge.	secular humanism: individual *reason* = scientific, liberal democracy. Ideological state apparatuses central dispensers of codified knowledge:schools and science especially	*pm of reaction* Neo-Nietzschean collapse of meaning, nihilism, schizo-cynicism; cultural whirlpool of Baudrillardian simulacra	*pm of resistance* Participatory, dialogic & pluralistic structures of authority. Non-dualistic, anti-hierarchical. Uprising of ex-centrics. Multiple sites from which the world is spoken. Feminism as "the quantum physics of postmodernism" (Kroker & Cook, 1986).
conception of individual	god-given, destined. Religious human	*Humanism:* Autonomous individualism, self-directive, natural rights, shapeable, potentially fully conscious, refusal to accept limits. Socio-political human, producer.	*Post-humanism:* De-centered subject, culturally inscribed/constructed, contradictory, relational, valorize unconscious; foreground limits. Cyborg: continously recreated & recreating via technology. Fractured, schizoid consumer	Subject-in-process, capable of agency & ego integration w/in fluidity.

material base	feudal economy	*Industrial Age* Navigation, gunpowder, printing press. Various forms of nation-state capitalism. Bureaucratic rationalization	*Information Age* Nuclear power and micro-electronic global capitalism.
view of history	static, divinely ordered	linear, progressive change = teleological. Ignorance-enlightenment-emancipation = inevitable trajectory. Doctrine of eventual *secular* salvation via human rationality, especially science	Non-linear, cyclical, indeterminant, discontinuous, contingent. Focus on the present as history, the past as a fiction of the present.
place of community/tradition	commitment to what is fixed and enduring	valorize change; dualism of individual vs. cultural embeddedness	Increased normalization & regulation. Multinational hyperspace. Difference without opposition. Beyond dualism of individual & social relatedness. Personal autonomy *and* social relatedness. Ecopolitics.

Coda: Seductions and Resistances

> [W]hy should the work of Foucault, Deleuze and others be becoming increasingly popular on the left? (Patton, 1983:56)

Taking this manuscript to New Zealand provided me with the opportunity to present a fairly finished document to colleagues from another part of the world, to test its receptions outside of the United States context so lately enamoured of poststructuralism as a theoretical adequation of contemporary times. Often feeling like something of a cheerleader for poststructuralism, I encountered some memorable reactions.

At the 1989 New Zealand women's studies conference, a keynote speaker termed poststructuralism a "virus" which threatened the coherency and effectivity of feminist work in the world. More than a few self-identified structuralist Marxists raised grave doubts about this latest theoreticism. "Attacks on the dialectic" were not well-received and the relativisms presumed attendant upon poststructuralism were especially troublesome for many. Many women branded it as a "male conspiracy" which both re-presents in obtuse jargon what feminists had already formulated and serves to mark the panic of the de-centered white male intellectual. Many raised concerns along the lines of Cock's (1989) observation that there is a tendency toward depoliticization of interests on the part of thought preoccupied with shades of grey in the social world, a kind of mental masturbation which, while great fun in terms of language play, siphons off intellectual energy that could be better spent.

On the other hand, as I spoke throughout New Zealand, others, both male and female, viewed these theoretic movements as a way to get "unstuck," a way to think and act outside of the logic which limits us in the face of right-wing discourses that have seized the imaginations and meaning-making of so much of the populations of both the U.S. and New Zealand. The available codes for conceptualizing radical political praxis seem inadequate: "One needs another language besides that of political liberation," Derrida answered his interviewer (Kearney, 1984:122) who asked, "can the theoretical radicality of deconstruction be translated into a radical political praxis?" (Ibid.:119). Western logocentrism with its dependence on oppositional relations with Otherness, its assumptions of self-presence, its pretensions toward mastery, totalization and certitude has begun to implode. The emancipatory projects are, in varying degrees, inscribed in such logic, adrift and looking for bridges from existent political codes to codes more adequate in terms of "harbour[ing] a future of meaning" (Derrida, in Kearney, 1984:110).

At a lecture I gave in Dunedin for New Zealand Women's Suffrage Day, I talked of three moves in the reception of postmodernism: unambiguous condemnation, unambiguous celebration, and deliberate ambivalence. Locating myself in the latter category, I see this ambivalence as a way to interrupt the contestatory discourses of the various feminisms, neo-Marxisms, minoritarianisms, and poststructuralisms in order to begin to move outside of both the logic of binary oppositions and the principle of non-contradiction. Situated in our multiple sites for movements of social justice, we can begin to "reinscribe otherwise" while avoiding the fall into an infinite regression of demystification. I grant that the extent to which we can invest in alternative discourses and practices and the kinds of alternatives we choose are affected by the differences within and between ourselves and our Others (Orner, 1989, personal correspondence). But it has been a central argument in these pages that both the seductions of and resistances to postmodernism can help us to "get smart" about the possibilities and limits regarding, specifically, political work through education, and, more generally, a basis for critical social theories less ensnared in phallocentric and logocentric assumptions.

Foucault refused to articulate tactics and strategies, leaving such questions to those directly involved. He argued that the role of dispersion, deviation and contingency in history via the complex consequences of the actions of subjects is far more interesting than "plans of reform" engineered by experts (Smart, 1986). Rather than "how to" guidelines, what I have tried to "sum up" here, instead, is the need for intellectuals with liberatory intentions to take responsibility for transforming our own practices so that our empirical and pedagogical work can be less toward positioning ourselves as masters of truth and justice and more toward creating a space where those directly involved can act and speak on their own behalf.

How to do so without romanticizing the subject and experience-based knowledge is, of course, the dilemma. The best solution I have been able to come up with in these pages is to do our thinking and our investigating in and through struggle and to learn the lessons of practice, one of which is that there is no "correct line" knowable through struggle. The struggle reconstitutes itself and any useful theories of social change must deal with this fluidity. Rather than a descent into anarchy/chaos, such theories celebrate the dispersion and fragmentation that has displaced the ideal of a global, totalizing project of emancipation which attempted to unify and solidify what is contradictory, diverse and changing.

> Turning and turning in the widening gyre
> The falcon cannot hear the falconer;
> Things fall apart; the centre cannot hold;
> (W.B. Yeats, 1919)

So begins William Butler Yeats' poem, "The Second Coming," written in response to the Russian Revolution. I often think of these words as I struggle with what postmodernism is and might mean for those of us contesting how the world is understood in ways that challenge hegemonic knowledges. Rather than the sense of loss and even fear at "And what rough beast, its hour come round at last,/Slouches towards Bethlehem to be born?" I end this book feeling poised at some opening that bodes well for those of us who want our intellectual engagement to matter in the struggle toward social justice. The conjunction in critical social theory of the various feminisms, neo-Marxisms and poststructuralisms feels fruitful ground for shifting us into ways of thinking that can take us beyond ourselves. This book is intended to both mark and propel that shift.

Notes

Series Editor's Introduction

1. Linda Hutcheon, *The Politics of Postmodernism* (New York: Routledge, 1989), p. 1.
2. Ibid., p. 3.
3. Ibid., p. 4.
4. Michael F. D. Young, ed., *Knowledge and Control* (London: Collier-Macmillan, 1971).
5. Samuel Bowles and Herbert Gintis, *Schooling in Capitalist America* (New York: Basic Books, 1976).
6. Michael W. Apple and Lois Weis, eds., *Ideology and Practice in Schooling* (Philadelphia: Temple University Press, 1983). See also Cameron McCarthy and Michael W. Apple, "Race, Class and Gender in American Educational Research," in Lois Weis, ed., *Class, Race and Gender in American Education* (Albany: State University of New York, 1988).
7. Michael W. Apple, *Ideology and Curriculum* (New York: Routledge, 1979; second edition, 1990), *Education and Power* (New York: Routledge ARK Edition, 1985), and *Teachers and Texts: A Political Economy of Class and Gender Relations in Education* (New York: Routledge, 1988).
8. Hutcheon, *The Politics and Postmodernism,* p. 2. See also, Elizabeth Ellsworth, "Why Doesn't This Feel Empowering?" *Harvard Educational Review,* 59 (August 1989), pp. 297–324.
9. Alison Jaggar, *Feminist Politics and Human Nature* (New Jersey: Rowman and Allenfield, 1983), p. 387.
10. These arguments are put most forcefully in Leslie Roman's work. For further discussion, see Leslie Roman and Michael W. Apple, "Is Naturalism a Move Away from Positivism?," in Elliot Eisner and Alan Peshkin, eds., *Qualitative Inquiry in Education* (New York: Teachers College Press, 1990).

Preface

1. Pluralizing each of these three critical discourses foregrounds the many varied and even antagonistic strands within each of them. While I make some effort in this book to not homogenize the feminism*s*, neo-Marxism*s* and poststructuralism*s* under study here, my focus is on how each functions simultaneously as both parallel and interruption to one another. Chapter 2 will deal with this in more detail.
2. I use discourse in the Foucauldian sense of a conceptual grid with its own exclusions and erasures, its own rules and decisions, limits, inner logic, parameters and blind alleys. A discourse is that which is beneath the writer's awareness in terms of rules governing the formation and transformation of ideas into a dispersal of the historical agent, the knowing subject.
3. Polkinghorne (1983) traces the history of the term "human science." He argues that "behavioral science" retains the spectre of behaviorism and its prohibition against including consciousness as a part of scientific study. "Social science" carries connotations of seeking a knowledge characteristic of the natural sciences in its law-seeking mode of inquiry. "Human science," he argues, is more inclusive, using multiple systems of inquiry, "a science which approaches questions about the human realm with an openness to its special characteristics and a willingness to let the questions inform which methods are appropriate" (p. 289).
4. This listing of positionality has long been normative in feminist scholarship. It is, however, much problematized by poststructuralist debates on the authority of meaning, specifically on the role of the author. Spivak (1989c) writes of "a kind of confessional attitudinizing . . . a confessional self-description" (p. 208) that denies "the difference between making a confessional declaration and inhabiting a subject position that is assigned to you" (p. 216). Additionally, poststructuralism brings into question the idea of a unified, stable "self" capturable via linguistic portrayal. For example, that I write from a position of heterosexual privilege is not unimportant, but "heterosexual" feels a thin term and an unattractive kind of closure to the complexity of my life. How to use such categories as provisional constructions rather than as systematic formulations and what this means in terms of identity politics remain largely unexplored territory. Chapter 6 will deal with this a bit more.

   Kipnis (1988) writes of "the resistance of first-world feminists to the dangerous knowledge that in a *world* system of patriarchy, upheld by an international division of labor, unequal exchange and the International Monetary Fund, we first-world feminists are also the beneficiaries" (p. 165).
5. Post-Marxism will be outlined in Chapter 2. Postmodernism is definitionally circled around in Chapters 1, 2 and, again, in 5. In terms of "postmodern materialist-feminism," Newton and Rosenfelt (1985) define materialist-feminism thusly: the social and economic circumstances of people's lives

are central to an understanding of culture; intellectual work is both product of and intervention in particular moments of history; the social construction of gender, class, race and sexual identity arises out of power relations that change with social and economic conditions, conditions that are simultaneously cause and effect of ideological relations. While their definition captures many of my basic assumptions, my reservations about "materialist" as a term of choice to describe my feminism are based on its embeddedness in the binary of idealism/materialism and its assumption of a reality prior to and independent of thought which the latter in some way merely reflects. All of this is both illustrated and complicated by Spivak's movement from "feminist Marxist deconstructivist" (1987:117) to "a feminist who is an old-fashioned Marxist" (1989a:269).

6. For background on and representatives of "new French feminisms" (as opposed to the "old French feminism" of Simone de Beauvoir), see: Irigaray, 1985; Delphy, 1984; Marks and de Courtivon, 1980; Jardine, 1985; Moi, 1985. See, also, *Signs,* 3 (4, 1978), entire issue, and *Ideology and Consciousness,* 4 (1978), entire issue. Jardine (1982) makes clear that the term "feminist" is problematic given that many of these women define themselves as beyond a feminism which is seen as "hopelessly anachronistic, grounded in a (male) metaphysical logic which [post]modernity has already begun to overthrow" (p. 64).

   Spivak (1987) terms much of this "French High 'Feminism' (p. 141) and "French high theory of the Female Body" (p. 241). The importance of such work is well argued in Haraway (1985), but it is oft critiqued as fraught with danger in its valorization of the female body. See Grosz (1989) for an argument to the contrary—that this charge of essentialism is a misreading of the fundamental antihumanism and materialism of these theorists, a misreading that ontologises what are discursive/deconstructive strategies.

1 Framing the Issues

1. Calinescu (1987) points out how the tendency to construct a "bad reactionary" postmodernism and "a good, resistant, anticapitalist variety" reproduces the very binaries to which postmodernism is purportedly other than (p. 292).
2. I put "paradigm" in quotes because part of the deconstructive argument is that we are in a "postparadigmatic" era. See Chapter 6.
3. Phrase used by Jean Anyon in a session of the annual meeting of the American Educational Research Association, Montreal, April 1984.
4. See Solomon-Godeau (1988) for an attempt to define "critical practice" within the context of art photography.
5. *Women's Ways of Knowing,* Belenky, et al. (1986) is an example of this psychologistic reductionism of what empowerment means.

6. In terms of the limitations of such a chart, Deleuze (1988) writes: ". . . forces are in a perpetual state of evolution; *there is an emergence of forces which doubles history,* rather envelopes it, according to the Nietzschean conception. This means that the diagram, in so far as it exposes a set of relations between forces, is not a place but rather 'a non-place': it is the place only of mutation" (p. 85, original emphasis).
7. Habermas' worry about postmodernity is an academic specialty in and of itself. For his own statements, see "Modernity vs. Postmodernity," *New German Critique,* 22 (1981), 3–14; "Modernity—An Incomplete Project," in *The Anti-Aesthetic: Essays on Postmodern Culture,* Hal Foster, ed. (1983); and *The Philosophical Discourse of Modernity* (1987). In essence, Habermas identifies poststructuralism with neo-conservatism and argues that the Enlightenment project is not failed, only unfinished. His polemical defense of universalism and rationality is positioned explicitly against what he sees as the "nihilism" of Foucault and Derrida and, implicitly, against Lyotard's challenge to the "great ideological fairy tales" that fuel Habermas' praxis of universal values and rational consensus (Calinescu, 1987:274). For an overview, see Kellner, 1988:262–266.
8. Barthes (1975) defined "readerly texts" as those which fulfill our expectations of the conventions that allow readers to be passive consumers. "Writerly texts," conversely, interrupt those conventions and require readers who participate in making meaning.
9. Thanks to Dr. Sherry O'Donnell, University of North Dakota, for this reading of my writing style.
10. Johnson (1981) foregrounds Derrida's insistence upon some "passage from three to four," some "violent but imperceptible displacement of the 'triangular'—Dialectical/Trinitarian, Oedipal—foundations of Western thought," "a warning to those who, having understood the necessity for a deconstruction of metaphysical binarity, might be tempted to view the number 'three' as a guarantee of liberation from the blindness of logocentrism" (p. xxxii).
11. Arguments regarding the inadequacies of dialectics are premised on the archaeological principle: to look at what makes controversies and opinions possible where the goal is "no synthesis, no resolution of tensions, no ultimate knowledge" (Jardine, 1985:18). Classical dialectics holds that any thesis contains its radical opposite; poststructuralists argue that there is that which is not dialectically recuperable. Such theorists argue that we must abandon dialectics for "a move to an affirmative thought of disjunction and multiplicity" (Hand, 1986:xliv). For Spivak's ideas about "the reinscription of the dialectic into deconstruction," see Harasym, 1988:67. See, also, Deleuze, *Nietzsche and Philosophy* (1983), "Against the Dialectic," pp. 8–10, and Section 5, "The Overman: Against the Dialectic," pp. 147–194.
12. Elshtain (1987) calls this "hardening of the categories" (p. 325).
13. My favorite experimenters and barrier-breakers are the poststructuralist anthropologists, e.g., Clifford and Marcus, 1986; Marcus and Fischer,

1986. Other examples of what might be termed "deconstructivist empirical work" include Mulkay, 1985; Mishler, 1984, 1986a,b; Zeller, 1987. Chapter 5 discusses much of this work.

14. For a critique of how issues of relativism get framed in the human sciences, see Chapter 6 of this book as well as Harding, 1987; Cherryholmes, 1988; John K. Smith, 1988; and Alcoff, 1989.

2 Postmodernism and the Discourses of Emancipation: Precedents, Parallels and Interruptions

1. Derrida writes, "In any case, I am very mistrustful whenever people identify historical breaks or when they say, 'This begins here' " (1985:84).
2. An example of this is "The Politics of Postmodernity" conference, Quebec City, May 28–30, 1989, sponsored by The Canadian Society for Hermeneutics and Postmodern Thought. See, also, *Boundary 2* symposium on "Engagements: Postmodernism, Marxism, Politics," in Arac, 1982–83.
3. Arun Bose (1975) claims to have coined the term "post-Marxian." By this he means a modern extension of Marxism which "validates some propositions of marxian political economy, extends others and discards a few" (p. 19). I would term this *neo-Marxism,* the twentieth-century efforts of Marxism to remain relevant.
4. Implosion is "an explosion toward the center" (Baudrillard, 1984:281), a collapsing inward, a self-consumption caused by the "alterity," the structuring absence, the shadow, the unsaid (and unsayable) present in every concept. Neo-Marxist media critic, Larry Grossberg (1988a), writes: ". . . Baudrillard talks about the supercession of reality by the image. . . . It is not merely that reality fails to give up its meaning to us, or even that it no longer has any meaning, but that it has *any* meaning which we give to it; reality has disappeared into its images" (p. 136). Recent American presidential media politics is a stellar example of this collapse of the distinctions between a medium of representation and the "real": "There is no longer any medium in the literal sense; it is now intangible, diffuse, and diffracted in the real, and it can no longer even be said that the latter is distorted by it" (Baudrillard, 1984:273).
5. Heteroglossia is a Bakhtinian (1984) term that means the proliferation of multiple "unofficial" linguistic practices.
6. There are varied ways of categorizing feminisms. Alison Jaggar's 1983 categories of liberal, orthodox Marxist, radical and socialist feminism had wide currency for awhile. Moi (1985), quite Eurocentrically, divides feminism into continental and Anglo-American. Ferguson (1988) posits categories of liberal humanist, gynocentric and linguistic feminisms. She stresses that each enables in some ways, constrains in others and celebrates the very multiplicity of feminisms "against the somnolent hand of totalization" (p.

18). Grosz's (1988) categories are liberal, structuralist and autonomy-oriented; by the latter, she means breaking out of a reactive pattern to male-centered theorizing and politics. Pringle (1988) finds the still generally hegemonic categories of liberal, radical and socialist no longer adequate and questions the obsession with labelling altogether. In the same vein, de Lauretis (1989) characterizes "the typological project" (p. 33) as constructing "an ascending scale of theoretico-political sophistication" (p. 4). Her term of choice is "non-denominational feminist theorist" (p. 9).

7. Simulacra: copies without originals. Images of the Virgin Mary are the archetypal simulacra. Another is the simulated economic prosperity of the Reagan era. Perhaps the contemporary simulacrum par excellence is the foetus as constructed by the New Right (Kroker, 1983). The Baudrillardian argument is that we have shifted from a culture of representations to one of simulacra. See Kroker and Cook, 1986. Simulacra function to mask the absence of referential finalities. Baudrillard's definition of simulacrum comes from Ecclesiastes, "The simulacrum is never that which conceals the truth—it is the truth which conceals that there is none. The simulacrum is true" (Baudrillard quoted in Bogard, 1988).
8. See, also, *Marxism Today,* October, 1988, special issue on post-Fordism, and January, 1989.
9. Thanks to many discussions with my former Mankato State University colleague, Dennis Crow, for this understanding of Derrida's "the always already," which is actually a Heideggerean concept. For Heidegger, "the always already" meant the implicit circularity of language (Lawson, 1985:72). For an extended comparison of Derrida and Heidegger's use of "the always already," see Gasche, 1987.
10. For black American and post-colonial readings of this, see, West, "Black Culture and Postmodernism," Wallace, "Reading 1968 and the Great American Whitewash," and Bhabha, "Remembering Fanon: Self, Psyche and the Colonial Condition," in Kruger and Mariani, 1989.
11. Logocentrism: as used in the work of Derrida, Western philosophy from Plato on associates the full word of truth with Reason as *Logos,* as transcendental signified. Logocentrism is the heart of Enlightenment belief that reason could set us free, an innocent reason that was universal, abstract and disinterested. Bhabha writes of "the strategic failure of . . . western idealism or logocentrism" (1986:151). Feminism, of course, has long protested the masculine bias of hegemonic meanings of reason (Harding, 1982), and Derrida's own work makes much of the phallus as center of our symbolic order, a condition he terms "phallogocentrism" (Rabine, 1988:15). See, also, Spanos, 1987:56–58.
12. Selma Greenberg, mid-year SIG/Research on Women in Education conference, session on the usefulness of postmodernism to feminist thought and practice, Hofstra University, Hempstead, New York, Nov. 10–12, 1988.

13. Personally, I had just about gotten enough on top of neo-Marxist and feminist literature to feel that perhaps I could get active in some social movement work. I had the local battered women's shelter in mind. Then I got caught up in an intellectual rush that rivaled my experiences of both feminist and neo-Marxist theory. I have yet to get my head above the water of the vast, transdisciplinary literature of postmodernism. Given the rate of its production, I wonder if I ever will.
14. Ashley (forthcoming a) quotes George A. Carver, a senior fellow at the Center for Strategic and International Studies in Washington, D.C., that the desire of many East Germans "to decamp for the West" was not an ideological victory but to be attributed to commercials on TV (*The New York Times*, Nov. 8, 1989).
15. Dowling (1984) uses this phrase in writing about Sartre's opinion of structuralism.
16. For feminist work in this area, see Flax, 1987; Harding, 1986, 1987; Haraway, 1988; Rabine, 1988; Scott, 1988; Spivak, 1987; Nicholson, 1989.
17. From literary criticism and cultural studies, see Ulmer, 1985; Nelson, 1986; Atkins and Johnson, 1985; Zavarzadeh and Morton, 1986–87; Naidus, 1987. From educational studies, see Orner and Brennan, 1989; Maher and Tetreault, 1989; Brodkey, 1987; Bowers, 1987; McLaren, 1986, 1988; Giroux, 1988; Kenway and Morda, 1989.
18. Cherryholmes' book ignores what Newton (1988) terms "the mother roots" of poststructuralism. For a review, see Lather, 1988b. In this regard, it is interesting to compare Cherryholmes' bibliography with those of Giroux (1988) and McLaren (1988). The latter are both other to Luke's discussion of how feminist work, when used by male theorists, often becomes "marginalia . . . in the burial site of the bibliography" (n.d., p. 23). For discussions of men in feminism, see Jardine and Smith (eds.), 1987.
19. The concept of "voice" is also problematized in Morton and Zavarzadeh, 1988–89.
20. Thanks to my Ohio State colleague, Mary Leach, for helping me work through this section.

3 Research as Praxis

1. Morgan (1983) distinguishes between positivist, phenomenological, and critical/praxis-oriented research paradigms. While my earlier work used the term "openly ideological" (Lather, 1986b), I find "praxis-oriented" better describes the emergent paradigm I have been tracking over the last few years. "Openly ideological" invites comparisons with fundamentalist and conservative movements, whereas "praxis-oriented" clarifies the critical and

empowering roots of a research paradigm openly committed to critiquing the status quo and building a more just society.

"Praxis-oriented" means "activities that combat dominance and move toward self-organization and that push toward thoroughgoing change in the practices of . . . the social formation" (Benson, 1983:338). Praxis is, of course, a word with a history. I use the term to mean the dialectical tension, the interactive, reciprocal shaping of theory and practice which I see at the center of an emancipatory social science. The essence of my argument, then, is that we who do empirical research in the name of emancipatory politics must discover ways to connect our research methodology to our theoretical concerns and political commitments. At its simplest, this is a call for critical inquirers to practice in their empirical endeavors what they preach in their theoretical formulations.

2. It was actually French philosopher Gaston Bachelard who originated this concept of epistemological break, which Althusser then applied to the work of Marx. See Lecourt, 1975. Epistemological break means a rupture in the established way of conceptualizing an issue, a rupture which essentially *inverts* meaning. Hesse (1980), for example, uses the term to characterize those who argue not only *against* the possibility of an "objective" social science but *for* the possibilities inherent in an explicitly value-based social science with emancipatory goals.
3. See Lather, 1986b, for a discussion of openly ideological research.
4. The basic assumptions of positivism are four: 1) the aims, concepts and methods of the natural sciences are applicable to the social sciences; 2) the correspondence theory of truth which holds that reality is knowable through correct measurement methods is adequate for the social sciences; 3) the goal of social research is to create universal laws of human behavior which transcend culture and history; and 4) the fact/value dichotomy, the denial of both the theory-laden dimensions of observation and the value-laden dimensions of theory creates the grounds for an "objective" social science. For an overview and critique of each of the three paradigms, the positivist, the interpretive and the critical/praxis-oriented, see Bredo and Feinberg (1982), Carr and Kemmis (1983), and Bernstein (1976).
5. See Wexler (1987) for an extensive critique of "the new sociology of education."
6. Two examples of the dangers of conceptual overdeterminism leading to theoretical imposition (the lack of a reciprocal relationship between theory and data) in the new sociology of education are correspondence theory which posited an overly deterministic mirror-image relationship between schools and the needs of corporate capitalism (Bowles and Gintis, 1976; Apple, 1979), and the wishful thinking which saw resistance in every inattentive student and recalcitrant teacher (for critiques, see Giroux, 1983; Bullough and Gitlin, 1985).

7. I first heard this term used in relation to social theory by James T. Sears, 1983.
8. See Roman and Apple (1990) for an update of his position on the role of theory in critical ethnography, a position articulated "largely by Leslie [Roman]" but "worked through with discussions and debate with me" (personal correspondence with Apple, August, 1989). Additionally, this paper is interesting for its attempts to textually display the "we" and the "I" of co-authorship. For a somewhat different approach to this problem, see Lewis and Simon (1986).
9. The inadequacies of an over-reliance on rationality in human behavior are eloquently captured in Ascher's letter to de Beauvoir, a letter written to "clear the air" after Ascher had written a biography of de Beauvoir: "I don't think you ever grasped sufficiently the way the unconscious can hold one back from grasping a freedom consciously chosen. Too often I see your sense of freedom being based on a rationalism that denies that murky inner world over which we have as little, or much, control as the world outside us. And, in fact, control would be your word, not mind. For I believe we have to love this deep inner self and try to be in harmony with it" (Ascher, De Salivo, Ruddick, 1984:93; Harding, 1982).
10. Issues of validity in openly ideological research are dealt with much more fully in Lather, 1986b.

4 Feminist Perspectives on Empowering Research Methodologies

1. This work was started under the auspices of a Bush Curriculum Development Grant, 1985–86, supplemented by Mankato State University Faculty Research Grants, 1986–88. I especially thank my colleagues who also teach the introductory course for opening up their classrooms for purposes of this research: Clare Bright, Sudie Hoffman, Marilee Rickard, Lisa Dewey Joyce-Child, Kim Luedtke and Carol Ann Lowinski.

   The data gathering was a collective effort on the part of my Feminist Scholarship classes (1985: Sandy Parsons, Sharon Anderson, Kim Luedtke, Brenda Winter, Barry Evans, Diane Finnerty, Max Hanson, Edna Wayne, Kathy Kea and Eileen Grady; 1986: John Edwards, John Eeten, Kay Hawkins, Sindy Mau, Jeanne Burkhart, Ruthe Enstad, Ann Halloran, Pat Hawley, Terri Hawthorne, Najma Siddiqui and Margaret Mara; 1987: Cherie Scricca, Tara Tull, Shelly Owen, Patty Wasson, Dorothy Quam, Signe Wieland, Lin Hamer, Seetha Anagol and Deb Harris).
2. Gray writes that Gilligan's initial concern was the shaky construct validity arising from hypothetical rather than real-life moral dilemmas. Intending to interview young men making draft resistance choices, she got an all-female sample quite by accident when the Vietnam War ended (1982:52). Abortion

had just been legalized and Gilligan soon recognized the moral dilemma of whether to carry a child to full-term as a real-life situation with great potential for expanding the methodology of moral development research beyond hypothetical situations.

3. I read of this project in *Participatory Research Newsletter,* Sept., 1985, published by the Participatory Research Group, 309–229 College St., Toronto, Ontario M5T 1R4. The present incarnation of this newsletter is published as NETWORK NOTES, Highlander Center, Rt. 3, Box 370, Newmarket, TN 37820. The project itself can be reached through: Laura Bush, Executive Director, Women's Economic Development Project, c/o Institute for Community Education and Training, P.O. Box 1937, Hilton Head Island, South Carolina 29925. 803–681–5095.
4. See Giroux's review of neo-Marxist theories of resistance, *Harvard Educational Review,* 53 (3), 1983, 257–292.
5. Raymond Williams makes a very helpful distinction between alternative and oppositional, with the former being one of many legitimate perspectives and the latter a clear intention of critique and transformation (1977:114).
6. Dr. Janet Lee, "The Effects of Feminist Education on Student Values," paper presented at the annual meeting of the National Women's Studies Association, June, 1988, Minneapolis, Minnesota.
7. For a lyrical exploration of the issues involved in empirical accountability in the area of historical/literary research, see Bunkers, 1987.
8. This argument is developed much more fully in Lather, 1987, where I look at how male neo-Marxist discourse on schooling largely obscures male privilege and the social construction of gender as central issues in the shaping of public school teaching.
9. See, Benton (1984) for a discussion of the limits of Althusser's self-criticisms.

5 Deconstructing/Deconstructive Inquiry: The Politics of Knowing and Being Known

1. Harding, 1986, 1987; Mulkay, 1985; Clifford and Marcus, 1986; Marcus and Fischer, 1986; Richardson, 1988; Nelson et al., 1987; Nicholson, 1990; Haraway, 1988; Longino, 1988.
2. Correspondence from Elizabeth Ellsworth, March 1, 1988.
3. This is not to say that the same questions have not been asked previously. See, for example, such materialist-feminist work as Acker, et al., 1983, and Roman, 1988.
4. A very interesting piece challenging the non-interventionist stance of interpretive ethnography *from the inside* is that of Campbell, where he traces his own awareness that ". . . all research approaches, including our own, reflect (more or less explicitly) assumptions about human nature and human

social relationships, and about ways of studying them. . . . [F]oreswearing interventionist intent merely leaves open the possibility of intervening by default. . . ."(1988:116–117).

5. Phone call from Gitlin, June, 1989. This was in response to my mailing him a draft of my critique of his work. All of this raises questions about how we use one another's reports of always in-process efforts to do inquiry more democratically without setting ourselves up as the "methodological police."
6. The politics of this sort of "radical constructivism" are beginning to be questioned. See Haraway, 1988, Longino, 1988, and Clifford's comments in *The Chronicle of Higher Education,* November 30, 1988, A5 and A8.

6 Reinscribing Otherwise: Postmodernism and the Human Sciences

1. The work of Guba and Lincoln (1981) and Lincoln and Guba (1985) was problematic in its collapsing of all alternative paradigms into one, the "naturalistic." That they have rethought this position is obvious in the framing of a March, 1989, conference on alternative paradigms of inquiry where they have moved from a one paradigm model to conceptualizing three alternative paradigms to positivism: postpositivist, critical and constructivist. This was in response to those concerned with what Guba terms the "parochialism" of the initial proposal for the conference (Feb. 8, 1988, correspondence with Egon Guba).
2. See Paul Feyerabend, the *enfant terrible* of philosophy of science, *Against method: Outline of an anarchistic theory of knowledge*. London: Verso, 1975.
3. Livingstone et al. (1987) combines both types of neo-Marxist inquiry and exemplifies both the more self-righteous ideology critique and the more self-reflexive work influenced by the linguistic turn in social theory.
4. These questions grow out of my very fruitful collaboration over the last few years with Ann Berlak and Janet Miller.
5. Coward and Ellis (1977) coined the phrase "the subject-ed subject."
6. A beautiful example of this complexity within one individual is Hall (1985). Pratt (1984) wrestles with the same issue of racial identity, but from the position of white privilege. For an incandescent critique of Pratt, see Martin and Mohanty (1986).
7. For a now somewhat embarrassing socialist-feminist critique of the Marxist search for a revolutionary subject, see Lather, 1984.
8. David Byrne, Talking Heads rock impressario, is oftentimes referred to as a "postmodern" artist. "Stop Making Sense" is both an album and a critically acclaimed rock concert movie.

7 Staying Dumb? Student Resistance to Liberatory Curriculum

1. For further breakdown of the survey data, see Lee, 1988.
2. Panel presentation, Teaching About and Doing Feminist Research, NWSA, Atlanta, Georgia, June, 1987.
3. Thanks to Dan DeMattis, Ken Hay, Myrna Packard and Michel Coconis. Each worked with parts of the data as an assignment for a course in the analysis of qualitative data that I taught at Ohio State University, Spring, 1989. When I presented a version of this paper in Alison Jones' 1989 University of Auckland third-year course on women and education, students raised the paradox of whose names I use and whose I don't. The names of high-status theorists are recirculated and doctoral students are named (with their permission, of course), while undergraduates are positioned as disembodied, unnamed, unnoted "data" sources. Much of this was done to protect confidentiality, but it bears thinking about. For a discussion of this issue within the context of collaborative research with teachers, see Shulman, in press.
4. A special thanks to Alison Jones for helping me work this through and to the other New Zealand colleagues who were helpful in my writing of this chapter, especially Sue Middleton and Louise Johnson.
5. One example from my own teaching is Charlotte Perkins Gilman's "The Yellow Wallpaper" which serves as a strategic site for contestation of dominant ideological subject identities. By moving the text around provisionally, unfixedly, we begin by discussing how different audiences respond to the story, elicit student assessments as to whether the narrator goes crazy or not and then explore WHY we interpret this so differently, how our interpretations are rooted in our own positionalities.
6. One might contrast this with the more traditional categorization process at work in *Women's Ways of Knowing,* Belenky et al., 1986.

Bibliography

Acker, Joan; Barry, Kate; and Essevold, Joke. 1983. Objectivity and truth: Problems in doing feminist research. *Women's Studies International Forum* 6:423–435.

Alcoff, Linda. 1987. Cultural feminism versus post-structuralism: The identity crisis in feminist theory. *Signs* 13 (3): 405–436.

———. 1989. Justifying feminist social science. In *Feminism and Science*, ed. Nancy Tuana, 85–103. Bloomington: Indiana University Press.

Althusser, Louis. 1971. Ideology and ideological state apparatuses. In *Lenin and philosophy and other essays*. New York: New Left Books.

———. 1976. *Essays in self-criticism*. Trans. Grahame Lock. Norfolk: New Left Books.

Anderson, Sharon. 1986. *A study of the resistance to liberatory education and liberatory ideology in re-entry women*. Unpublished M.S. thesis, Mankato State University.

Anyon, Jean. 1980. Social class and the hidden curriculum of work. *Journal of Education* 62:67–92.

———. 1982. Adequate social science, curriculum investigations, and theory. *Theory into Practice* 21 (1): 34–37.

———. 1983. Accommodation, resistance, and female gender. In *Gender and education*, ed. Stephen Walker and L. Burton, 19–38. Sussex, England: Falmer Press.

Apple, Michael. 1979. *Ideology and curriculum*. Boston: Routledge and Kegan Paul.

———. 1980–81. The other side of the hidden curriculum: Correspondence theories and the labor process. *Interchange* 11 (3): 5–22.

———. 1982. *Education and power*. Boston: Routledge and Kegan Paul.

Arac, Jonathan, 1982–83. Introduction to engagements: Postmodernism, Marxism, politics. Special issue of *Boundary 2* 11 (1–2): 1–4.

———, ed. 1986. *Postmodernism and politics*. Theory and History of Literature Series, vol. 28. Minneapolis: University of Minnesota Press.

Arato, Andres and Gebhardt, Eike, eds. 1985. *The essential Frankfurt School reader*. New York: Continuum.

Aronowitz, Stanley. 1981. *The crisis in historical materialism: Class, politics and culture in Marxist theory*. New York: Praeger.

Aronowitz, Stanley and Giroux, Henry. 1985. Radical education and transformative intellectuals. *Canadian Journal of Political and Social Theory* 9 (3): 48–63.

Ascher, C.; De Salvio, L.; and Ruddick, S., eds. 1984. *Between women*. Boston: Beacon Press.

Ashley, David. Forthcoming, a. Playing with the pieces: The fragmentation of social theory. In *Critical Theory Now,* ed. Philip Wexler. London: Falmer Press.

———. Forthcoming, b. Marx and the excess of the signifier: Domination as production and as simulation. *Sociological Perspectives*.

Atkins, G. Douglas, and Johnson, Michael L. 1985. *Writing and reading differently: Deconstruction and the teaching of composition and literature*. Lawrence: University of Kansas Press.

Atkinson, Paul; Delamont, Sara; and Hammersley, Martyn. 1988. Qualitative research traditions: A British response to Jacob. *Review of Educational Research* 58 (2): 231–250.

Atwood, Margaret. 1986. *The Greenfield Review* 13 (3, 4): 5.

Bakhtin, Mikhail. 1981. *The dialogic imagination: Four essays*. Trans. Caryl Emerson and M. Holquist. Austin: University of Texas Press.

———. 1984. *Problems of Dostoevsky's poetics*. Trans., ed. Caryl Emerson. Minneapolis: University of Minnesota Press.

Ball, Steven, ed. Forthcoming. *Foucault and education*. London: Routledge.

Bannett, Eve Tavor. 1989. *Structuralism and the logic of dissent: Barthes, Derrida, Foucault, Lacan*. Chicago: University of Chicago Press.

Barthes, Roland. 1975. *The pleasure of the text*. Trans. Richard Miller. New York: Hill and Wang.

Baudrillard, Jean. 1981. *For a critique of the political economy of the sign*. Trans. Charles Levin. St. Louis: Telos Press.

———. 1984. The precession of simulacra. In *Art after modernism: Rethinking representation,* ed. Brian Wallis, 253–281. Boston: David Godine Pub.

Bazerman, Charles. 1987. Codifying the social scientific style: The *APA Publication Manual* as a behaviorist rhetoric. In *The rhetoric of the human sciences,* ed. Nelson, et al., 125–144. Madison: University of Wisconsin Press.

Bauman, Zygmunt. 1989. Sociological responses to post modernity. *Thesis Eleven* 23:35–63.

Beechley, Veronica and Donald, James, eds. 1985. *Subjectivity and social relations: A reader*. Philadelphia: Open University Press.

Belenky, Mary Fields; Clinchy, B.; Goldberger, N.; and Tarule, J. (1986). *Women's ways of knowing: The development of self, voice, and mind*. New York: Basic Books.

Bennington, Geoff. 1987. Demanding history. In *Post-structuralism and the question of history,* ed. Derek Altridge, G. Bennington, and R. Young, 15–29. Cambridge: Cambridge University Press.

Benson, J. K. 1983. A dialectical method for the study of organizations. In *Beyond method: Strategies for social research,* ed. G. Morgan, 331–346. Beverly Hills: Sage.

Benton, Ted. 1984. *The rise and fall of structural Marxism: Althusser and his influence*. London: Macmillan.

Berlak, Ann. April, 1983. The critical pedagogy of skilled post-secondary teachers: How the experts to it. Paper delivered to annual conference of the American Educational Research Association, New Orleans, Louisiana.

———. October, 1986. Teaching for liberation and empowerment in the liberal arts: Towards the development of a pedagogy that overcomes resistance. Paper delivered at the eighth annual Curriculum Theorizing Conference, Dayton, Ohio.

———. 1989. Teaching for outrage and empathy in the liberal arts. *Educational Foundations* 3 (2): 69–93.

Berlak, Ann, and Berlak, H. 1981. *Dilemmas of schooling: Teaching and social change*. New York: Methuen.

Berman, Marshall. 1982. *All that is solid melts into air: The experience of modernity*. New York: Viking Penguin.

Bernstein, Basil. 1977. *Class, codes and control*. London: Routledge and Kegan Paul.

Bernstein, Richard. 1976. *The restructuring of social and political theory*. New York: Harcourt Brace Jovanovich.

———. 1983. *Beyond objectivism and relativism: Science, hermeneutics, and praxis*. Philadelphia: University of Pennsylvania Press.

———. 1985. Introduction to *Habermas and modernity,* 1–32. Cambridge: M.I.T. Press.

Bhabha, Homi K. 1986. The other question: Difference, discrimination and the discourse of colonialism. In *Literature, politics and theory,* eds. Francis Barker, Peter Hulme, Margaret Iverson, and Diana Loxley, 148–172. New York: Methuen.

———. 1989. Remembering Fanon: Self, psyche, and the colonial condition. In *Remaking history,* ed. Barbara Kruger and Phil Mariani, 131–148. Seattle: Bay Press.

Bloom, Allan. 1987. *The closing of the American mind: How higher education has failed democracy and impoverished the souls of today's students.* New York: Simon and Schuster.

Bogard, William. April, 1988. Sociology in the absence of the social: The significance of Baudrillard for contemporary social thought. Paper delivered at the Pacific Sociological Association annual conference, Las Vegas, Nevada.

Bogdan, Robert, and Biklen, Sari. 1982. *Qualitative research for education: An introduction to theory and methods.* Boston: Allyn and Bacon.

Bookman, Ann, and Morgan, Sandra, eds. 1988. *Women and the politics of empowerment.* Philadelphia: Temple University Press.

Bordo, Susan. 1989. Feminism, postmodernism and gender-skepticism. In *Feminism/postmodernism,* ed. Linda Nicholson, 133–156. New York: Routledge.

Bose, Arun. 1975. Marxian and post-Marxian political economy: An Introduction. Hamondsworth, England: Penguin Books.

Bottomore, Tom. 1978. Marxism and sociology. In *A history of sociological analysis,* ed. T. Bottomore and R. Nisbet, 118–148. London: Hunemann.

———. 1983. *A dictionary of Marxist thought.* Oxford: Blackwell Reference.

Bowers, C. A. 1984. *The promise of theory: Education and the politics of cultural change.* New York: Longman.

———. 1987. *Elements of a post-liberal theory of education.* New York: Teacher's College Press.

———. 1988. *The cultural dimensions of educational computing: Understanding the non-neutrality of technology.* New York: Teacher's College Press.

Bowles, Gloria, and Duelli-Klein, Renata, eds. 1983. *Theories of women's studies.* Boston: Routledge and Kegan Paul.

Bowles, S., and Gintis, H. 1976. *Schooling in capitalist America: Educational reform and the contradictions of economic life.* New York: Basic Books.

Bredo, Eric, and Feinberg, Walter, eds. 1982. *Knowledge and values in social and educational research.* Philadelphia: Temple University Press.

Britzman, Deborah. February, 1989. The terrible problem of "knowing thyself"; Toward a poststructural account of teacher identity. Paper presented at the Ethnography and Education Research Forum, University of Pennsylvania.

Brodkey, Linda. 1987. Postmodern pedagogy for progressive educators: An essay review. *Journal of Education* 196 (3): 138–143.

Bromley, Hank. 1989. Identity politics and critical pedagogy. *Educational Theory* 39 (3): 207–223.

Brown, Dave and Tandom, R. 1978. Interviews as catalysts. *Journal of Applied Psychology* 63 (2): 197–205.

Buckingham, David. 1986. Against demystification: A response to *Teaching the Media*. *Screen* 27:80–95.

Buker, Eloise. Forthcoming. Hermeneutics: Problems and promises for doing feminist theory. *Social Epistemology*.

Bullough, Robert, and Gitlin, Andrew. 1985. Beyond control: Rethinking teacher resistance. *Education and society* 3 (1): 65–73.

Bullough, Robert; Goldstein, S.; and Holt, L. 1982. Rational curriculum: Teachers and alienation. *Journal of Curriculum Theorizing* 4 (2): 132–143.

Bunch, Charlotte, and Pollack, Sandra. 1983. *Learning our way: Essays in feminist education*. New York: The Crossing Press.

Bunkers, Suzanne. 1987. "Faithful friends": Nineteenth-century midwestern American women's unpublished diaries. *Women's Studies International Forum* 10 (1): 7–17.

Calinescu, Matei. 1987. *Five faces of modernity: Modernism, avant-garde, decadence, kitsch and postmodernism*. Durham: Duke University Press.

Callaway, Helen. 1981. Women's perspectives: Research as re-vision. In *Human Inquiry*, ed. Peter Reason and John Rowan, 457–472. New York: John Wiley.

Campbell, Douglas. 1988. Collaboration and contradiction in a research and staff-development project. *Teacher's College Record* 90 (1): 99–121.

Campioni, Mia, and Gross, Elizabeth. 1983. Love's labours lost: Marxism and feminism. In *Beyond marxism: Interventions after Marx*, ed. S. Allan and P. Patton, 113–141. Leichardt: Intervention Pub.

Caputo, John. 1987. *Radical hermeneutics: Repetition, deconstruction, and the hermeneutic project*. Bloomington: University of Indiana Press.

Carr, Wilfred, and Kemmis, Stephen. 1986. *Becoming critical: Education, knowledge and action research*. London: The Falmer Press. First published as *Becoming critical: Knowing through action research*. Australia: Deakin University Press, 1983.

Carr-Hill, Roy. 1984. Radicalizing survey methodology. *Quality and Quantity* 18:275–292.

Carson, Tom. May 12, 1987. The Long Way Back. *The Village Voice*. 17–30.

Cherryholmes, Cleo. 1988. *Power and criticism: Poststructural investigations in education*. New York: Teacher's College Press.

Christian, Barbara. 1987. The race for theory. *Cultural Critique* 6:51–63.

———. 1988. Response to "Black women's texts." *NWSA Journal* 1 (1): 32–36.

Clark, David. 1985. Emerging paradigms in organizational theory and research. In *Organizational theory and inquiry: The paradigm revolution,* ed. Y. Lincoln, 43–78. Beverly Hills: Sage.

Cleveland, Harlan. 1985. The twilight of hierarchy: Speculations on the global information society. *Public Administration Review* 45 (1): 185–195.

Clifford, James. 1983. On ethnographic authority. *Representations* 1 (2): 118–146.

———. 1988. *The predicament of culture: Twentieth-century ethnography, literature and art*. Cambridge: Harvard University Press.

Clifford, James, and Marcus, George. 1986. *Writing culture: The poetics and politics of ethnography*. Berkeley: University of California Press.

Cocks, Joan. 1989. *The oppositional imagination: Feminism, critique and political theory*. New York: Routledge.

Collins, James. 1987. Postmodernism and cultural practice: Refining the parameters. *Screen* 28 (2): 11–26.

———. 1989. *Uncommon cultures: Popular culture and post-modernism*. New York: Routledge.

Comstock, Donald. 1982. A method for critical research. In *Knowledge and values in social and educational research,* ed. Eric Bredo and Walter Feinberg, 370–390. Philadelphia: Temple University Press.

Corrigan, Philip. 1987. In/forming schooling. In *Critical pedagogy and cultural power,* ed. David Livingstone, 17–40. South Hadley, Massachusetts: Bergin and Garvey.

Cott, Nancy. 1987. *The grounding of modern feminism*. New Haven: Yale University Press.

Coward, Rosalind, and Ellis, John. 1977. *Language and materialism: Development in semiology and the theory of the subject*. London: Routledge and Kegan Paul.

Cronbach, Lee. 1975. Beyond the two disciplines of scientific psychology. *American Psychologist* 30:116–127.

———. 1980. Validity on parole: Can we go straight? *New Directions for Testing and Measurement* 5:99–108.

Cronbach, Lee and Meehl, P. 1955. Construct validity in psychological tests. *Psychological Bulletin* 52:281–302.

Culler, Jonathan. 1982. *On deconstruction: Theory and criticism after structuralism*. Ithaca: Cornell University Press.

Culley, Margo, and Portuges, Catherine. 1985. *Gendered subjects: The dynamics of feminist teaching*. Boston: Routledge and Kegan Paul.

Davies, Bronwyn. 1989. *Frogs and snails and feminist tales*. Sydney: George Allen and Unwin.

de Lauretis, Teresa. 1987. *The technologies of gender: Essays on theory, film, and fiction*. Bloomington: Indiana University Press.

———. 1989. The essence of the triangle or, taking the risk of essentialism seriously: Feminist theory in Italy, the U.S., and Britain. *differences* 1 (2): 3–37.

Deleuze, Giles. 1983. *Nietzsche and philosophy*. Trans. Hugh Tomlinson. London: The Athlone Press. Originally pub. in French in 1962.

———. 1988. *Foucault*. Trans., ed. Sean Hand. Minneapolis: University of Minnesota Press.

Delphy, Christine. 1984. *Close to home: A materialist analysis of women's oppression*. Amherst: University of Massachusetts Press.

Derrida, Jacques. 1978. Structure, sign and play in the discourse of the human sciences. In *Writing and difference,* trans. Alan Bass, 278–293. Chicago: University of Chicago Press.

———. 1981. *Positions*. Trans. Alan Bass. Chicago: University of Chicago Press.

———. 1982. *Margins of Philosophy*. Trans. Alan Bass. Chicago: University of Chicago Press.

———. 1985. *The ear of the other: Texts and discussions with J. Derrida*. Ed. Christi V. McDonald, trans. Peggy Kamuf. New York: Schocken Books.

Dews, Peter. 1987. *Logics of disintegration: Poststructuralist thought and claims of critical theory*. London: Verso.

Dickens, David R. 1983. The critical project of Jurgen Habermas. In *Changing social science,* ed. D. Sabina and J. Wallulis, 131–155. Albany: State University of New York Press.

Doll, William E. Jr. 1989. Foundations for a post-modern curriculum. *Journal of Curriculum Studies* 21 (3): 243–253.

Donald, James. 1985. Beacons of the future: Schooling, subjection and subjectification. In *Subjectivity and social relations: A reader,* ed. Veronica Beechey and James Donald, 214–249. Philadelphia: Open University Press.

Dowling, William C. 1984. *Jameson, Althusser, Marx: An introduction to the political unconscious*. Ithaca: Cornell University Press.

Dreyfus, Hubert, and Rabinow, Paul. 1983. *Michael Foucault: Beyond structuralism and hermeneutics*. Second Edition. Chicago: University of Chicago Press.

Dubiel, Helmut. 1985. *Theory and politics: Studies in the development of critical theory*. Trans. Benjamin Gregg. Cambridge: M.I.T. Press.

Du Bois, Barbara. 1983. Passionate scholarship: Notes on values, knowing and method in feminist social science. In *Theories of Women's Studies,* ed. Gloria Bowles and Renate Duelli Klein, 105–116. Boston: Routledge and Kegan Paul.

Ebert, Teresa. 1988. The romance of patriarchy: Ideology, subjectivity, and postmodern feminist cultural theory. *Cultural Critique* 10:19–57.

Eco, Umberto. 1989. *Foucault's pendulum*. London: Secker and Warburg.

Eichler, Margrit. 1980. *The double standard*. New York: St. Martin's Press.

Eisenstein, Hester. 1983. *Contemporary feminist thought*. Boston: G. K. Hall.

Eisner, Elliot. 1983. Anastasia might still be alive, but the monarchy is dead. *Educational Researcher* 12 (5): 13–14, 23–24.

———. 1988. The primacy of experience and the politics of method. *Educational Researcher* 17 (5): 15–20.

Ellsworth, Elizabeth. 1987. The place of video in social change: At the edge of making sense. Unpublished paper.

———. 1989. Why doesn't this feel empowering? Working through the repressive myths of critical pedagogy. *Harvard Educational Review* 59 (3): 297–324.

Ellsworth, Elizabeth; Larson, Margot Kennard; and Selvin, Albert. 1986. MTV presents: Problematic pleasures. *Journal of Communication Inquiry* 10 (1): 55–69.

Elshtain, Jean Bethke. 1987. Feminist political rhetoric and women's studies. In *The rhetoric of the human sciences,* ed. John S. Nelson et. al., 319–340. Madison: University of Wisconsin Press.

Epstein, Steven. 1987. Gay politics, ethnic identity: The limits of social constructionism. *Socialist Review* 92–93, 17 (3, 4): 9–54.

Everhart, Robert. 1977. Between stranger and friend: Some consequences of "long term" fieldwork in schools. *American Educational Research Journal* 14 (1): 1–15.

———. 1983. *Reading, writing and resistance: Adolescence and labor in a junior high school*. Boston: Routledge and Kegan Paul.

Fay, Brian. 1975. *Social theory and political practice*. London: George Allen and Unwin Ltd.

———. 1977. How people change themselves: The relationship between critical theory and its audience. In *Political theory and praxis,* ed. Terence Ball, 200–233. Minneapolis: University of Minnesota Press.

———. 1987. *Critical social science*. Ithaca: Cornell University Press.

Fekete, John, ed. 1987. *Life after postmodernism: Essays on value and culture*. New York: St. Martin's Press.

Ferguson, Kathy. 1988. Subject centeredness in feminist theory. Paper presented at the annual meeting of the National Women's Studies Association, Minneapolis.

Feinberg, Walter. 1983. *Understanding education: Toward a reconstruction of educational inquiry*. New York: Cambridge University Press.

Femia, Walter. 1975. Hegemony and consciousness in the thought of Antonio Gramsci. *Political Studies* 23 (1): 29–48.

Feyerabend, Paul. 1975. Against method: Outline of an anarchistic theory of knowledge. London: Verso.

Finlay, Marike. 1987. Technology as practice and (so) what about emancipatory interest? *Canadian Journal of Political and Social Theory* 11 (1–2): 198–214.

Fiske, Donald W., and Shweder, Richard A., eds. 1986. *Metatheory in social science: Pluralisms and subjectivities*. Chicago: University of Chicago Press.

Flax, Jane. 1978. Critical theory as a vocation. *Politics and society* 8 (2): 202–223.

———. 1987. Postmodernism and gender relations in feminist theory. *Signs* 12 (4): 621–643.

Foster, Hal. 1985. *Recodings: Art, spectacle, cultural politics*. Washington: Bay Press.

———. 1988. Wild signs: The breakup of the sign in seventies' art. In *Universal abandon: The politics of postmodernism,* ed. A. Ross, 251–268. Minneapolis: University of Minnesota Press.

Foucault, Michael. 1977. The political function of the intellectual. *Radical Philosophy* 17:12–14.

———. 1979. *Discipline and punishment*. New York: Vintage Books.

———. 1980. *Power/knowledge: Selected interviews and other writings, 1972–1977*. Ed. Colin Gordon, trans. Gordon et al. New York: Pantheon.

———. 1984. What is enlightenment? In *The Foucault Reader,* ed. Paul Rabinow, 32–50. New York: Pantheon.

Fox-Keller, Evelyn. 1985. *Reflections on gender and science*. New Haven: Yale University Press.

Fox, Mike. 1988. Plain talk: on empowerment talk. *The Ladder* 27 (August/Sept.): 2. Washington, D.C.: PUSH Literacy Action Now.

Fraser, Nancy. 1987. What's critical about critical theory? The case of Habermas and gender. In *Feminism as critique,* ed. Seyla Benhabib and D. Cornell, 31–56. Minneapolis: University of Minnesota Press.

———. 1989. *Unruly practices: Power, discourse & gender in contemporary social theory*. Minneapolis: University of Minnesota Press.

Fraser, Nancy, and Nicholson, Linda. 1988. Social criticism without philosophy: An encounter between feminism and postmodernism. In *Universal abandon: The politics of postmodernism,* ed. A. Ross, 83–104. Minneapolis: University of Minnesota Press.

Freire, Paulo. 1973. *Pedagogy of the oppressed*. New York: Seabury.

———. 1985. *The politics of education: Culture, power and liberation*. Massachusetts: Bergin and Garvey.

Fuss, Diana. 1989. Reading like a feminist. *differences* 1 (2): 77–92.

Gasche, Rodolphe. 1987. Introduction. *Reading in interpretation: Holderlin, Hegel, Heidegger, Andrzej Warminsk*. Minneapolis: University of Minnesota Press.

Gebhardt, Eike. 1982. Introduction to Part III, A Critique of Methodology. In *The essential Frankfurt School reader,* ed. Andrew Arato and Eike Gebhardt, 371–406. New York: Continuum.

Geertz, Clifford. 1980. Blurred genres. *The American Scholar* 49:165–179.

Giddens, Anthony. 1979. *Central problems in social theory*. Berkeley: University of California Press.

Gilligan, Carol. 1982. *In a different voice*. Cambridge: Harvard University Press.

Gilman, Charlotte Perkins. 1892. The yellow wallpaper. *New England Magazine* 5:647–659. Reprinted by The Feminist Press, Old Westbury, New York, 1973.

Giroux, Henry. 1981. *Ideology, culture and the process of schooling*. Philadelphia: Temple University Press.

———. 1983a. *Theories of resistance in education: A pedagogy for the opposition*. Massachusetts: Bergin and Garvey.

———. 1983b. Theories of reproduction and resistance in the new sociology of education: A critical analysis. *Harvard Educational Review* 53 (3): 257–292.

———. 1988. Border pedagogy in the age of postmodernism. *Journal of Education* 170 (3): 162–181.

Giroux, Henry, and Simon, Roger. 1988. Schooling, popular culture, and a pedagogy of possibility. *Journal of Education* 170 (1): 9–26.

Gitlin, Andrew; Siegel, Marjorie; and Boru, Kevin. April, 1988. Purpose and method: Rethinking the use of ethnography by the educational left. Paper presented at the annual meeting of the American Educational Research Association.

Gitlin, Todd. Nov. 6, 1988. Hip-deep in postmodernism. *The New York Times Book Review* 1:35–36.

———. 1989. Post-modernism: The stenography of surfaces. *New Perspectives Quarterly* 6 (1): 56–59.

Glaser, Barney, and Strauss, A. 1967. *The discovery of grounded theory: Strategies for qualitative research*. Chicago: Aldine Pub.

Gleick, James. 1987. *Chaos*. New York: Viking.

Goddard, David. 1973. Max Weber and the objectivity of social science. *History and Theory* 12:1–22.

Gonzalvez, Linda. 1986. The new feminist scholarship: Epistemological issues for teacher education. Unpublished paper.

Gouldner, Alvin. 1970. *The coming crisis of Western sociology*. New York: Basic Books.

Gramsci, Antonio. 1971. *Selections from the prison notebooks of Antonio Gramsci*. Ed., trans. Quintin Hoare and G. Smith. New York: International Pub.

Gray, Elizabeth Dodson. 1982. *Patriarchy as a conceptual trap*. Massachusetts: Roundtable Press.

Green, Bill, and Bigum, Chris, n.d. *Quantum curriculum and chaotic classrooms: Re-framing educational computing*. Unpublished manuscript, Deakin University.

Grossberg, Lawrence. 1987. The in-difference of television or, mapping TV's popular economy. *Screen* 28 (2): 28–47.

———. 1988a. Rockin' with Reagan, or the mainstreaming of postmodernity. *Cultural Critique* 10:123–149.

———. 1988b. Putting the pop back into postmodernism. In *Universal abandon: The politics of postmodernism,* ed. A. Ross, 167–190. Minneapolis: University of Minnesota Press.

Grosz, Elizabeth A. 1988. The in(ter)vention of feminist knowledges. In *Crossing boundaries: Feminisms and the critique of knowledges,* ed. Barbara Caine, E. A. Grosz, and Marie de Lepervanche, 92–104. Sydney: Allen and Unwin.

Grosz, Elizabeth. 1989. *Sexual subversions: Three French feminists*. Sydney: Allen and Unwin.

Grundy, S. 1982. Three modes of action research. *Curriculum Perspectives* 3 (2): 22–34.

Guba, Egon, and Lincoln, Yvonna. 1981. *Effective evaluation*. San Francisco: Jossey-Bass.

Gwin, Minrose. 1988. A theory of black women's texts and white women's readings, or . . . the necessity of being other. *NWSA Journal* 1 (1): 21–31.

Habermas, Jurgen. 1971. *Theory and practice*. Boston: Beacon Press.

———. 1975. *Legitimation crisis*. Boston: Beacon Press.

———. 1981. Modernity versus postmodernity, *New German Critique* 22:3–14.

———. 1983. Modernity—An incomplete project. In *The anti-aesthetic: Essays on postmodern culture,* ed. Hal Foster, 3–15. Washington: Bay Press.

———. 1987. *The philosophical discourse of modernity*. Cambridge: M. I. T. Press.

Hall, Budd. 1975. Participatory research: An approach for change. *Prospects* 8 (2): 24–31.

———. 1981. The democratization of research in adult and non-formal education. In *Human Inquiry,* ed. P. Reason and J. Rowan, 447–456. New York: John Wiley.

Hall, Stuart. 1985. Signification, representation, ideology: Althusser and the post-structuralist debates. *Critical Studies in Mass Communication* 2 (2): 91–114.

———. 1988. Brave new world. *Marxism Today* (Oct. 1988): 24–29.

Hand, Sean. 1986. Translating theory, or the difference between Deleuze and Foucault. Introduction to *Foucault,* Gilles Deleuze. Trans., ed. Sean Hand, xli–xliv. Minneapolis: University of Minnesota Press.

Hanmer, Jalna, and Saunders, Shelia. *Well-founded fear: A community study of violence to women*. London: Hutchinson.

Harasym, Sarah. 1988. Practical politics of the open end: An interview with Gayatri Spivak. *Canadian Journal of Political and Social Theory* 12 (1–2): 51–69.

Haraway, Donna. 1985. A manifesto for cyborgs: Science, technology and socialist feminism in the 1980s. *Socialist Review* 80:65–107.

———. 1988. Situated knowledges: The science question in feminism and the privilege of partial perspective. *Feminist Studies* 14 (3): 575–599.

Harding, Sandra. 1982. Is gender a variable in conceptions of rationality? *Dialectica* 36:225–242.

———. 1986. *The science question in feminism*. Ithaca: Cornell University Press.

———. 1987. *Feminism and methodology*. Bloomington: Indiana University Press.

Hargreaves, Andy. 1982. Resistance and relative autonomy theories: Problems of distortion and incoherence in recent Marxist analyses of education. *British Journal of Sociology of Education* 3:107–126.

Hariman, Robert. 1989. The rhetoric of inquiry and the professional scholar. In *Rhetoric in the human sciences,* ed. Herbert Simons, 211–232. London: Sage.

Harland, Richard. 1987. *Superstructuralism: The philosophy of structuralism and post-structuralism*. New York: Methuen.

Harste, J.; Woodward, V.; and Burke, C. 1984. *Language stories and literacy lessons*. New Hampshire: Heinemann.

Hartmann, Heidi. 1981. The unhappy marriage of Marxism and feminism: Towards a more progressive union. In *Women and revolution,* ed. L. Sargent, 1–41. Boston: South End Press.

Hartsock, Nancy. 1987. Rethinking modernism: minority vs. majority theories. *Cultural Critique* 7:187–206.

Harvey, David. 1989. *The condition of postmodernity*. Oxford: Basil Blackwell.

Hassan, Ihab. 1987. *The postmodern turn: Essays in postmodern theory and culture*. Columbus: The Ohio State University Press.

Haug, Frigga, ed. 1987. *Female sexualization*. Trans. Erica Carter. London: Verso.

Heath, Stephen. 1978–79. Difference. *Screen* 19 (4): 51–112.

Hendrick, Clyde. 1983. A middle-way metatheory. (Review of *Toward transformation in social knowledge* by Kenneth J. Gergen.) *Contemporary Psychology* 28 (7): 504–507.

Henriques, Julian; Holloway, Wendy; Unwin, Cathy; Venn, Couze; and Walkerdine, Valerie. 1984. *Changing the subject: Psychology, social regulation and subjectivity*. London: Methuen.

Heron, John. 1981. Experimental research methods. In *Human Inquiry,* ed. Reason and Rowan, 153–166. New York: John Wiley.

Hesse, Mary. 1980. *Revolution and reconstruction in the philosophy of science*. Bloomington: Indiana University Press.

Hooker, C. A. 1982. Understanding and control: An essay on the structural dynamics of human cognition. *Man-Environment Systems* 12:121–160.

Hooks, Bell. 1984. *Feminist theory: From margin to center*. Boston: South End Press.

Hutcheon, Linda. 1988a. *A poetics of postmodernism: History, theory, fiction*. New York: Routledge.

———. 1988b. A postmodern problematics. In *Ethics/Aesthetics: Post-modern positions,* ed. Robert Merrill, 1–10. Washington, D.C.: Maisonneuve Press.

———. 1989. *The politics of postmodernism*. New York: Routledge.

Huyssen, Andreas. 1987. Foreword: The return of Diogenes as postmodern intellectual. *Critique of cynical reason,* Peter Sloterdijk. Trans. Michael Eldred, ix–xxv. Minneapolis: University of Minnesota Press.

Inglis, Fred. 1988. *Popular culture and political power*. New York: Harvester-Wheatsheaf.

Irigaray, Luce. 1985. *Speculum of the other woman*. Trans. Gilian Gill. Ithaca: Cornell University Press.

Jaggar, Alison. 1983. *Feminist politics and human nature*. New Jersey: Rowman and Allanheld.

Jameson, Frederic. 1984. Postmodernism, or the cultural logic of late capitalism. *New Left Review* 146:53–92.

JanMohamed, Abdul R., and Lloyd, David. 1987. Introduction: Toward a theory of minority discourse. *Cultural Critique* 6:5–12.

Jardine, Alice. 1982. Gynesis. *Diacritics* 12:54–65.

———. 1985. *Gynesis: Configurations of women and modernity*. Ithaca: Cornell University Press.

Jardine, Alice and Smith, Paul, eds. 1987. *Men in feminism*. New York: Methuen.

Jauss, Hans Robert. 1988–89. The literary process of modernism: From Rousseau to Adorno. *Cultural Critique* 11 (Winter): 23–61.

Johnson, Barbara. 1981. Translator's introduction to *Dissemination,* Jacques Derrida, vii–xxxiii. London: The Athlone Press.

———. 1987. *A world of difference*. Baltimore: Johns Hopkins University Press.

Johnson, Richard. 1986–87. What is cultural studies anyway? *Social Text* 16:38–80.

Johnston, John. 1990. Ideology, representation, schizophrenia: Toward a theory of the postmodern subject. In *After the future: Postmodern times and places,* ed. Gary Shapiro, 67–95. Albany: State University of New York Press.

Johnston, Marilyn. 1990. Experience and reflections on collaborative research. *Qualitative Studies in Education, 3* (2), 173–183.

Joycechild, Lisa Dewey. March, 1987. Emergent highlights from the preliminary report. Women's Studies faculty in-service document.

Joycechild, Lisa Dewey. 1988. *Presenting feminism: Toward a reflexive pedagogy in the introductory women's studies course*. Unpublished M.S. thesis. Mankato State University.

Kamarovsky, Mira. 1981. Women then and now: A journey of detachment and engagement. *Women's Studies Quarterly* 10 (2): 5–9.

Kaplan, Abraham. 1964. *The conduct of inquiry: Methodology for behavioral sciences*. San Francisco: Chandler.

Kappeler, Susanne. 1986. *The pornography of representation*. Cambridge: Polity Press.

Kearney, Richard. 1984. *Dialogues with contemporary continental thinkers: The phenomenological heritage*. Manchester: Manchester University Press.

Kellner, Douglas. 1975. The Frankfurt School revisited. *New German Critique* 4:131–152.

———. 1978. Ideology, Marxism, and advanced capitalism. *Socialist Review* 42:37–65.

———. 1988. Postmodernism as social theory. *Theory, Culture and Society, 5* (2–3), 239–269.

Kendall. 1990. Theatre and theory (review of *Feminine focus: The new women playwrites). The Women's Review of Books* 7 (4): 15–16.

Kenway, Jane, and Modra, Helen. 1989. Feminist pedagogy and emancipatory possibilities. *Critical Pedagogy Newsletter,* Deakin University, 1–17.

Kidder, Louise. 1982. Face validity from multiple perspectives. In *New directions for methodology of social and behavioral science: Forms of validity in research*. Vol. 12, ed. D. Brinberg and L. Kidder, 41–57. San Francisco: Jossey-Bass.

Kipnis, Laura. 1988. Feminism: The political conscience of postmodernism? In *Universal abandon: The politics of postmodernism,* ed. A. Ross, 149–166. Minneapolis: University of Minnesota Press.

Kirby, Vicki. 1989. Capitalizing difference: Feminism and anthropology. *Australian Feminist Studies* 9:1–24.

Klotz, Heinrich. 1988. *The history of postmodern architecture*. Cambridge: M. I. T. Press.

Kritzman, Lawrence D., ed. 1988. *Michael Foucault: Politics, philosophy, culture: Interviews and other writings, 1977–1984*. New York: Routledge.

Kroker, Arthur. 1983. The disembodied eye: Ideology and power in the age of nihilism. *Canadian Journal of Political and Social Theory* 7 (1–2): 194–234.

Kroker, Arthur, and Cook, David. 1986. *The postmodern scene: Excremental culture and hyper-aesthetics*. New York: St. Martin's Press.

Krueger, Marlis. 1981. In search of the "subjects" in social theory and research. *Psychology and Social Theory* 1 (2): 54–61.

Kruger, Barbara, and Mariani, Phil, eds. 1989. *Remaking history*. Seattle: Bay Press.

Kuhn, Thomas. 1970. *The structure of scientific revolutions*. Chicago: University of Chicago Press.

Kushner, Saville, and Norris, Nigel. 1980–81. Interpretation, negotiation and validity in naturalistic research. *Interchange* 11 (4): 26–36.

Laclau, Ernest, and Mouffe, Chantal. 1985. *Hegemony and socialist strategy: Towards a radical democratic politics*. Trans. Winson Moore and Paul Cammack. London: Verso.

Lanser, Susan S. 1989. Feminist criticism, "The Yellow Wallpaper," and the politics of color in America. *Feminist Studies* 15 (3): 415–441.

Laslett, Barbara, and Rapoport, Rhona. 1975. Collaborative interviewing and interactive research. *Journal of Marriage and the Family* 37: 968–977.

Lather, Patti. 1983. *Women's studies as counter-hegemonic work: The case of teacher education*. Unpublished dissertation, Indiana University.

———. 1984. Critical theory, curricular transformation and feminist mainstreaming. *Journal of Education* 66 (1): 49–62.

———. 1986a. Research as praxis. *Harvard Educational Review* 56 (3): 257–277.

———. 1986b. Issues of validity in openly ideological research: Between a rock and a soft place. *Interchange* 17 (4): 63–84.

———. 1986c. Issues of data trustworthiness in openly ideological research. Paper presented at annual meeting of the American Educational Research Association, San Francisco, California.

———. 1987. Patriarchy, capitalism and the nature of teacher work. *Teacher Education Quarterly* 14 (2): 25–38.

———. 1988a. Feminist perspectives on empowering research methodologies. *Women's Studies International Forum* 11 (6): 569–581.

———. 1988b. Review of *Power and criticism: Poststructural investigations in education,* Cleo Cherryholmes, Teacher's College Press. *Journal of Curriculum Theorizing*. 8 (4): 127–134.

———. 1989. Postmodernism and the politics of enlightenment. *Educational Foundations* 3 (3): 7–28.

Lattas, Judy. 1989. Feminism as a proper name. *Australian Feminist Studies* 9:85–96.

Lawson, Hilary. 1985. *Reflexivity: The post-modern predicament*. Illinois: Open Court.

Lauder, Hugh, and Kahn, G. I. A. R. 1988. Democracy and the effective schools movement in New Zealand. *International Journal of Qualitative Studies in Education* 1 (1): 51–68.

Lecourt, Dominique. 1975. *Marxism and epistemology*. London: National Labor Board.

Lee, Janet. June, 1988. The effects of feminist education on student values.

Paper presented at the annual conference of the National Women's Studies Association, Minneapolis.

Lerner, Gerda. 1987. Where biographers fear to tread. *Women's Review of Books* 4 (12): 11–12.

Lewis, Magda, 1988. Without a word: Sources and themes for a feminist pedagogy. Unpublished dissertation, University of Toronto.

———. March, 1989. Problems of practice in radical teaching: A feminist perspective on the psycho/social/sexual dynamics in the mixed gender classroom. Paper presented at the annual meeting of the American Educational Research Association, San Francisco.

Lewis, Magda and Simon, Roger. 1986. A discourse not intended for her: Learning and teaching within patriarchy. *Harvard Educational Review* 56 (4): 457–472.

Lincoln, Yvonna. 1990. The making of a constructivist: A remembrance of transformations past. In the Paradigm dialog: options for social science inquiry, Egon Guba (ed.). Beverly Hills: Sage.

Lincoln, Yvonna, and Guba, Egon. 1985. *Naturalistic inquiry*. Beverly Hills: Sage.

Livingstone, David, ed. 1987. *Critical pedagogy and cultural power*. Massachusetts: Bergin and Garvey.

Longino, Helen. 1986. Can there be a feminist science? Working paper No. 163, Wellesley Center for Research on Women, Wellesley, Massachusetts 02181. A revised version is in *Feminism and science,* ed. Nancy Tuana, 45–57. Bloomington: Indiana University Press, 1989.

———. 1988. Science, objectivity, and feminist values (a review essay). *Feminist Studies* 14 (3): 561–574.

Lorde, Audre. 1984. *Sister outsider*. New York: Crossing Press.

Lugones, Maria. 1987. Playfulness, "world"-travelling, and loving perception. *Hypatia* 2 (2): 3–19.

Lugones, Maria, and Spelman, Elizabeth. 1983. Have we got a theory for you! Feminist theory, cultural imperialism and the demand for "the woman's voice." *Women's Studies International Forum* 6 (6): 573–581.

Luke, Carmen. n.d. Feminist politics in radical pedagogy. Unpublished manuscript.

Lusted, David. 1986. Why pedagogy? *Screen* 27 (5): 2–14.

Lyotard, Jean-Francois. 1984. *The postmodern condition: A report on knowledge*. Trans. Geoff Bennington and Brian Massumi. Minneapolis: University of Minnesota Press.

Macdonell, Diane. 1986. *Theories of discourse: An introduction*. Oxford: Basil Blackwell.

Maguire, Patricia. 1987. *Doing participatory research: A feminist approach*. Amherst: The Center for International Education, School of Education, University of Massachusetts.

Maher, Frinde, and Tetreault, Mary Kay. March, 1989. Feminist teaching: Issues of mastery, voice, authority and positionality. Paper presented at the annual meeting of the American Educational Research Association, San Francisco.

Marcus, George, and Fischer, Richard. 1986. *Anthropology as cultural critique*. Chicago: University of Chicago Press.

Marcus, Jane. 1986. Of method and madness. *Women's Review of Books* 3 (11): 1, 3–4.

Marks, Elaine, and de Coutivon, Isabell, eds. 1980. *New French feminisms*. Amherst: University of Massachusetts Press.

Marsh, Dave. 1987. *Glory days: Bruce Springsteen in the 1980s*. New York: Pantheon.

Martin, Biddy, and Mohanty, Chandra Talpade. 1986. Feminist politics: What's home got to do with it? In *Feminist studies/critical studies,* ed. Teresa de Lauretis, 191–212. Bloomington: Indiana University Press.

Martin, Luther; Gutman, Huch; and Hutton, Patrick, eds. 1988. *Technologies of the self: A seminar with Michael Foucault*. Amherst: University of Massachusetts Press.

Masemann, V. 1982. Critical ethnography in the study of comparative education. *Comparative Education Review* 26:1–15.

McLaren, Peter. 1986. Review article—Postmodernity and the death of politics: A Brazilian reprieve. *Educational Theory* 36 (4): 389–401.

———. 1988. Schooling the postmodern body: Critical pedagogy and the politics of enfleshment. *Journal of Education* 170 (3): 53–83.

McCloskey, Donald. 1983. The rhetoric of economics. *Journal of Economic Literature* 21:481–517.

McNeil, Linda. April, 1984. Critical theory and ethnography in curriculum analysis. Paper presented at the annual meeting of the American Educational Research Association, New Orleans.

McRobbie, Angela. 1978. Working class girls and the culture of femininity. In *Women take issue: Aspects of women's subordination,* Women's Study Group, 96–108. London: Hutchinson.

———. 1982. The politics of feminist research: Between talk, text and action. *Feminist Review* 12:46–57.

Meese, Elizabeth. 1986. *Crossing the double-cross: The practice of feminist criticism*. Chapel Hill: University of North Carolina Press.

Merck, Mandy. 1987. Difference and its discontents. *Screen* 28 (1): 2–9.

Merquior, J. G. 1986. *A critique of structuralist and poststructuralist thought*. London: Verso.

Mies, Maria. 1984. Towards a methodology for feminist research. In *German feminism: Readings in politics and literature,* ed. Edith Altbach, et al., 357–366. Albany: State University of New York Press.

Miles, Matthew, and Huberman, Michael. 1984. *Qualitative data analysis: A sourcebook of new methods*. Beverly Hills: Sage.

Miller, Janet. 1986. Women as teachers: Enlarging conversations on issues of gender and self-control. *Journal of Curriculum and Supervision* 1 (2): 111–121.

———. October, 1987. Points of dissonance in teacher/researchers: Openings into emancipatory ways of knowing. Paper presented at the Bergamo Curriculum Theorizing Conference, Dayton, Ohio.

Minh-ha, Trinh T. 1989. *Woman native other*. Bloomington: Indiana University Press.

Mishler, Elliott. 1979. Meaning in context: Is there any other kind? *Harvard Educational Review* 49 (1): 1–19.

———. 1984. *The discourse of medicine: Dialectics of medical interviews*. New Jersey: Ablex Pub.

Mitchell, W. J. T., ed. 1983. *The politics of interpretation*. Chicago: University of Chicago Press.

Mitroff, Ian, and Kilmann, R. 1978. *Methodological approaches to social science*. San Francisco: Jossey-Bass.

Moi, Toril. 1985. *Sexual/textual politics: Feminist literary theory*. New York: Methuen.

———. 1988. Feminism, postmodernism, and style: Recent feminist criticism in the United States. *Cultural Critique* 9:3–22.

Moon, J. Donald. 1983. Political ethics and critical theory. In *Changing social science,* ed. D. Sabia and J. Wallulis, 171–188. Albany: State University of New York Press.

Moraga, Cherrie, and Anzaldua, Gloria, eds. 1983. *This bridge called my back: Writings by radical women of color*. New York: Kitchen Table Press.

Morgan, Gareth, ed. 1983. *Beyond method: Strategies for social research*. Beverly Hills: Sage.

Morris, Meaghan. 1988. *The pirate's fiancee: Feminism, reading, postmodernism*. London: Verso.

Morton, Donald, and Zavarzadeh, Mas'ud. 1988–89. The cultural politics of the fiction workshop. *Cultural Critique* 11:115–173.

Mulkay, Michael. 1985. *The word and the world: Explorations in the form of sociological analysis*. London: George Allen and Unwin.

Naidus, Beverly. 1987. The artist/teacher as decoder and catalyst. *Radical Teacher* (Sept.): 17–20.

Namenwirth, Marion. 1986. Science through a feminist prism. In *Feminist approaches to science,* ed. Ruth Bleir, 18–41. New York: Pergamon.

Nelson, Cary, ed. 1986. *Theory in the classroom*. Urbana: University of Illinois Press.

Nelson, John S. 1987. Seven rhetorics of inquiry: A provocation. In *The rhetoric of the human sciences,* ed. Nelson et al., 407–434. Madison: University of Wisconsin Press.

Nelson, John S.; Megill, Allan; and McCloskey, Donald N., eds. 1987. *The rhetoric of the human sciences: Language and argument in scholarship and public affairs*. Madison: University of Wisconsin Press.

Newton, Judith. 1988. History as usual? Feminism and the "new historicism." *Cultural Critique* 9 (Spring): 87–121.

Newton, Judith, and Rosenfelt, Deborah, eds. 1985. *Feminist criticism and social change: Sex, class and race in literature and culture*. New York: Methuen.

Nicholson, Linda. 1986. *Gender and history: The limits of social theory in the age of the family*. New York: Columbia University Press.

———. 1990. *Feminism/postmodernism*. New York: Routledge.

Norris, Christopher. 1982. *Deconstruction: Theory and practice*. London: Methuen.

Nowotny, Helga, and Rose, H., eds. 1979. *Counter-movements in the sciences: The sociology of the alternatives to big science*. Boston: D. Reidel.

Oakley, Ann. 1981. Interviewing women: A contradiction in terms. In *Doing feminist research,* ed. Helen Roberts, 30–61. Boston: Routledge and Kegan Paul.

O'Brien, Mary. 1984. The commatization of women: Patriarchal fetishism in the sociology of education. *Interchange* 15 (2): 43–60.

Ogbu, John. 1981. School ethnography: A multilevel approach. *Anthropology and Education Quarterly* 12:3–29.

Orner, Mimi, and Brennan, Marie. March, 1989. Producing collectively: Power, identity and teaching. Paper presented at the annual meeting of the American Educational Research Association, San Francisco.

Owens, Craig. 1983. The discourse of others: Feminism and postmodernism.

In *The anti-aesthetic: Essays on postmodern culture,* ed. H. Foster, 57–82. Washington: Bay Press.

Patai, Daphne. 1988. Constructing a self: A Brazilian life story. *Feminist Studies* 14 (1): 143–166.

Patton, Paul. 1983. Marxism in crisis: No difference. In *Beyond Marxism: Interventions after Marx,* ed. S. Allen and P. Patton, 47–72. Leichardt: Intervention Pub.

Peller, Gary. 1987. Reason and the mob. The politics of representation. *Tikkun* 2 (3): 28–31, 92–95.

Penley, Constance. 1986. Teaching in your sleep: Feminism and psychoanalysis. In *Theory in the classroom,* ed. Cary Nelson, 129–148. Urbana: University of Illinois Press.

Peshkin, Alan. 1988. In search of subjectivity–One's own. *Educational Researcher* (October): 17–21.

Peters, Michael. 1989. Techno-science, rationality, and the university: Lyotard on the "postmodern condition." *Educational Theory* 39 (2): 93–105.

Peters, Michael, and Robinson, Viviane. 1984. The origins and status of action research. *The Journal of Applied Behavioral Sciences* 20 (2): 113–124.

Phillips, D. C. 1983. After the wake: Postpositivistic educational thought. *Educational Researcher* 12 (5): 4–12.

———. 1987. *Philosophy, science, and social inquiry: Contemporary methodological controversies in social science and related applied fields of research.* New York: Pergamon Press.

Polanyi, M. 1967. *The tacit dimension.* New York: Anchor Books.

Polkinghorne, Donald. 1983. *Methodology for the human sciences: Systems of inquiry.* Albany: State University of New York Press.

Poovey, Mary. 1988. Feminism and deconstruction. *Feminist Studies* 14 (1): 51–65.

Popkewitz, Thomas. 1984. *Paradigm and ideology in educational research: The social functions of the intellectual.* New York: Falmer Press.

Poster, Marc. 1987–88. Foucault, the present and history. *Cultural Critique* 8:105–121.

———. 1989. *Critical theory and poststructuralism: In search of a context.* Ithaca: Cornell University Press.

Pratt, Minnie Bruce. 1984. Identity: Skin, blood, heart. In *Yours in struggle: Three feminist perspectives on anti-semitism and racism,* Elly Bulkin, Minnie Bruce Pratt and Barbara Smith, 11–63. New York: Long Haul Press.

Pringle, Rosemary. 1988. Socialist-feminism in the eighties: Reply to Curthoys. *Australian Feminist Studies* 6:25–30.

Rabine, Leslie. 1988. A feminist politics of non-identity. *Feminist Studies* 14(1): 11–31.

Rajchman, John. 1985. *Michael Foucault: The freedom of philosophy*. New York: Columbia University Press.

Ramsay, Peter. 1983. A response to Anyon from the Antipodes. *Curriculum Inquiry* 13 (3): 295–320.

Reason, Peter. 1981. Patterns of discovery in the social sciences by Paul Diesing: An appreciation. In *Human Inquiry,* ed. Reason and Rowan, 183–189. New York: John Wiley.

Reason, Peter, and Rowan, John. 1981. Issues of validity in new paradigm research. In *Human Inquiry,* ed. Reason and Rowan, 239–252. New York: John Wiley.

Reinharz, Shulamit. 1979. *On becoming a social scientist.* San Francisco: Jossey-Bass. Reissued in paperback, New Jersey: Transaction, 1984.

———. 1983. Experiential analysis: A contribution to feminist research. In *Theories of women's studies,* ed. G. Bowles and R. Duelli-Klein, 162–191. Boston: Routledge and Kegan Paul.

———. 1985. *Feminist distrust: A response to misogyny and gynopia in sociological work*. Unpublished manuscript.

Reiss, Timothy J. 1988. *The uncertainty of analysis: Problems in truth, meaning and culture*. Ithaca: Cornell University Press.

Repo, Satu. 1987. Consciousness and popular media. In *Critical pedagogy and cultural power,* ed. D. Livingstone, 77–98. Massachusetts: Bergin and Garvey.

Reynolds, D. 1980–81. The naturalistic method and educational and social research: A Marxist critique. *Interchange* 11 (4): 77–89.

Rich, Adrienne. 1975. The burning of paper instead of children. *Poems: Selected and new, 1950–1974*. New York: W. W. Norton.

———. 1979. *On lies, secrets and silence: Selected prose. 1966–1978*. New York: W. W. Norton.

Richardson, Laurel. 1988. The collective story: Postmodernism and the writing of sociology. *Sociological Focus* 21 (3): 199–208.

———. Forthcoming. Value constituting practices, rhetoric, and metaphor in sociology: A reflexive analysis. *Current perspectives on social theory*. J. A. I. Press.

Riley, Denise. 1988. *"Am I that name?" Feminism and the category of "women" in history*. Minneapolis: University of Minnesota Press.

Roberts, Helen, ed. 1981. *Doing feminist research.* London: Routledge and Kegan Paul.

Roman, Leslie. 1987. *Punk femininity: Young women's formation of their gender identification and class relations within the extra-mural curricula of a contemporary sub-culture*. Unpublished dissertation. University of Wisconsin-Madison.

———. 1988. Intimacy, labor, and class: Ideologies of feminine sexuality in the punk slam dance. In *Becoming feminine: The politics of popular culture*, ed. Leslie Roman and Linda K. Christian-Smith, 143–184. New York: The Falmer Press.

Roman, Leslie, and Apple, Michael. 1990. Is naturalism a move away from positivism? Materialist and feminist approaches to subjectivity in ethnographic research. In *Qualitative inquiry in education: the continuing debate*, ed. Elliot Eisner and Alan Peshkin, 38–73. New York: Teachers College Press.

Rorty, Richard. 1979. *Philosophy and the mirror of nature*. New Jersey: Princeton University Press.

Rose, Hilary. 1979. Hyper-reflexivity—A new danger for the counter-movements. In *Counter-movements in the sciences*, ed. H. Nowotny and H. Rose, 277–289. Boston: D. Reidel.

Ross, Andrew, ed. 1988. *Universal abandon: The politics of postmodernism*. Minneapolis: University of Minnesota Press.

Rushdie, Salman. 1982. *Midnight's Children*. New York: Avon Books.

Ryan, Michael. 1982. *Marxism and deconstruction: A critical articulation*. Baltimore: Johns Hopkins Press.

Sabia, D., and Wallulis, J., eds. 1983. *Changing social science: Critical theory and other critical perspectives*. Albany: State University of New York Press.

Said, Edward. 1975. *Beginnings: Intention and method*. New York: Basic Books.

———. 1986. Orientalism reconsidered. In *Literature, politics and theory*, ed. Francis Barker, et al., 210–229. New York: Methuen.

———. 1989. Representing the colonized: Anthropology's interlocutors. *Critical Inquiry* 15:205–225.

Salamini, Leonardo. 1981. *The sociology of political praxis: An introduction to Gramsci's theory*. London: Routledge and Kegan Paul.

Sarup, Madan. 1983. *Marxism/structuralism/education: Theoretical developments in the sociology of education*. London: Falmer Press.

Sawicki, Jana. 1988. Identity politics and sexual freedom: Foucault and feminism. In *Feminism and Foucault: Reflections on resistance*, ed. Irene Diamond and Lee Quinby, 177–191. Boston: Northeastern University Press.

Schmitz, Betty. 1985. *Integrating women's studies into the curriculum: A guide and a bibliography*. New York: The Feminist Press.

Scholes, Robert. 1989. Eperon strings. *differences* 1 (2): 93–104.

Schrift, Alan D. 1990. The becoming-postmodern of philosophy. In *After the future: Postmodern times and places,* ed. Gary Shapiro, 99–113. Albany: State University of New York Press.

Schwartz, Peter, and Ogilvy, J. April, 1979. *The emergent paradigm: Changing patterns of thought and belief.* Analytical Report: Values and Lifestyles Program. Menlo Park: Stanford Research Institute (S. R. I.) International.

Scott, Joan. 1987. Critical tensions. (Review of Teresa de Lauretis, *Feminist studies/critical studies.*) *Women's Review of Books* 5 (1): 17–18.

———. 1988. Deconstructing equality-versus-difference: Or, the uses of post-structuralist theory for feminism. *Feminist Studies* 14 (1): 33–50.

———. 1989. History in crisis? The others' side of the story. *The American Historical Review* 94 (3): 680–692.

Sears, James. October, 1983. Black holes of critical theory: Problems and prospects of ethnographic research. Paper presented at Fifth Annual Curriculum Theorizing Conference, Dayton, Ohio.

Shapiro, Gary, ed. 1990. *After the future: Postmodern times and places.* Albany: State University of New York Press.

Shapiro, Svi. 1989. Towards a language of educational politics: The struggles for a critical public discourse of education. *Educational Foundations* 3 (3): 79–100.

Sharp, Rachael, and Green, A. 1975. *Education and social control: A study in progressive primary education.* Boston: Routledge and Kegan Paul.

Sheridan, Alan. 1980. *Michael Foucault: The will to truth.* London: Tavistock.

Sheridan, Susan. 1988. Introduction. In *Grafts: Feminist cultural criticism,* 1–9. London: Verso.

Sherman, Julia. 1983. Girls talk about mathematics and their future: A partical replication. *Psychology of Women Quarterly* 7:338–342.

Sholle, David J. 1988. Critical studies: From the theory of ideology to power/knowledge. *Critical Studies in Mass Communication* 5:16–41.

Shor, Ira. 1980. *Critical teaching and everyday life.* Boston: South End Press.

Shrewsbury, Carolyn. 1987. What is feminist pedagogy? *Women's Studies Quarterly* 15 (3, 4): 6–14. See, also, Feminist pedagogy: A bibliography, 116–124.

Shulman, Judith H. In press. Now you see them, now you don't: Anonymity versus visibility in case studies of teachers. *Educational Researcher.*

Simon, Roger. 1987. Work experience. In *Critical pedagogy and cultural power,* ed. D. Livingstone, 155–178. Massachusetts: Bergin and Garvey.

Simon, Roger, and Dippo, Donald. 1986. On critical ethnographic work. *Anthropology and Education Quarterly* 17 (4): 195–202.

Simons, Herbert. 1989. Introduction. In *Rhetoric in the human sciences,* ed. H. Simons, 1–9. London: Sage.

Sloterdijk, Peter. 1987. *The critique of cynical reason.* Minneapolis: University of Minnesota Press.

Smart, Barry. 1983. *Foucault, Marxism and critique.* London: Routledge and Kegan Paul.

———. 1986. The politics of truth and the problem of hegemony. In *Foucault: A critical reader,* ed. David Couzens Hoy, 157–173. New York: Basil Blackwell.

Smith, Barbara, ed. 1983. *Home girls: A black feminist anthology.* New York: Kitchen Table Press.

Smith, John K. 1983. Quantitative vs. qualitative research: An attempt to clarify the issue. *Educational Researcher* 12 (3): 6–13.

———. 1984. The problem of criteria for judging interpretive inquiry. *Education Evaluation and Policy Analysis* 6 (4): 379–391.

———. 1988. The evaluator/researcher as person vs. the person as evaluator/researcher. *Educational Researcher* 17 (2): 18–23.

Smith, John K., and Heshusius, Lous. 1986. Closing down the conversation: The end of the quantitative-qualitative debate among educational inquirers. *Educational Researcher* 15 (1, January): 4–12.

Smith, Paul. 1988. *Discerning the subject.* Minneapolis: University of Minnesota Press.

Snitow, Ann. 1989. Textual intercourse. (Review of *Thinking through the body,* Jane Gallop.) *The Women's Review of Books* 7 (1): 13–14.

Sollers, Philippe. 1983. *Writing and the experience of limits.* Ed. David Hayman, trans. Philip Barnard and David Hayman. New York: Columbia University Press.

Solomon-Godeau, Abigail. 1988. Living with contradictions: Critical practices in the age of supply-side aesthetics. In *Universal abandon: The politics of postmodernism,* ed. A. Ross, 191–213. Minneapolis: University of Minnesota Press.

Spanier, Bonnie; Bloom, Alexander; and Boroviak, Darlene. 1984. *Toward a balanced curriculum: A sourcebook for initiating gender integration projects.* Massachusetts: Schenkman.

Spanos, William. 1987. *Repetitions: The Postmodern occasion in literature and culture.* Baton Rouge: Louisiana State University Press.

Spender, Dale. 1981. *Men's studies modified: The impact of feminism on the academic disciplines*. New York: Pergamon Press.

Spivak, Gayatri, 1985. Three women's texts and a critique of imperialism. *Critical Inquiry* 12:243–261.

———. 1987. *In other worlds: Essays in cultural politics*. New York: Methuen.

———. 1987b. Speculations on reading Marx: After reading Derrida. In *Post-structuralism and the question of history,* ed. Derek Attridge, Geoff Bennington and Robert Young, 30–62. Cambridge: Cambridge University Press.

———. 1989a. Who claims alterity? In *Remaking History,* ed. Barbara Kruger and Phil Mariani, 269–292. Seattle: Bay Press.

Spivak, Gayatri, with Rooney, Ellen. 1989b. In a word. Interview. *differences* 1 (2): 124–156.

Spivak, Gayatri. 1989c. A response to "The difference within: feminism & critical theory." *In the difference within: Feminism and critical theory,* ed. Elizabeth Meese and Alice Parker, 207–220. Amsterdam/Philadelphia: John Benjamins Pub. Co.

Stam, Robert. 1988. Mikhail Bakhtin and left cultural critique. In *Postmodernism and its discontents: Theories, practices,* ed. E. Ann Kaplan, 116–145. New York: Verso.

Stanley, Liz, and Wise, Sue. 1983. *Breaking out: Feminist consciousness and feminist research*. Boston: Routledge and Kegan Paul.

Stephanson, Anders. 1987. Regarding postmodernism—A conversation with Frederic Jameson. *Social Text* 17:29–54. Reprinted in *Universal abandon: The politics of postmodernism,* ed. A. Ross, 3–30. Minneapolis: University of Minnesota Press, 1988.

———. 1988. Interview with Cornel West. In *Universal abandon: The politics of postmodernism,* ed. A. Ross, 269–286. Minneapolis: University of Minnesota Press.

Storr, Robert. October 6, 1987. Other "others." *Village Voice*. Fall Art Supplement 3 (2): 15–17.

Thompson, E. P. 1963. *The making of the English working class*. New York: Parthenon.

———. 1978. *The poverty of theory and other essays*. New York: Monthly Review Press.

Treichler, Paula A. 1989. AIDS and HIV infection in the third world: A first world chronicle. In *Remaking History,* ed. Barbara Kruger and Phil Mariani, 31–86. Seattle: Bay Press.

Tripp, David. 1983. Co-authorship and negotiation: The interview as act of creation. *Interchange* 14 (3): 32–45.

———. 1984. Action research and professional development. Paper presented at the Australian College of Education Project, Murdoch University, Australia.

Tschumi, Bernard. 1989. De-, dis-, ex-. In *Remaking History,* ed. Barbara Kruger and Phil Mariani, 259–267. Seattle: Bay Press.

Tyler, Stephen. 1985. Ethnography, intertextuality, and the end of description. *American Journal of Semiotics* 3 (4): 83–98.

———. 1987. *The unspeakable: discourse, dialogue, & rhetoric in the postmodern world.* Madison: University of Wisconsin Press.

Ulmer, Gregory. 1985. *Applied grammatology: Post(e)-pedagogy from Jacques Derrida to Joseph Beuys.* Baltimore: Johns Hopkins University Press.

Unger, Rhoda K. 1982. Advocacy versus scholarship revisited: Issues in the psychology of women. *Psychology of Women Quarterly* 7: 5–17.

———. 1983. Through the looking glass: No wonderland yet! (The reciprocal relationship between methodology and models of reality). *Psychology of Women Quarterly* 8 (1): 9–32.

———. In press. Personal epistemology and personal experience. *Journal of Social Issues.*

Van Maanen, John. 1988. *Tales of the field: On writing ethnography.* Chicago: University of Chicago Press.

Walker, Alice. 1983. My father's country is the poor. In *In search of our mothers' gardens: Womanist Prose,* 199–222. New York: Harcourt Brace Jovanovich.

Walker, J. C. 1985. Rebels with our applause: A critique of resistance theory in Paul Willis' ethnography of schooling. *Journal of Education* 167 (2): 63–83.

Walkerdine, Valerie. 1981. Sex, power and pedagogy. *Screen Education* 38:14–24.

———. 1984. Developmental psychology and child-centered pedagogy. In *Changing the subject,* ed. J. Henriques, et al., London: Methuen, 153–202.

———. 1985. On the regulation of speaking and silence: Sexuality, class and gender in contemporary schooling. In *Language, gender and childhood,* ed. C. Steedman, C. Urwin and V. Walkerdine, 203–242. London: Routledge.

———. 1986. Post-structuralist theory and everyday social practices: The family and the schools. In *Feminist Social Psychology: Developing Theory and Practice,* ed. Sue Wilkinson, 57–76. Milton Keynes: Open University Press.

Warminsk, Andrzej. 1987. *Reading in interpretation: Holderlin, Hegel, Heidegger.* Minneapolis: University of Minnesota Press.

Wax, Rosalie. 1952. Reciprocity as a field technique. *Human Organization* 11:34–41.

Weedon, Chris. 1987. *Feminist practice and poststructuralist theory*. Oxford: Basil Blackwell.

Weinstein, Jeff. September 29, 1987. The postmodern mini. *The Village Voice*.

West, Cornell. 1987. Postmodernism and black America. *Zeta Magazine* 1 (6): 27–29.

Westkott, Marcia. 1977. Conservative method. *Philosophy of Social Sciences* 7:67–76.

———. 1979. Feminist criticism of the social sciences. *Harvard Educational Review* 49 (4): 422–430.

Wexler, Philip. 1982. Ideology and Education: From critique to class actions. *Interchange* 13 (1): 53–78.

———. 1987. *Social analysis of education: After the new sociology*. New York: Routledge and Kegan Paul.

Wexler, Philip; Martusewicz, Rebecca; and Kern, June. 1987. Popular educational politics. In *Critical pedagogy and cultural power,* ed. David Livingstone, 227–243. Massachusetts: Bergin and Garvey.

White, Hayden, 1973. Foucault decoded: Notes from underground. *History and Theory* 12:23–54.

Whitson, Tony. 1988. The politics of "non-political" curriculum: Heteroglossia and the discourse of "choice" and "effectiveness." In *Contemporary curriculum discourses,* ed. William Pinar, 279–330. Arizona: Gorsuch Scarisbrick.

Williams, Raymond. 1977. *Marxism and literature*. Oxford: Oxford University Press.

Willis, Paul. 1977. *Learning to labor: How working class kids get working class jobs,* 88–95. New York: Columbia University Press.

———. 1980. Notes on method. In *Culture, media, language,* ed. Stuart Hall et al., 88–95. London: Hutchinson.

Winter, Pamela. October, 1989. Departmental seminar paper, Sociology Dept., University of Waikato, Hamilton, New Zealand.

Wright, Erik Olin. 1978. *Class, crisis and the state*. London: National Labor Board.

Yeats, W. B. 1950. *The collected poems of W. B. Yeats*. London: Macmillan.

Yeo, Michael. 1989. Review of M. C. Dillon's *Merleau-Ponty's ontology*. In *Bulletin* of the Canadian Society for Hermeneutics 4 (1): 7–10.

Yudice, George. 1988. Marginality and the ethics of survival. In *Universal abandon: The politics of postmodernism,* ed. A. Ross, 214–236. Minneapolis: University of Minnesota Press.

Zavarzadeh, Mas'ud, and Morton, Donald. 1986–87. Theory pedagogy politics: The crisis of "the subject" in the humanities. *Boundary 2* 15 (1–2): 1–21.

Zeller, Nancy. 1987. *A rhetoric for naturalistic inquiry.* Unpublished dissertation, Indiana University.

Index